AWAKENING THE SENSES TO ART AND MUSIC

William Greiner
Neal McMullian

Learning Solutions

New York   Boston   San Francisco
London   Toronto   Sydney   Tokyo   Singapore   Madrid
Mexico City   Munich   Paris   Cape Town   Hong Kong   Montreal

Cover Art: "Spring Morning" by William Greiner

Pearson Learning Solutions, 501 Boylston Street, Suite 900, Boston, MA 02116
A Pearson Education Company
www.pearsoned.com

Printed in the United States of America

4 5 6 7 8 9 10 V0CR 15 14 13 12 11

000200010270566949

MP/JS

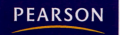

ISBN 10: 0-558-73686-6
ISBN 13: 978-0-558-73686-6

CONTENTS

ACKNOWLEDGEMENTS

Mr. Greiner would like to acknowledge the following for their help and support on the art section of this project:

Editorial Assistant: Gena Olson
Technical Editors: Lauren Edwards, Rachel Rhule
Selected Photography: Lisa Pesavento, Raul Rubiera
Senior Acquisitions Editor: Anthony Howard, Pearson Publishing

I want to *"Thank"* my wife Kathy for encouraging and supporting me during the time I was preoccupied with re-writing, editing and thoroughly enjoying the process.

I would like to personally *"Thank"* Gena Olson who gave inspiration throughout the art sections of this book. Gena's help was immeasurable! She worked tirelessly for many evenings and weekends. She captured the vision of and made suggestions that make the art section of this book more fluent and organized.

Neal McMullian would like to thank Gena Olson for all of her help with this project. I would also like to thank my wife, Cathy, for her help in proof-reading and for her continued support throughout this process.

PREFACE

Whether we go to museums or just watch television commercials at home, it all boils down to ART. It can be said that the definition of art is a record of human experience. It holds no meaning unless we, as the viewers, have some human experience to relate to the image. It also holds true that each culture presents its own experience through their art. For example the Egyptians built the pyramids that would last for centuries; the Greeks created statues; and painters have documented their culture for generations. As we look at any given culture, their art is a reflection of their experiences. As viewers we need to draw upon our own experiences while relating to those of the past. The important aspect of all types of art is our ability to understand an image. In all cultures there are symbols with various meanings that are particular to that culture.

How did we get to digital media from the ancient Egyptians? The art section of this book will explain the process of architecture and the development of statues along with an understanding of the elements of art. The art section concludes with a brief history of art from Renaissance through Post Modernism.

Artists define their culture by creating images that depict their time in history. Being able to understand these images requires the viewer to actively participate, seeing not only with the eyes, but with one's life experiences. Our world is filled with ever-changing symbols. We surround ourselves with media or rather media surrounds us, we have no choice but to participate. The result is a unique interplay of reality versus fiction. Images, both concrete and subliminal, create a wealth of instructional data.

We are constantly bombarded by information via various media, the internet, mp3 players, cell phones and the like. Televisions have become the icon of our culture. More channels, more news, more of whatever the viewer wants can be found around the clock somewhere on the "tube." Our culture has moved from the traditional way of receiving images, going to museums, reading the newspaper to receiving the majority of their information via the internet. The popular Apple iphone was designed slim and sleek with state-of-the-art technology that appeals to the current culture. On the highway, billboards advertise information about where to shop, the location of the nearest mall, or how to contact a favorite insurance agent. Images are very important in the grand scheme of marketing and selling.

Television commercials are a direct link to our society. They instruct us on how and where to eat, which fashions and accessories are needed, and the best ways to travel from place to place. Commercials have changed over the past several decades to fit the times. In the 1950's and early 1960's cigarette and car ads were the popular product features of the day. Most advertisers used a spokesperson, an actor or celebrity that the audience could associate with the product. The idea of a spokesperson remains the same but in many cases the spokesperson is selling their own line of merchandise today.

Most of us certainly have favorite television commercials; they make us laugh and cause us to think. They create a series of images that respond to our psyche, therefore capturing our attention. The marvel of television commercials is that they are mini movies with a beginning, middle and an end, all in 30 seconds.

The Post Modern society we live in today has moved into a new realm of advertising venue, the internet. Popular websites such as Facebook and YouTube are not only sites for entertainment but also advertisement. Rhett and Link (see figure below) have combined the two entities into what they call "Internetainers." They are a North Carolina based comedy duo that has developed an international following for their internet videos. Rhett and Link support themselves through sponsorships and brand integration. They write, shoot and produce their own videos that have been seen over 40 million times.

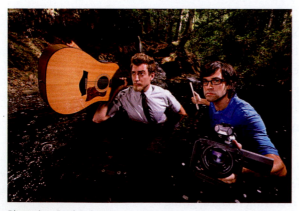

Photo by: Paul Rubiera

They produce quality songs and web videos of just about any genre. One notable video is the "Taco Bell Song" (http://rhettandlink.com/blog/fast-food-folk-song). They wrote their order in the form of a folk song to be sung into the drive-through ordering box. While singing their order, the employee on the inside actually began taking their order! When the song is over the employee repeats the order back. Much to their surprise, the employee has gotten the entire order correct! We can see the amazed expressions on the faces of Rhett and Link. The video captures a common occurrence of our culture, something we all do on a regular basis, order fast food. Their humorous take on the process is what speaks to the two million plus viewers on YouTube. The employee processing the order takes it as fast as they dish it out; instead of being mad at having someone sing a huge order into the drive-through box, he accepts the order as if it were an everyday happening at Taco Bell.

"The Red House" (http://rhettandlink.com/videos/redhousefurniture) is a local commercial produced by Rhett and Link. It is a statement on racial tension done in a humorous fashion. The parody's subject is black and white people talking about how comfortable the furniture is for a black person, white person or any person. Rhett and Link are trying to make sense of racial tension in a nonsensical manner, showing the viewers the ridiculousness of racism. The furniture does not care what color you are, it is comfortable for everyone.

Rhett and Link continue making "local commercials" across the country for small businesses. Their videos can be seen at http://rhettandlink.com. Those wishing to see more and join their "Kommunity" can go to www.RhettandLinKommunity.com.

ART

1

ARCHITECTURE

Since the beginning of time man, as a species, has needed a place to live. And though the dwelling space has changed radically, as have the building materials, the function remains the same. Our concept of architecture relates to the buildings that we inhabit and work within.

PREHISTORIC DWELLINGS

In Paleolithic times prehistoric people lived in cave dwellings. Eventually, rock huts called dolmans were built. These **dolmans** (Fig. 1.1) were nothing more than rock slabs placed together as walls and a roof, but they certainly fulfilled the purpose as a place of shelter and safety from an untamed environment. Thus the earliest form of architecture was created. As man became more domesticated and began living in settlements, his housing needs changed. People began building communal living quarters by constructing a fortification system made of branches, earth and rocks next to and on top of one another. These early settlements were built in close proximity to a fresh water supply. In addition, they protected the people from neighboring threats as their town grew. Another benefit of a permanent settlement was communal hunting, gathering and farming abilities. Many elements from early dwellings have remained. In cities today, many people live in what primitive man would have called communal quarters, modern day apartments.

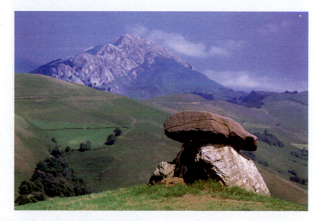

Fig. 1.1 The Gaystenia dolmen (photo) by Mendive, France/© SGM/The Bridgeman Art Library.

What is architecture? This chapter looks into the development of architecture from the dolmans to modern day skyscrapers. What is immediately apparent is how building materials have changed, styles have changed, and ways in which dwellings are built have changed. With all the changes, one thing has remained consistent; the basic function of the dwelling—living within and developing human comforts—has not changed that much since prehistoric times. The simple definition of architecture is: **a dwelling for human needs.**

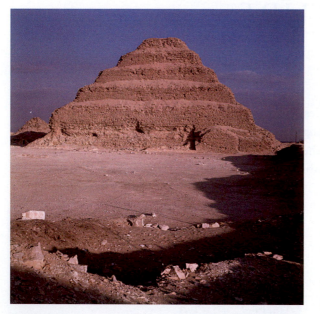

Fig. 1.2 Step Pyramid (Alistair Duncan © Dorling Kindersley).

EGYPTIAN PYRAMIDS

The early pyramids were made of **mud brick**, which is mud and straw mixed together, then formed into bricks and hardened in the sun. One of the earliest pyramids is that of King Djoser, a major ruler of Egypt's third dynasty. Djoser's pyramid (Fig. 1.2) is a **step pyramid**, so called because it rises out of the ground as if it were built in steps. To the Egyptians this type of pyramid appeared to hesitate as it rose to the sun god Ra. For the Egyptians, architecture was not necessarily focused on dwellings as homes, but rather as tombs, dwelling places for the dead.

The Step Pyramid of Djoser was designed by **Imhotep** whose name was found recorded on statues within the complex. Imhotep was an overseer to the pharaoh and must have been a very intelligent individual with great abilities. He was known as an astronomer and even a healer. Imhotep is regarded as the first architect and even today architects remember the important ideas and building style Imhotep began.

Successors to Djoser would move away from the step pyramid into the smooth sided pyramid that we are all familiar with today. Accomplishing this feat took several generations of architects. The pyramids' function was to house the dead pharaoh's **Ka** and keep the deceased protected to enjoy eternal life. The Ka was an individual's life-force, or their soul. The Egyptian philosophy was that *"life on Earth was a road to the grave."*

Gazing at the great pyramids (Fig. 1.3) of Egypt, particularly the pyramids of Giza built in the 4th dynasty (2575–2465 B.C.), they appear to lie dormant and silent across the vast desert. In reality they were not isolated structures at all; they were used as temples and places of rituals that were held during a pharaoh's lifetime and after. In fact, pyramids were placed within a funerary district called Necropolis as a sort of 'living quarters' for the deceased, along with their wives, families and servants, complete with all the accessories needed throughout eternity.

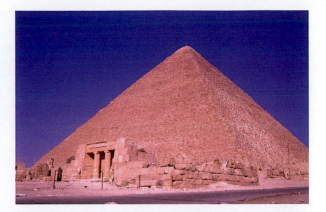

To attempt to understand how the Egyptians constructed these monumental tombs, modern day man was faced with a simple, yet astounding question: which came first, the height or the length? For centuries the answer was elusive. Finally, one day at Giza archeologists measuring the pyramid realized the length was two times height. The formula which most, if not all, pyramids are based on is summarized as:

Length or Base = 2 × Height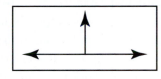

The mathematical formula is quickly found to be Pi or 3.14. Pi is most closely associated with the circle; however the circle fits inside the square. There has been much debate over the years on how the Egyptians arrived at a sophisticated mathematical equation for architectural dimensions. Some have speculated that aliens from outer space were involved. However, scientists have concluded that the Egyptians were very functional people who did not choose to overwork or burden themselves with unnecessary labor. They came up with the formula in their basic need to find the easiest way to build structures. Their construction methods consisted of log rollers, sand, levers and weights to position the stones into place.

The Great Pyramid at Giza is one of the earliest and largest pyramids ever built. Originally it would have had an outer casing of 'dressed' stone which has disappeared except for the middle pyramid, that of Kahfre. Dressed stone was used for the outer casing of the pyramid and sanded to a smooth finish. This gave the pyramid a very polished look versus the stepped-look that we see today. In the final stages of building the pyramid the Egyptians laid the stones in what looked like a step formation and then put a white soft stone on top. Then chiselers started at the top and smoothed the white stone, creating a flat sided tomb.

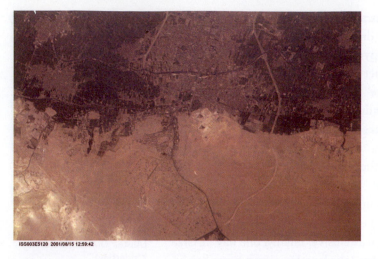

ISS003E5120 2001/08/15 12:59:42

Fig. 1.4 Pyramids at Giza seen from space station (Courtesy of Earth Sciences and Image Analysis Laboratory at Johnson Space Center).

The Great Pyramid has remarkable statistics. First, it was built 6,550 years ago on a thirteen acre base. This pyramid was the tallest structure built for 4,300 years. It was finally beat out by the Eiffel tower in 1889 and is still the largest stone structure ever built. Five of the world's largest cathedrals would fit inside the base of the Great Pyramid. They used 2.3 million blocks of stone, weighing an average of 2.5 tons each. Upon close inspection of the pyramids, one finds the stones have been chiseled so tightly together that a piece of tissue paper cannot be pressed between the stones. The Great Pyramid was originally 488 feet high. Today it stands 455 feet high and is equivalent to a 40-story skyscraper. In fact, the Great Pyramid is so large that when men landed on the moon in 1969 they saw the pyramid from the moon's surface (Fig. 1.4). It is estimated that it took 20 years to build with 100,000 laborers working at any given time. Although the Egyptians had and used slaves, it is believed the pyramids were built by farmers and local townspeople. Egyptians would have considered it a civic duty to the pharaoh; it would have been an honor to serve the pharaoh with hard labor.

As vast symbols of an ancient society, the pyramids served as a visible reminder of the wealth of the pharaoh and his kingdom. If it is true that pyramids are burial chambers and an attempt to safeguard the pharaoh's Ka, then they must be considered failures. Each pyramid housed thousands of precious objects of gold, and commodities to ensure the pharaoh would enjoy the same afterlife as was experienced on earth. Great care was taken to protect all of the valuables through trap doors, secret passageways and even false burial chambers. However, most pyramids were plundered within the first year of completion, perhaps by the very same people who built them. Workers, having built and finished the technical accomplishment, knew of their hidden secrets and false passageways. Most known pyramids were emptied of their vast treasures thousands of years ago. Although considered failures in regard to their function, the world will always marvel at the size, the accomplishment, and the design of one of the great wonders of the world. In fact, the Great Pyramid at Giza is the only surviving wonder of the 7 Wonders of the Ancient World. To have built something 6,500 years ago that today remains among the largest structures built is testimony to Egyptian civilization's efforts and beliefs in an after-life. (www.unmuseum.org/wonders.htm)

Shortly after the great pyramids were built, architects began design-ing smaller pyramids, even placing them in the sides of mountains and hills in an attempt to make them more secure. The goal was to create a tomb that could be hidden rather than exposed for all to find. Today we realize there are many pyramids around Giza and the Valley of the Kings near Thebes that were built in this way. Interestingly, the only tomb found still completely intact was that of **Tutankhamen**, as it was buried in and below the side of a hill.

ARCHITECTURE OF THE GREEKS

Early significant temples of the Greek culture were shrines to protect their gods. Unlike the Egyptian temples, the Greeks temples were not tombs. They were places for worship and celebrations honoring their many gods. The buildings were conceived as sculptures that evoke human responses, which was not an architectural concept. As architecture developed, more adornment was added to the temples, until it was believed that the gods embodied the temples themselves. The Greeks even increased the impor-tance of the temples by placing them on elevated sites. The temples were built with much embellishment and sculptures on the outside. The inside of the temple usually housed the god for which that temple was erected. The temples were not a place for public worship but rather generally reserved for the high priests and their rituals.

One of the interesting manifestations of Greek Art (Architecture) was a wide ranging series of issues regarding humanistic and reli-gious questions. The Greek civilization believed strongly that order and disorder were all part of this world's existence. Many aspects of Greek life dealt in those oppositions. For example, **Order** which represents the cosmos was the opposite of **Disorder**, or chaos. These opposites are a constant in Greek culture.

It was the Greeks who developed order in architecture (Fig. 1.5). These orders created pro-portion in architecture, sculpture and pottery. Our country's capitol, Wash-ington, D.C., looked to these Orders to build a foundation that would reflect the ideas started by the Greeks centuries ago.

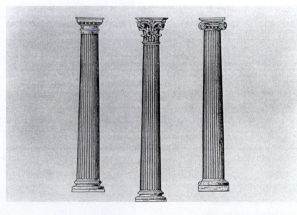

Fig. 1.5 The three orders of architecture
(Courtesy of the Library of Congress).

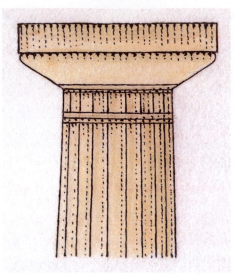

Fig. 1.6 Doric order column (Rob Shone © Dorling Kindersley).

The **Doric order** (Fig. 1.6) is considered a masculine order. It is the oldest order and can hold the most weight of all the orders. Doric columns are found on the outside of Greek buildings where they wanted emphasis to be placed. It originated from the Dorian people who came from islands off the coast of Greece. Doric architecture refers to the standard that constitutes the outside of any Doric building. When looking at the Doric column, the **capital**, which is the top of the column, is simple with no adornment. The column has no base and rests directly on the **platform**. A platform is generally the base foundation of a building upon which the column would sit. Doric columns are marked by 20 shallow vertical grooves known as **flutes**. The Doric column tapers radically at the top to give the appearance of stability. The Greeks called this **refinement**.

A prime example of the Doric order is the **Parthenon** (Fig. 1.7), the largest temple on the Greek mainland. It was dedicated to the virgin goddess Athena, the patron of the city of Athens. The word "Parthenon" means "The Virgin's Place," and refers to a particular room inside the Parthenon where the goddess' statue stood. Construction was started in 447 B.C. and completed in 432 B.C. Iktinos and Kallikrates, along with a

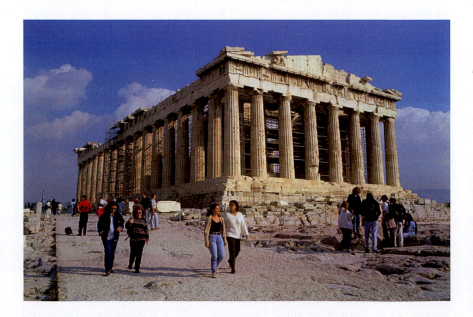

Fig. 1.7 Greece, Athens. Parthenon is located on Acropolis (Copyright © Rob Reichenfeld/Dorling Kindersley).

designer, Phidians were the architects of the Parthenon temple. The Parthenon measures an impressive 228 feet by 101 feet. The Parthenon is a typical Greek structure with several stairs that lead up to the Doric columns. The tapering at the top of the column is visible even in photographs. This temple is somewhat unconventional in that the floor is convex to allow drainage of weather elements. The graceful balance of the structure is still evident even in its ruined state. It was a building of festivals and great celebration.

The Parthenon has an unusual significance, as it is the only temple known to have served four different faiths. After its demise as a temple for Athena, it became a Byzantine church then a Catholic church. During those early Christian years, a statue of the Virgin Mary replaced the statue of Athena. It became a Turkish mosque in the 1400's. The Ottoman Turks then used it as an ammunition dump. It was severely damaged on September 26, 1687 when it was bombed by Venetians.

The next order is **Ionic** (Fig. 1.8) which originated in the mid 6th century B.C. in the southwest coastland settled by Ionian Greeks where an Ionian dialect was spoken. The Ionic order was perfected in the 5th century B.C. by mainland Greeks. The Ionic column is believed to have its origins in Egyptian architectural papyrus half columns called **pilasters**. Ionic columns are lighter and more graceful than Doric columns; they lack the muscular quality of the Doric columns. The Ionic column has a **volute**, a scroll-like capital, and a small base at the bottom. The column is more slender and holds less weight than its Doric counterpart. It is more fluid than Doric, meaning that this style works better within the architecture. It remains more flexible and its features are more striking than that of the Doric order. The longer lasting Ionic column at the Temple of Artemis at Ephesus was one of the 7 Wonders of the Ancient World.

The **Erechtheum** (Fig. 1.9A) is an excellent example of the Ionic order. It served several religious functions in ancient times, mainly because it housed four rooms. The exact purpose of each room has long been disputed. The Erechtheum has an irregular shape because of the sloping sight on which it was built. Interestingly, it features a side porch with female statues as columns. These female figures are called **Caryatids**

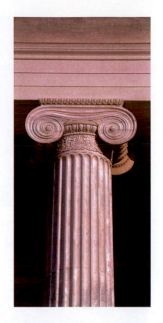

Fig. 1.8 Ionic order column (Nigel Hicks © Dorling Kindersley).

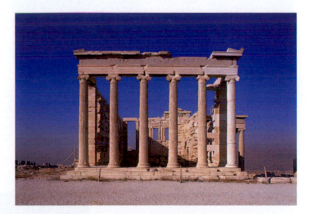

Fig. 1.9A Erechtheum (Courtesy of Rob Reichenfeld/Dorling Kindersley. Copyright © Archaeological Receipts Fund [TAP]).

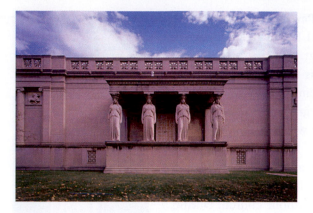

Fig. 1.9B Caryatids
(Copyright © Andrew Leyerle/
Dorling Kindersley).

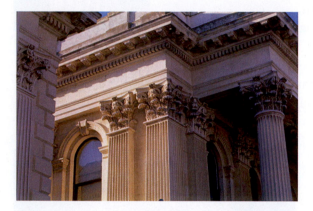

Fig. 1.10 Corinthian order
column
(Lloyd Park © Dorling
Kindersley).

(Fig. 1.9B). A Caryatid is a sculpted female figure serving as an architectural support replacing the traditional column. The term Caryatid literally means "maidens of Karyai." These figures are draped and posed from archaic Greece. The porch is a structure attached to the temple, forming a covered entrance to a vestibule or doorway.

All six of the Caryatids which help support the roof of the southern porch have been removed for preservation and replaced by copies.

The final order, **Corinthian,** (Fig. 1.10) did not appear until after the 5th century B.C. and actually appeared on the inside of the temple before it was used on the outside. The Corinthian column is considered the feminine order, the counterpart to the Doric order because it holds very little weight. Its **capital** is very ornate with a small base at the bottom. The Corinthian order's name is derived from the Greek city of Corinth, though it first appeared externally at Athens. Although it is of Greek origin, the Corinthian order was actually seldom used in Greek architecture. It came into its own in Roman practice. The Corinthian order came to be used as the standard order in most Roman buildings such as the Pantheon (Fig. 1.11).

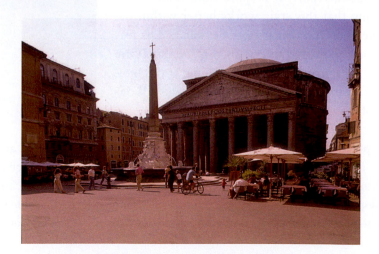

Fig. 1.11 Pantheon
(Copyright © John Heseltine/
Dorling Kindersley).

Over the centuries these three orders have been considered the true basis for architecture worldwide. As well as creating the three orders, Greek architects formulated sets of proportions that are in perfect agreement. They had achieved near perfection by creating a harmony of nature in their architecture and in their art. Later architects would use these standards to create buildings with new dynamics. Today, modern architects cannot surpass but only adapt what the ancient Greeks once perfected.

ROMAN ARCHITECTURE

The Romans, who saw themselves as the divinely appointed rulers of the world, admired the Greeks for their art and architecture; they wanted to create their own style. Building on the Greek influence and philosophy of functionality of architecture, the Romans made great strides in architecture and made buildings more suitable for the needs of man.

One of their greatest contributions to modern civilization is their architecture and city planning. The most ingenious artists tremendously gifted in planning and organization found an outlet and excelled in creating large architectural structures. The Romans exceeded in urban design, creating new systemized construction methods which allowed them to build utilitarian and civic structures on a large scale. These were gathering places for people to talk about the news, apartment structures where they lived, even public bath houses.

The enormous impact of Romans on our culture is the result of their industrious determination to fulfill their mission as they spread their culture from the north of England to Africa and from Spain to India. At one point it was thought that Rome controlled one-third of the known world. Rome was a well planned city where people wanted to live. They enjoyed the luxuries the city offered with its modern design. The Romans knew that if the people were well cared for, they would be happy citizens, and the military force could lessen its hold over them. They knew well planned cities would maintain peace and increase security at the same time. This plan for good government resulted in more time for military accomplishments.

An extraordinary architectural element that the Romans would adapt was the arch. It was the Romans who would maximize the functionality of arches, although Greeks and previous cultures had used the arch to some degree. The Romans excelled in architectural designs for everyday use. The plan was to establish individual family apartments with a cooking area, living space, and separate sleeping quarters.

A particularly impressive innovation was the plan to bring water into the city for everyday use. Water was plentiful in the mountains anywhere from five miles to thirty-five miles away from the city. Water needed to be brought into the city free flowing and in constant supply to bath houses and to various other locations within the city for drinking and cooking. The Romans' answer to the water problem was the **aqueduct** (Fig. 1.12). The aqueduct is a water supply or navigable channel constructed to convey water. In modern engineering the term is used for any system of pipes, ditches, canals and other structures used for this purpose. To more restrict the use, aqueduct applies to any bridge or viaduct that transports water across a large gap. Remarkably, these large aqueducts are currently in use in the United States to supply some of our country's biggest cities. For example the Catskill Aqueduct carries water to New York City over a distance of 120 miles. The Catskill Aqueduct is dwarfed by aqueducts in the western half of our country, most notably the Colorado River Aqueduct which supplies the Los Angeles area with water from the Colorado River 248 miles away. These otherwise uninhabitable waterless areas are made into productive cities because of the use of Roman ingenuity. The water was contained in the aqueduct until it arrived in the city where it was distributed to numerous access locations throughout the city. The slope of the aqueduct from the mountain to the city was the secret of maintaining gravity to move the water along. The arch was used to its full potential in the aqueduct, none more impressive than the Pont du Gard (Fig. 1.13) in the southern part of France.

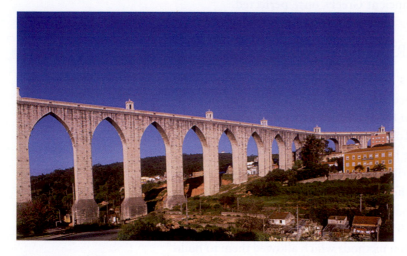

Fig. 1.12 Aqueduct (Linda Whitwam © Dorling Kindersley).

Commissioned by Marcus Agrippa to carry water over thirty miles, the **Pont du Gard** has proven its astonishing durability; it is still in use today, roughly two thousand years later. This aqueduct uses all three orders: the Doric on the bottom, Ionic in the middle and Corinthian on top. In this structure the arch replaces the column, and the weight being carried determines the order. The Doric arch is heavy and holds all the weight, while the Corinthian order is much smaller holding only its own weight. The Pont du Gard aqueduct was built approximately fifty feet in the air in order to keep warring factions from blocking water flow and holding the city captive.

Where the Greeks gave us exteriors, the Romans gave us impressive interior spaces. The **Pantheon** (Fig. 1.14) is an amazing Roman engineering feat. It is the only ancient building still in use today. It is made of brick and concrete, a material developed and perfected by the Romans. The Pantheon's design is a combination of simple geometric elements—a circle and a rectangle. It was built as a pagan church to house the seven planetary gods. The word "Pantheon" means "every god" and was a temple for all of the gods of ancient Rome. People speculate that the name comes from the statues of gods placed around the building, or from the resemblance of the dome to the heavens. In 609 A.D. the pope removed the pagan images and replaced them with Christian symbols. Today it is a Christian church.

Since the Renaissance the Pantheon has been used as a tomb. Among those buried there are the painters Raphael and Carracci, the composer Corelli and the architect Peruzzi. Also interesting, architect Brunelleschi

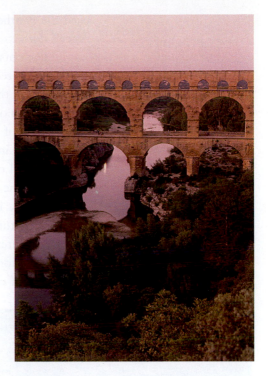

Fig. 1.13 Pont du Gard (Max Alexander © Dorling Kindersley).

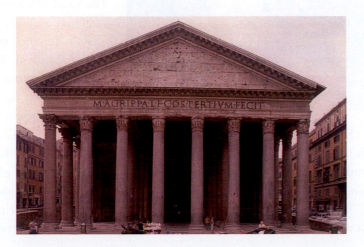

Fig. 1.14 Pantheon (Copyright © Mike Dunning/ Dorling Kindersley).

used the Pantheon as an influence when designing the Cathedral of Florence's dome.

The outside of the Pantheon consists of two parts: the rectangular traditional Greek temple **portico**, or front porch, with massive granite columns, and the circular **rotunda**. The building is circular with a portico of three ranks of huge granite Corinthian columns (8 in the first rank, and two groups of 4 columns behind) under a pediment opening into the rotunda. The inside space gives way to a **coffered** (concrete dome) vault with a central opening, known as an oculus, to the sky. The height from the floor to the oculus and the diameter of the interior circle are the same measurement, 142 feet. It was and remains today an impressive yet odd looking structure.

The interior is awe-inspiring with an enormous domed rotunda, the construction of which was made possible by the slow drying concrete. 5,000 tons of concrete was used during construction in a small span of

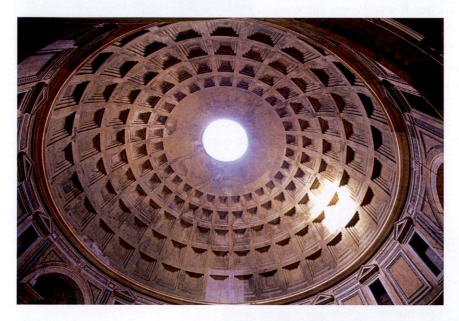

space, 150 feet. It was the largest dome in the world for 18 centuries. The huge domed interior space gives way to form and function. The **vault,** or ceiling, is approximately four feet thick at the top to ensure against collapse. The vault has a **coffered** design, (Fig. 1.15) which means sunken panels, that creates a lighter appearance as one looks up. A ceiling made of stone is known as a

Fig. 1.15, 1.16, 1.17 Pantheon Interior Coffered Ceiling and Oculus (Copyright © Cosmo Condina/Stock Connection).

vault (Fig. 1.16) in architecture. At the top is an **oculus**, (Fig. 1.17, 17A) which is a round opening in the ceiling. The oculus serves to let light in the building. The Romans did not insert windows in the walls of their buildings because they feared it would undermine its structural integrity.

The Pantheon construction was started in 27B.C. by Agrippa to reflect a celestial order. The hole in the ceiling (oculus), was conceived as a sundial that symbolized the union between earth and heaven. The opening is a huge 29 feet across and is the only light source and source of fresh air for the building. The base of the opening is 29 feet across made of hard basalt stone. It is the only five feet across at the top opening, which is made of lightweight pumice concrete. The oculus lets in the rain and snow that drains into well hidden drain holes integrated into the floor pattern.

Today the dome shape in architecture represents the heavens in churches throughout the world. The Pantheon holds the original majestic dome that Christian churches are known for today. The arch, vault and dome are used in one building to show the strength and durability of Roman design and genius.

The arch became an essential element in Roman architecture, emphasizing strength while creating massive usable space. The **Coliseum** (Fig. 1.18), the sports center of the city, was such a building. It was capable of seating 50,000 spectators. It was an oval shaped structure with a center floor that was sunken several feet to allow stadium seating up to four stories high. The stage area of the floor was covered with wooden boards, sand and straw to collect the blood and gore left behind by contests and public spectacles. The Coliseum had restrooms and snack bars. People would purchase tickets in the form of cracked pottery shells and had an assigned seat with ramps and stairways to allow the 50,000

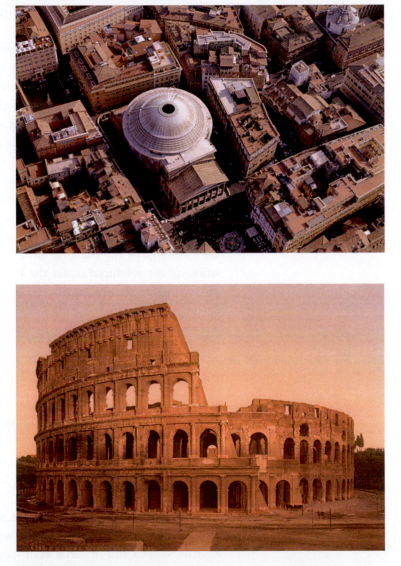

Fig. 1.17A Pantheon in Rome, World Heritage Site, Italy (Georg Gerster/Photo Researchers, Inc.).

Fig. 1.18 Coliseum (Library of Congress).

spectators to enter and exit efficiently. Some of the exhibitions displayed at the Coliseum were Gladiator games, mock sea battles, executions, re-enactments of famous battles, along with, dramas from classical mythology. It is estimated that about 500,000 people and over 1 million animals died in coliseum solely for the enjoyment of the crowd. During its inauguration alone it is estimated that over 9,000 wild animals were killed.

The Coliseum was built entirely by using the arches that integrate and unite the design by rhythmic horizontal and vertical repetition. This creates an aesthetically interesting overall design. Many modern professional buildings reflect the design of the Roman Coliseum.

Concrete was used very efficiently by the Romans, though they weren't certain it would stand the test of time. Thus, it was used mostly on the foundation and walls. With all the revolutionized architecture, the Romans were able to build over large areas using load-bearing structures. Before the discovery of concrete, architecture was simply a structural mass, but now space could be designed and manipulated to whatever form was required. The Romans' ingenuity assured the ability to meet structural needs for the design of any building form. The term 'Roman' may be used for all works of art produced under the Roman rule, but architecture sets them apart from their predecessors and counterparts. The world learned from the Romans and developed plans based off their buildings. When the Christians were ready to build churches, architecture was ready and waiting.

ROMANESQUE ARCHITECTURE

In 323 A.D. Constantine the Great made a fateful decision that affects us even today. He made Christianity an official religion. He decided to move the Roman Empire to the Greek town of Byzantium and renamed the town Constantinople. Today it is called Istanbul. These early churches were called **Romanesque**, identifying them as a debased form of Roman architecture.

When Christianity became the official religion, Jesus' status changed also. Christians needed a place to worship and the combination of the Roman Basilica and Imperial Hall would make the transverse design. The basilica plan featured a long hall with side aisles to house the worshippers. The first church built was Old St. Peter's church built from 324–400 A.D. (Fig. 1.19) (called 'old' because it was completely replaced by a new building in the sixteenth century) in Rome over the grave of St. Peter. It would be the monumental building to house the spiritual leader that later would become the Pope. The long basilica type church had four side aisles, two on each side of the **nave,** or main body of the church. The nave was lined with columns to support the structure. A **transept,** a crossing of the nave at a right angle to form a cross, would meet the needs in terms of space for the large numbers of worshippers. This church held 14,000 worshippers and remained the largest Christian church until the 11th century. It illustrate the various elements of the church, from the **atrium, narthex,** nave, transept and **apse** in the rear of the church. The worshipper would enter the church from the west and move towards the east, the direction Jesus would rise on judgment day.

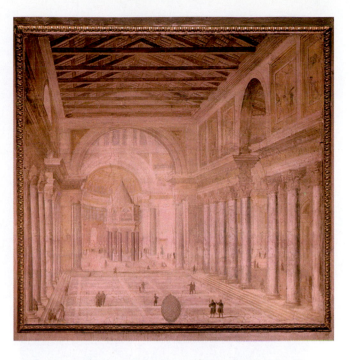

Fig. 1.19 Old St. Pete's Cathedral (Courtesy of Scala/ Art Resource, NY).

The term Romanesque Architecture stems from the medieval Europe characterized by rounded arched. There is no exact beginning date of the Romanesque style, but many agree it began sometime between the 6th and 10th centuries. Each building is known by its massive quality, its thick walls, rounded arches, barrel vaults, large towers and decorative facades. These buildings are frequently symmetrical in plan giving the overall appearance of simplicity.

At the beginning of the eleventh century Europe was experiencing many changes with a feudal system and an economy based on labor and trade. The one power that remained strong was the Christian church. It had been perfecting its spiritual and temporal power. The **cathedral,** a grander building that appeared to rise to the heavens, was used as the seat of the Bishop.

These massive cathedrals were needed across Europe because of the unprecedented growth in the number of worshipers traveling from one cathedral to the next seeking out the relics housed in each of the different cathedrals. These worshipers were called pilgrims. They would wear a typical pilgrim hat and a cockle shell around their waist as a common symbol of their humility. One of the beginning places of pilgrimage was Santiago de Compostela in Spain. From there the pilgrims would travel

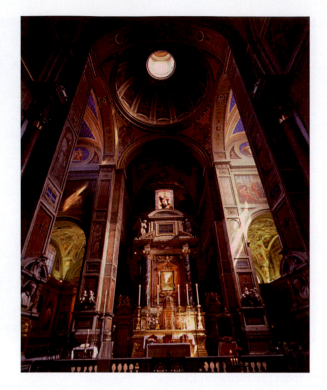

Fig. 1.20 Romanesque rounded arches
(Courtesy of Oliviero Olivieri/Getty Images).

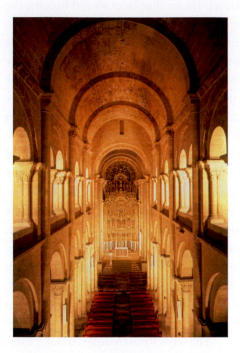

Fig. 1.21 Barrel vault. Old Cathedral,
Coimbra, Portugal
(Courtesy of Paulo Magalhaes/Getty Images).

on one of several pilgrimage trails. Some of the more famous pilgrimage routes were Canterbury in England and Speyer in Germany. Relics were often stolen from their cathedrals. In order to protect the relics, a military order was created known as Knights Templar.

Relics were often religious items from the past that medieval people thought held miraculous power. Today notable relics are the head of John the Baptist, the arm of St. Steven, a piece of wood from the true cross, the tunic of the Virgin Mary and the bones of St. Mary Magdalene. The pilgrims thought these relics could heal their ailments and forgive them of their sins. The more important the relic, the more important the cathedral became. The town would prosper from the large number of pilgrims traveling from place to place.

As the faithful began going on pilgrimages, towns of 1,500 built churches that would hold as many as 10,000 pilgrims who came to worship in their Cathedral. Romanesque churches were designed with rounded arches (Fig. 1.20) and blunt heavy walls with geometric regularity that resembled ancient Roman architecture. They had an overall blocky appearance with simple geometric masses of rectangles, cubes and squares. The massive blunt heavy buildings were appreciated for their strength, acoustical properties and the fire resistance of their masonry. The rounded vaults helped carry the sound from one end of the church to the other. The vaults were a series of rounded arches butted up to each other creating a **barrel vault** (Fig. 1.21) that became a standard in the Romanesque churches. The stone ceilings created another problem of support. The vault was so heavy it would crush the walls. The medieval architects supported the weight by building thick massive interior supports called **buttresses** (Fig. 1.22) The buttressing reinforced the walls at critical points and allowed for the walls to be taller. Most Romanesque churches are built with two levels, the nave and the **ambulatory** (Fig. 1.23) or covered walkway. The ambulatory was located on the second level and went around the church from the nave to the apse. The space was approximately 8 feet wide. The ambulatory was not only a place of worship but was also a means of crowd control allowing people to move from one place to another in the overcrowded church. The interior columns were massive as well, supporting much of the interior weight while the buttresses supported the outer weight of the stone ceiling.

The Saint Sernin church (Fig. 1.24) in Toulouse, France is a typical example of the blocky Romanesque architecture and its characteristics. The ceiling is vaulted with a single rib, which was a new innovation in supporting and distributing the weight of the barrel vaulted ceiling. Saint Sernin has characteristics common to most Romanesque churches: geometric regularity within the structure, a rounded vault, rounded arches, and buttressing within the walls for support. The Saint Sernin is a former abbey church and was rebuilt in the Romanesque style sometime around 1080 to 1120. It is located on the site of a previous basilica from the 4th century which contained the body of Saint Sernin, the first bishop of Toulouse in circa 250. The basilica contains a large three-manual

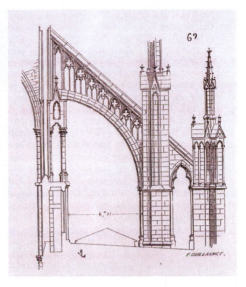

Fig. 1.22 Romanesque cathedral buttress illustration
(RIBA Library Photographs Collection).

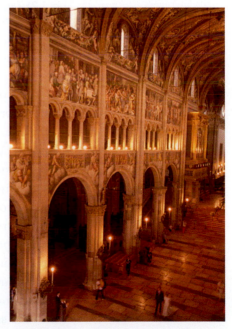

Fig. 1.23 Romanesque second level, ambulatory
(©Bob Sacha/Corbis).

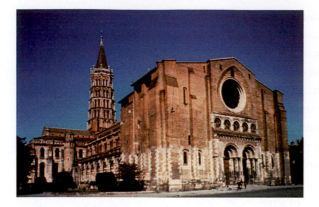

Fig. 1.24 Saint Sernin
(Courtesy of The French Government Tourist Office).

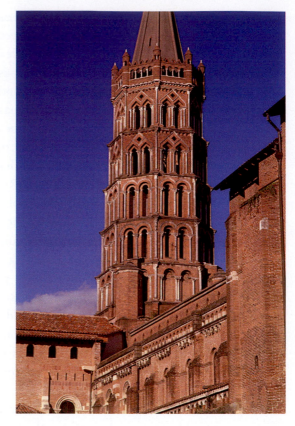

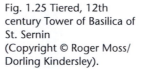

Fig. 1.25 Tiered, 12th
century Tower of Basilica of
St. Sernin
(Copyright © Roger Moss/
Dorling Kindersley).

Cavaille-Coll pipe organ built in 1888; this is considered to be one of the most important organs in all of France.

The exterior of most Romanesque churches have different roof levels that set off the nave and the transept against the side aisles. This causes the relationships of the exterior aesthetics to be enhanced. At the crossing of the transept and nave, a tower, which is called the **lantern,** allows light to filter in over the altar (Fig. 1.25). The blunt heavy architectural features of the buttressing within the outer walls are visible as square columns that act as supports. Behind the altar at the east end of the church is the apse, which originated with the secular Roman basilica. The apse is usually raised as the altar area is generally raised which sets apart this semi-circular architectural feature. Around the apse area there are **radiating chapels,** which are small rooms around the apse. Throughout Romanesque cathedrals the windows are generally small with rounded arches and are emphasized by decorative framing. The overall shape of the Romanesque cathedral is that of a Latin cross. In Latin cross construction the length is longer than the width.

The interior of Romanesque churches are dark except where the lantern creates a light-filled altar area. The vaulting of the nave served several purposes, among them elimination of a fire hazard and creating a temperature control system. Romanesque architecture explored the limits of the possible versus the impossible both structurally and aesthetically. Each element used in construction strained to make the nave as tall as possible.

GOTHIC CATHEDRALS

Gothic architecture represents an outpouring of labor, skill and faith. This is a style of architecture which flourished during the height of the medieval period. It evolved from Romanesque architecture and would be succeeded by Renaissance architecture. Originating in France lasting into the 15th century, Gothic architecture was known during this period as "The French Style." The term Gothic first appeared during the latter part of the Renaissance as an insult to its characteristics including pointed arches, rib-groin vaults and flying buttressing. There was a tremendous sense of change; nowhere was that change felt more strongly than in architecture. The population was booming and more space was needed for worship. In the short time span during the height of the Gothic period (1100–1300 approximately), more stone was quarried than in all of Egypt's reign (almost 8,000 years). During that time more than 100 cathedrals and thousands of churches were built.

Gothic cathedrals featured pointed arches with **ribbed-groin vaults** (Fig. 1.26). Massive Romanesque walls gave way to an illusion of weightlessness where the walls seem to disappear giving one a sense of being in God's heavenly kingdom. The once dark cathedral became a vast

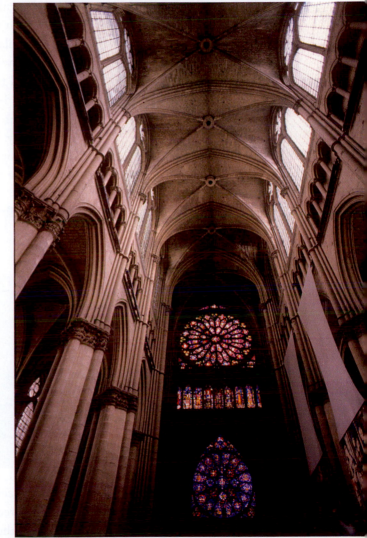

Fig. 1.26 Rib Groin Vault (Courtesy of Vanni/ Art Resource, NY).

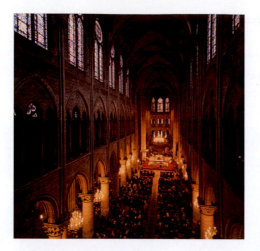

Fig. 1.27 Notre Dame Clerestory
(Photo by Bruce Dale/National Geographic/
Getty Images).

space filled with light because of large windows in the third story elevation called **clerestory** (Fig. 1.27) or clear-story of windows. The ambulatory or second elevation, of the Romanesque cathedral was replaced with a **triforium**, which is no longer a covered walkway but more of an aesthetic decoration to the cathedral. The triforium is a shallow gallery of arches within the thickness of the inner wall, which stands above the nave in a church or cathedral. The ambulatory was used as a place of worship and crowd control, whereas a triforium is a much narrower passage. The word triforium is derived from Latin *tres (*3) indicating a third level within the Gothic structure. People would no longer worship on the triforium as they did on the ambulatory. The heavy buttressing that supported the massive weight of the stone vault was now moved to the outside of the church and was called **flying buttressing** (Fig. 1.28).

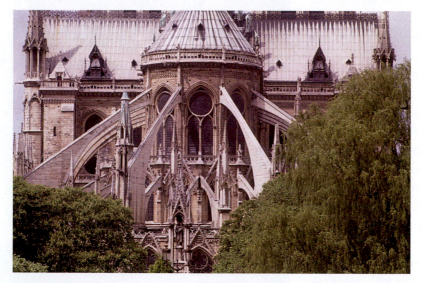

Fig. 1.28 Flying buttress
(Neil Lukas © Dorling
Kindersley).

Flying buttressing is a two part structural system. Where buttressing was previously within the exterior wall of Romanesque churches it is now moved to the outside of the building attached to an arm (flying) which pushed against the side of the wall supporting the weight of the vault. This allowed the interior space to appear as if the architect had created a weightless environment. The Gothic architect was now free to create walls of vast windows from floor to ceiling. To enhance the light, they used stained glass to create multicolored interiors representing the heavens. The Gothic cathedrals still used the geometric regularity of the Romanesque as a standard measure for creating the overall dimension of the building.

The new development of flying buttressing created a whole new dimension in architecture. Medieval man was no longer restrained by massive thick walls but rather was able to create very thin translucent walls or even could give the illusion that the walls had disappeared. The columns flanked on either side of the nave and side aisles were more slender than those of the Romanesque. The stone ceiling still provided a major obstacle for the architect. The solution was to put the heavy stone columns, buttress, on the outside of the building with arms spanning to the buttressing as a support from the straining weight of the vaulted ceiling. These structures were called "heavy bones" or a structural skeleton. Immediately people saw the flying buttressing as ugly and distracting to the outside aesthetics of the cathedral. Today they are considered beautiful and pleasing to the eye, a marvel of medieval construction techniques.

The most famous Gothic cathedral is actually part Romanesque but mostly Gothic. **Notre Dame** (Fig. 1.29) was designed as a Romanesque church, but as construction was underway, the Gothic era began and the architects changed the design into Gothic. Notre Dame is one of the most famous buildings in architectural history, with its curious mixture of old and new elements. Construction began in 1163 and was finished almost a century later. Notre Dame has all the standard elements of Gothic architecture including a triforium, a clerestory, pointed arches and, of course, the use of flying buttressing to support the nave walls. The lantern is still there, however, it is much thinner because its function is less important, due to the clerestory than it would have been in a Romanesque church. Another new feature is that the transept is much shorter. The west **façade**, which is the outer wall of a building, houses two large bell towers. The entrance contains three sets of doors that allow for large numbers to enter but also is a symbol of the trinity. The west façade has some basic features of Gothic design, that being reinforced corners of the towers, the façade divided into three main parts and the three story elevation of the church. The Notre Dame cathedral is rich with sculptural design around the façade.

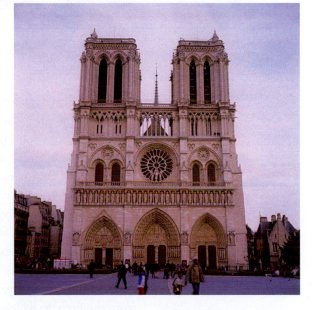

Fig. 1.29 Notre Dame Entrance (Courtesy of Panoramic Images/Getty Images).

The vast expanse and complexity of the flying buttresses around the nave and apse area are visible. These flying buttresses allow the interior of Notre Dame (Fig. 1.30) to achieve its characteristic light and airy appearance. Another standard feature of Gothic cathedrals is the use of **gargoyles**

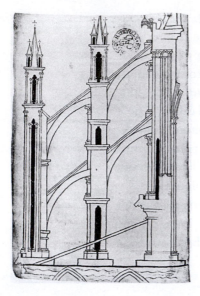

Fig. 1.30 Flying buttress illustration
(Library of Congress).

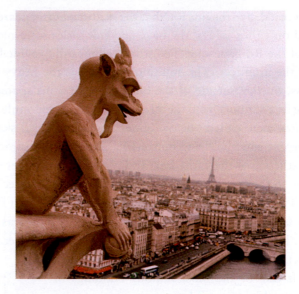

Fig. 1.31 Notre Dame Gargoyle
(Courtesy of Photodisc/Getty Images).

(Fig. 1.31). These give the appearance of demons, but are actually a method to convey the rain water away from the side of the building. Preventing rain water from ruining the masonry walls is important because the running water erodes the mortar between the stone blocks. Architects often used multiple gargoyles to divide the flow of rain water off the roof to minimize the potential damage from a rain storm. A trough is cut in the back of the gargoyle typically allowing the water to exit through the open mouth. Gargoyles are usually an elongated fantastic animal because the length of the gargoyle determines how far the water is thrown from the wall. When gothic flying buttresses were used, aqueducts were sometimes cut into the buttress to divert water over the aisle walls. The term gargoyle originates from the French, which originally meant throat or gullet, which represents the gurgling sound, made when large amounts of water pass through the opening. Gargoyles were thought to spiritually and symbolically wash the church from evil by allowing water to pour out of their mouths.

Skyscrapers

The business leaders of our industrial world presented a new problem for architects to solve during the early decades of the 20th century. As architects looked to the future, a new philosophy was needed to take advantage of the latest building techniques and materials that were available to the modern architect. With the advent of the industrial revolution large cities grew at such a rapid rate that new innovations in business housing were needed. How would architects allievate the overcrowded conditions the large cities were experiencing? Stack 'em up! An inventor, Henry Bessemer began a process of mass producing steel, essentially beginning the development of skyscrapers during the early to mid 1800's. William Kelly had a patent for a system of air-blowing the carbon out of pig iron, another method of steel production. Kelly would later sell his patent to Bessemer who developed it further into a decarbonization process utilizing the blast of air around 1855. Modern steel is based on Bessemer's process. George Fuller worked on solving problems of load bearing capacities of tall buildings. He created the first structure where the outside walls did not carry the weight of the building. Using Bessemer's steel beams Fuller was able to create steel cages that would support the weight in the tall buildings we know as skyscrapers. The term "Skyscraper" was coined during the 1880's after the first 10–20 story buildings were built in the United States. This was made possible by the innovations of steel structure, elevators, central heating, electrical plumbing pumps and the telephone. Skyscrapers began to dominate the American skyline at the turn of the century. This quest to shape modern society for the better, however, created many problems from faulty engineering to structural problems based on architecturally abstract ideas. The United States didn't share the excitement of skyscrapers until the 1920's with the impact of the International Style. When the skyscraper was envisioned it caused a stir among modern architects in Europe and around the world as the embodiment of an idea born in America. Very quickly architecture became an American form based on the skyscrapers of the 1930's, the most famous of which are the Empire State Building (Fig. 1.32) in New York and Willis Tower, formerly Sears Tower (Fig. 1.33) in Chicago.

An innovation that caused skyscrapers to become a reality was something created by a little known individual by the name of Elisha Otis who had invented the elevator in 1853 and went on to perfect an automated stopping safety feature. It is estimated that the equivalent of the world's population travel in Otis elevators, escalators and moving walkways every three

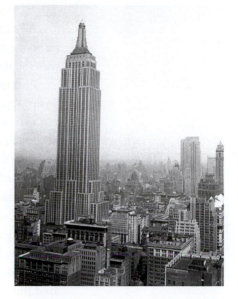

Fig. 1.32 The Empire State Building—New York City
(Courtesy of AP Images).

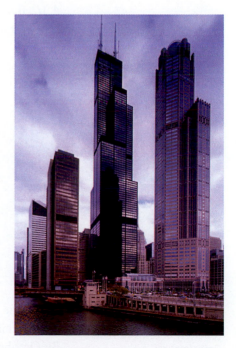

Fig. 1.33 Willis Tower, Chicago.
(Copyright © Andrew Leyerle/ Dorling Kindersley).

days. Once architects utilized the elevator along with modern day materials their imagination was unlimited. Before the elevator, a five to ten story building was the extent of the height of a building mainly because that was the number of floors anyone would want to climb by stairs.

Another important element discovered was that of the I-beam as a basic structural member. I-beams are commonly made of structural steel but may also be made from aluminum or other materials. The most common type of I-beam is the rolled steel joist because they are available in a wide variety of standard sizes. Common attributes to I-beams are deflection or stiffness of the I-beam, vibration or the stiffness chosen to prevent unacceptable vibrations particularly in offices, and bending failures by buckling sideways or through the entire structural beam. The I-beam could rise along the entire height of a building creating the skeletal structure that would be hidden from viewers. The effect would be similar to the Gothic cathedrals where the space seemed to give way to height. The harmony created through these ideals is the results of the underlying characteristics of modern architecture.

On March 17, 1930 construction on the Empire State Building began (Fig. 1.34). The building's steel frame was constructed at a rate of 4 1/2 floors per week. Interestingly, the building's main components were built in factories and later put together on site. This was done to facilitate the speed of construction. It is estimated that 60,000 tons of steel was brought in from Pennsylvania 300 miles away, by trains, barges and trucks. The Empire State Building was built during the depression as a competition between two corporate giants to see which could build the tallest building. The architect was chosen because his design was influenced by a common everyday item, the pencil. William Lamb, the architect, was inspired by its clean simple lines to design the modern skyscraper. He also decided that he would not use stone but opted for the newly invented steel I-beam method of construction. The steel cages were covered by a skin of stone, giving the building a more traditional appearance. Another element used was aluminum because of its lightweight yet durable construction panels. By October of 1930, 88 floors had been finished. The top floors have a

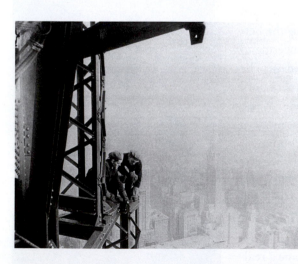

Fig. 1.34 Construction of the Empire State Building (Courtesy of Lewis W. Hine/ Getty Images).

very distinctive tower of glass, steel and aluminum. That tower today is roughly 200 feet high. When originally constructed the Empire State Building was topped with a mooring mast for dirigible landing. Dirigibles are more commonly known as Blimps. After several unsuccessful attempts, it was apparent that the wind speed at an elevation of 1,350 feet created conditions considered too hazardous. Today the mast is a TV tower. The Empire State Building is a modern marvel that still intrigues people from around the world.

As the flying buttress was to Gothic architecture, the steel beams were to the Eiffel Tower (Fig. 1.35) with its exposed structure embodies the 19th century belief in technological progress made possible from the Gothic era by Gustave Eiffel. The Eiffel Tower dominates the skyline in Paris as the towers of Notre Dame had before. The Eiffel Tower, which at the time of its construction was the tallest structure in the world, was built for the Universal Exposition of 1889. Eiffel won a competition for his design of a monument that would symbolize the French industrial revolution. The public loved the tower but it was hated by architects and artists, who considered it ugly and useless. It is composed of iron reinforced by four huge legs and trussed arches (bracing). An elevator allows passengers to go to the top 984 feet high.

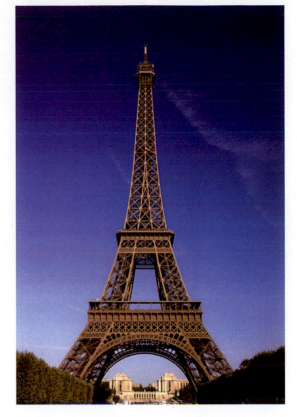

Fig. 1.35 Eiffel Tower (Courtesy of Photodisc/ Getty Images).

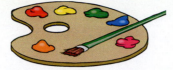

Name: _____

Class time: _____

Chapter 1 Homework
Architecture
50 Points Possible

Complete **one** of the following three projects. **Staple** all additional papers to this page. (**No bent corner-type attachments accepted**). Check which project you are completing.

Size restrictions: 8½ × 11 only. All work MUST be typed using complete sentences and correct punctuation to earn full credit.

Project 1: _____ **Design A Pyramid**

In your own words, write a paragraph explaining why the pyramids are considered a failure if they are still standing today and how your design would be better. Be as detailed as possible (25 points possible)

Design your own unique pyramid with interior views of each room, including booby traps, secret passages and whatever is necessary to keep your mummy happy (if your mummy ain't happy, no one's happy). (25 points possible)

Explanation 25 points possible	
Drawing Criteria 25 points possible	
Total Points	

Project 2: _____ **Greek Order Architecture**

Find and attach an image of a modern day building, built in the last 100 years that uses the Greek orders of architecture (one building for each order—30 points possible). Along with the images include: the name of each building, its location, year it was built and the architect. (5 points possible for each element.)

Images of Orders 30 points possible	
Building Name 5 points possible	
Location 5 points possible	
Year Built 5 points possible	
Architect 5 points possible	
Total Points	

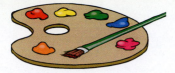

Chapter 1 Homework
Architecture
50 Points Possible

Project 3: _____ **Romanesque and Gothic Cathedrals**

Find and attach one Romanesque **and** one Gothic cathedral image from the list below. State the name of the cathedrals chosen (10 points possible). Discuss the features of each cathedral including images of each of the following: stained glass windows (10 points possible), type of columns used (10 points possible), the type of vaulted ceiling (explain the type) (10 points possible), and gargoyle examples (10 points possible).

Romanesque	Gothic
Santa Maria Maggiore	Notre Dame
San Sernin	St. Etienne
San Vitale	Chartres
St. Foy	Ely Cathedral
San Nicola	Florence Cathedral

Cathedral Images 10 points possible	
Stained Glass Images 10 points possible	
Column Type 10 points possible	
Ceiling Explanation 10 points possible	
Gargoyle Examples 10 points possible	
Total Points	

2

SCULPTURE
FROM STONE TO STEEL

EGYPTIAN 3500 B.C. TO 654 B.C.

Artists portray reality based on their own human experiences and emotions. They are, in a sense, creating a reality that is both fictional and non-fictional. The works of ancient Egyptians serve as perfect examples of fictional and non-fictional representation. Ancient Egyptians had very specific ways of portraying a human body in a work of art. The reasons for this representation (or reality) of the human body are unknown. To the Egyptians, it was not a priority. It would be several millennia before the realistic perspective of human rendering was rationalized and developed.

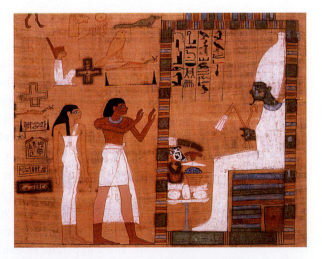

Fig. 2.1 Egyptian Art
(Courtesy of De Agostini
Editore Picture Library).

The Egyptians portrayed figures posed in profile. (Fig. 2.1) Upon inspection, the head, shoulders, legs and feet are in strict profile, while the eye is facing in a frontal view. This was known as **convention**. The convention is a system of rule or law in their visual language for depicting an image. The typical statue will be posed with arms at their side and fists clinched, the left leg moving forward, and the eyes are in a far-away stare. This positioning is symbolic of

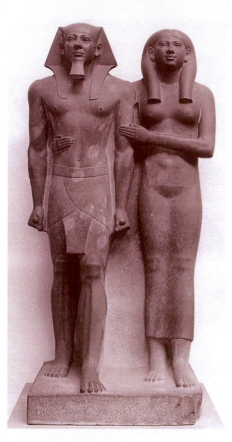

Fig. 2.2 King Menkaure and his Queen
(Courtesy, Museum of Fine Arts, Boston. Reproduced with permission. © 2008 Museum of Fine Arts, Boston. All Rights Reserved).

the figure walking from this world into the next. If the queen or a female figure is represented she will be slightly behind the male figure or the pharaoh. Another characteristic is that the stone is unfinished on the back. The space between the legs, the arms and between the figures themselves would remain uncarved in fear that the statue would be weak from removing excess stone. When one sees these distorted forms it is recognized immediately as ancient Egyptian. They understood it was not correct but it was the best possible view they could accomplish.

What the Egyptians achieved through this convention of pictorial representation was a static figure, particularly regal and ritual in nature. This style lasted thousands of years through the Egyptian culture and was seen as "true reality" in visual format. This contrasts what we know to be true today, that it is anatomically impossible for a human to stand in that particular pose. Egyptians would lay out a grid on the surface of a stone to be sculpted. The **grid** would represent the proportions for the figure creating a relationship between the grid and the stone to establish a natural pose of Egyptian standards.

GREEKS

When the Greeks viewed Egyptian sculptures, they found them very static. The Greek artists felt the need to capture the entire figure. At the beginning of the archaic period, 600 B.C. to 480 B.C., the Greeks developed free standing statues. This was a first in history, since Egyptian statues had been more block oriented and two sided, the front and side view only (Fig. 2.2). In contrast, archaic Greek sculptures were meant to be seen from all directions. They were able to perfect the art of sculpting humans. Within a 30 year period they were producing naturally posed figures.

In Greek statuary a young male was called **Kouros** (Fig. 2.3). The Kouros was typically nude. The Greeks chose to typify their culture through the athletic muscular physique of their statues. The influence of the Egyptians is evident in the statues with clenched hands at his sides, the left leg advances forward, and his eyes look straight ahead in a far-off stare. The Greeks sculptures were free standing with **negative space**. Negative space is the carved away area around the figure, such as between the legs.

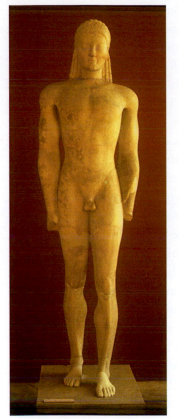

Fig. 2.3 Kouros–Greek
(Dorling Kindersley
© Archaeological Receipts
Fund (TAP)).

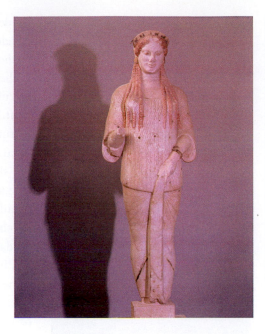

Fig. 2.4 Kore–Greek
(Werner Forman/Art
Resource, NY).

The female counter-part to a Kouros would be the **Kore** or young maiden (Fig. 2.4). Kore statues are typically clothed in Greek dress according to the style of the day. Where the Kouros is muscular, the Kore is delicate with the softer treatment of the flesh. She would have the far-away stare and wig-like hair typical of the Kouros. The sculptors would render intricate patterns and folds of material to indicate a more life-like contemporary statue.

What do these statues represent? The terms Kouros and Kore are non-committal names that gloss over the difficulty of identifying who they are. These figures did not represent an individual but rather they are generic representations of the society as a whole. These statues have been found on graves but because of their anonymity they do not represent an individual but the deceased only in an idolized sense. It's simply a grave marker. Both the Egyptian statues and archaic Greek statues are idealized not realized. In other words, the archaic statues do not represent any individual but rather the male/female form as a general statement.

The Greeks moved from the archaic into a transitional or early classical period, 480 B.C. to 450 B.C. It was during this time that techniques in

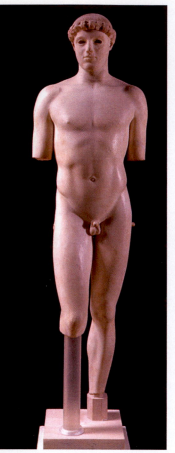

Fig. 2.5 *Kritios Boy*
(Nimatallah/Art Resource,
NY).

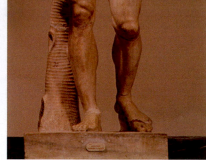

Fig. 2.6 *Doryphoros*
(Scala/Art Resource, NY).

modeling and casting of bronze developed more complex poses. One of the main discoveries of this period is the ***Kritios Boy***, (Fig. 2.5) which features, for the first time, '**weight shift.**' The figure still has idealized features of a young nude male, but what is distinctly different is that he has shifted his weight to his left leg. The sculptor has integrated natural details into the work to indicate that his shoulders are adjusted to accommodate his weight shift via his spine. His hips have compensated for that same shift to create a more natural appearance than the earlier Egyptian or Kouros-type sculptures. This is a major step in understanding the human form and the skeletal workings without dissection.

The Greeks further developed a new convention called a **canon** of proportions. Canon is Greek for measure, rule or law. A canon is a system for representing human form in relation to the scale of a whole figure. The Greek sculptor **Polykleitos** (450–400 B.C.) wrote a treatise in which he created an advanced theory of symmetry. From this he derived a proposed ideal system by which one could sculpt the human form using the harmony of the universe. The *Doryphoros* (spear bearer) (Fig. 2.6) is an example of Polykleitos' canon. This sculpture illustrates the Greeks' study of the human figure by using the set of proportions as a guideline to create a balanced generalized ideal figure, with all proportions exacting that of a human. Polykleitos and other sculptors of the time sought beauty not in the human figure, but in the mathematical definitions applied to the human form. There are mathematical relationships between each part on the figure, and this allows the possibility of replicating a human form to

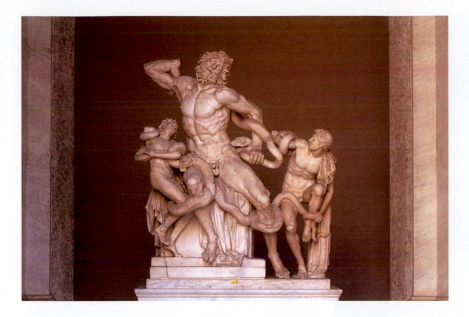

Fig. 2.7 *Laocoön and Sons* (Copyright © John Heseltine/ Dorling Kindersley).

perfection. Leonardo Da Vinci created a series of drawings relating to the measurements discovered by the Greeks and found them to be correct. He carefully recorded the various measurements as he discovered them. For more on this, see chapter four.

Later on, Greeks challenged the classical canon of proportion by creating sculptures in a swirl of lines, suggesting motion that was once restricted by the limited techniques of sculpting. An excellent example of this twisting motion in sculpture is ***Laocoön and Sons*** (Fig. 2.7) It's a product of the Hellenistic period, 323 B.C. to 30 B.C., which portrays a Trojan priest and his two sons being eaten by serpents sent by Poseidon. The story is told that Laocoön warned his fellow Trojans of the wooden horse. The god Poseidon, who supported the Greeks, attempted to destroy him. This grouping is very theatrical in that it displays the drama within the scene. The agony on the faces of Laocoön and his sons is apparent and the expressiveness with which these figures move within the group can be vividly seen and understood. Today this realistic sculpture, which clearly conveys human emotion in a natural form, is considered perfection.

Interestingly, *Laocoön and Sons* was discovered in the latter part of the 1400's. In 1501 Michelangelo was called to help excavate the sculpture from its earthly tomb. Perhaps the sight of *Laocoön and Sons* set Michelangelo on the path of sculpting which would become his life's passion.

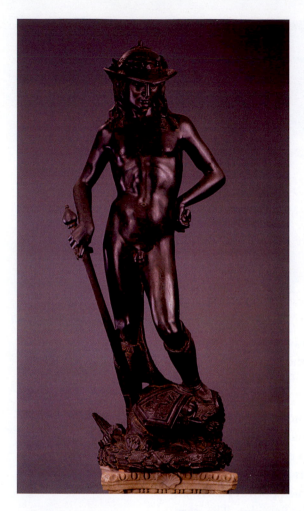

Fig. 2.8 *David*, c.1440
(bronze) by Donatello
(c.1386–1466) (Museo
Nazionale del Bargello,
Florence, Italy/The
Bridgeman Art Library).

DONATELLO (1386–1466)

Donatello was a master of sculpture in both marble and bronze. He is considered one of the greatest sculptors of the early Italian Renaissance period. He seemed to be a man of simple means. It is said that he was hard to deal with and a demanding individual. Donatello was a connoisseur of the ancient arts, and was inspired by their visual examples.

Donatello's interpretation of *David* (Fig. 2.8) departs somewhat from the Bible and suggests a more narrative story of David and Goliath. Donatello's *David* was one of the first life size (5 feet 2¼ inches) nudes since antiquity and is depicted as an adolescent youth. What is striking about *David* is the classical manner in which Donatello depicts the relaxed **contrapposto stance.** Contrapposto is the balance of opposites within a figure in a work of art. It creates a counter positioning of the body within the central axis generally shifting the weight to one foot or the other. Donatello's remarkable talent for naturalism shows in *David's* apathetic pose with his left foot on Goliath's severed head. This went against all the traditional styles of the early Renaissance.

At what moment does David become a hero in battling Goliath? Artists throughout history depicted David with various poses and emotional overtones trying to answer the simple question of heroism. Donatello chose to depict the moment of heroism at which David has severed the head and now stands victorious over Goliath.

Later in the chapter we will look at Michelangelo's and Bernini's depiction of the same theme. Michelangelo's point of heroism isn't the moment David kills Goliath but rather it is the moment David makes the fateful decision to pick up the stone and prepare for battle. On the other hand Bernini's *David* will show heroism within the act of slinging the stone at Goliath. Each of these represents the influence of the culture showing the moment of heroism can change from generation to generation. It's not to say one is superior over the other but simply represents the cultural style of the day. Donatello's *David* influences the other two.

MICHELANGELO (1475–1564)

Georgio Vasarie wrote about Michelangelo in his book *Lives of the Living Artist* in 1550

"While the artists were doing their best to imitate and to understand nature, bending every faculty to increase that high comprehension sometimes called intelligence, the Almighty Creator took pity on their often fruitless labor. He resolved to send to Earth a spirit capable of supreme expression in all the arts, one able to give form to painting, perfection to sculpture and grandeur to architecture. The Almighty also graciously endowed this chosen one with an understanding of philosophy and with the grace of poetry. And because He had observed that in Tuscany men were more zealous in study and more diligent in labor than in the rest of Italy, He decreed that Florence should be the birth place of this divinely endowed spirit."

Michelangelo was an unequaled master, a faithful Renaissance humanist with ideals of physical perfection and beauty in sculpture. Perhaps no other artist's passion for the untouched stone was more clearly understood than Michelangelo's. His approach was a "taking away" method which he saw as equal to brush strokes in painting. He would labor to free the figure, which was born in his mind, from the confines of the marble block. Michelangelo spent hours if not days inspecting the stone for fissures, defects and imperfections to get a clearer understanding of where the figure was hiding within the stone.

One of the greatest works of art is Michelangelo's sculpture *Pieta* (Fig. 2.9) (1498–1500) which was completed when he was only 23 years old. Pieta literally means pity or sorrowful and in this case it was his interpretation of Mary holding a dead Christ in her arms. He worked using a round drill, a tool that he would later abandon in favor of a claw chisel.

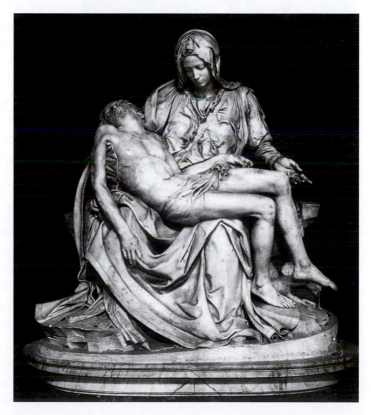

Fig. *2.9 Pieta* by Michelangelo (Alinari/Art Resource, NY).

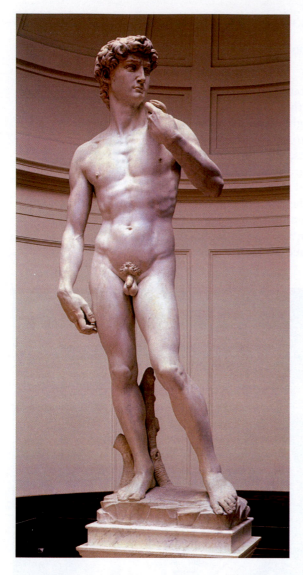

Fig. 2.10 *David* by Michelangelo (Scala/Ministero per i Beni e le Attività culturali/Art Resource, NY).

The Virgin's face appears peaceful and it is her left hand turned upward in helpless resignation that conveys the true depth of emotion, indeed the intensity of her grief. The dead Christ exhibits the very perfection of Michelangelo's past research of cadavers in every muscle, vein and nerve. The veins and muscles are carved with such precision that one cannot help but marvel at the hand of this artist. Michelangelo convinces us of the divine quality and the significance of these figures by means of Earthly beauty and perfection by human standards. We are here face to face not only with pain as a condition of redemption, but rather with absolute beauty of one of its consequences.

While the *Pieta* was on display in Rome Michelangelo overheard people discussing his recently completed sculpture, saying that the work was exquisite and could not have been made by a Florentine artist, that it must have been sculpted by an artist north of the Alps who were considered superior to Italian artists. In a moment of rage he carved his name in the ribbon across the Virgin's chest. Regretting that he signed it in a fit of prideful anger, he vowed never to sign his own work again.

In 1501 the Florentine Republic commissioned Michelangelo to create a gigantic model of a heroic youth for one of the buttresses of the Duomo, or cathedral, a structure of enormous civic and spiritual significance to the city of Florence. A large block of marble was given to Michelangelo which had been abandoned 40 years earlier by another sculptor who had badly damaged it. Michelangelo's predicament was to carve a *David* (Figure 2.10) while avoiding the damaged area of the stone. The completed *David* stands 13 feet 5 inches tall. It's an example of pent up energy. *David* is shown with a sling over his shoulder and a rock in his hand, eyeing the Goliath, the Philistine warrior. At one moment he is outwardly calm but at the next moment he will be in motion slinging the stone. The hint of intensity in *David* is seen in the eyes and the furrowing of his brow. This is a symbol of strength and wrath, two important virtues idolized by the new Republic. The Florentine Republic, it has been said, should govern justly and defend itself bravely with eyes watchful and *David* embodies that sensibility of force tempered by intellect.

The final sculpture to discuss sculpted by Michelangelo is *Moses* (Fig. 2.11). It was carved about a decade after *David*. *Moses* was part of a vast sculptural project for the tomb of Pope Julius II. This sculpture is meant to be seen from below. His pose is both watchful and meditative suggesting that Moses understood the conflict between God and man. Michelangelo's interpretation reveals his concept of the relationship between God and Moses. The figure has a long torso with a dramatic expression. *Moses'* arms and shoulders are clearly illustrating the strength of the seated figure. The beard of *Moses* is one of the most magnificent ever carved. The locks framing the broad angular face recall the images of God from the Sistine Ceiling which Michelangelo finished just before the *Moses* project began. The knowledge Michelangelo gained from the ceiling reflected a new vision in his sculptural pieces not seen in his earlier sculptures.

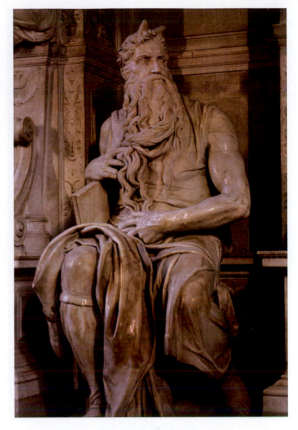

Fig. 2.11 *Moses* by Michelangelo (Vanni/Art Resource, NY).

The horns on *Moses'* head comes from a mistranslation of the Bible by St. Jerome. In the book of Exodus it says . . . Moses came down from Mt. Sinai with "rays of light," garen, beaming from his head. St. Jerome transposed the vowels in the word "garen" to "geran" which read Moses came down from Mt. Sinai with horns beaming from his head. Michelangelo and contemporaries of his day understood the misinterpretation but Michelangelo honored the old Saint by sculpting the horns on top of Moses' head.

BERNINI (1598–1680)

A notable sculptor and architect of the Baroque Period (1600–1700) was Gianlorenzo Bernini. He had a long and prolific career fusing architecture and sculpture in several major building designs. By 1620 he had caught a single view point, bursting into the spectator's space. Bernini's sculptures were revolutionary for exploring a variety of extreme mental states, such as the anger that we see in an early work of *David* (Fig. 2.12). Bernini conceived and carved his *David* in seven months; an amazing achievement for any sculptor.

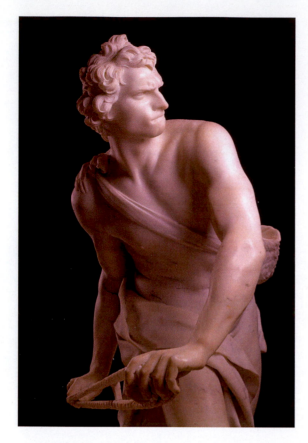

Fig. 2.12 *David* by Bernini
(Courtesy of Alinari/
Art Resource, NY).

Bernini was at the forefront of the revolution of sculpture in the Baroque Period, a period where sculptures were dramatic, implied sequences, and frozen in action. An early sculpture by Bernini was *David* which stands 5 feet 7 inches tall. In comparison to other *David's*, Bernini paid much attention to the Biblical text and tried to follow it as closely as possible. His emotion packed *David* appears to be moving through both time and space in an expansive and theatrical pose. *David's* face is frowning and even biting his lower lip in a contorted and fiercely concentrated effort. Bernini's *David* has a shepherds pouch around his neck which contains rocks. The upper part of *David's* body is posed immediately after he has taken a wind-up and is eyeing the Goliath. At one moment the torso is twisted and strains physically, indicating in the next moment his body will be in an opposite direction. The tension in Bernini's *David's* is spring-like with that split second before releasing the stone to kill Goliath. Historians have sought to locate a Goliath, thinking that this *David* is so realistic that Bernini must have carved a Goliath as well.

Bernini knew his *David* would be compared to other works in the sculptural tradition. Donatello's depiction is a very static figure standing over the head of Goliath where Michelangelo's depiction is that of pent up energy. Bernini countered with the dramatic theme and took his inspiration from an earlier Greek gladiator sculpture. Bernini's appears to be specifically interested in the depiction of the slaying of Goliath by a youthful *David*. This was not the objective of the other sculptures.

Generally considered to be one of Bernini's sculptural masterpieces is the **Ecstasy of St. Teresa** (1645–1652; Fig. 2.13). The sculpture is currently located in the interior of the Coronado Chapel of the Roman church Santa Maria della Vittoria. This sculptural grouping is 11 feet 6 inches in height. Teresa is shown lying on a cloud in full surrender to the angel as her cloak is pulled back ever so gently. The angel is at the ready to pierce her heart as we witness the Divine apparition. The work is a prime example of Bernini's vision: a decorative whole combining different materials and colors within an architectural space. Bernini specifically conceived and designed the alcove where the sculptural group is set within the chapel. It is illuminated by natural light through a hidden window in the dome.

Teresa was a Spanish Carmelite nun who established numerous convents in Spain. Her personality was unique in combining common sense with strong spiritual elements. Among her many writings Teresa reports . . .

"I saw in his hand spear of gold, and at the iron's point there seemed to be a little fire. He appeared to me to be thrusting it at times into my heart and to pierce my very entrails . . . to leave me all on fire with a great love of God. The pain is not bodily, but spiritual; though the body shares in it. It is a caressing of love so sweet which now takes place between my soul and God . . ."

Thus the symbolic taking of her life by God through His divine love calling her into heaven is represented by Bernini's famous sculpture.

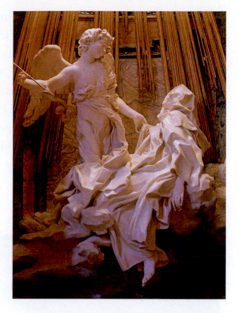

Fig. 2.13 *Ecstasy of St. Theresa* (marble) (detail) by Giovanni Lorenzo Bernini (1598–1680) Santa Maria della Vittoria, Rome, Italy (Alinari/The Bridgeman Art Library).

JEAN ANTOINE HOUDON (1741–1828)

Houdon studied and worked in Rome and even though the art around him was not influential, he did use life models to serve as the inspiration for his statues. After ten years of study he would return to his home country of France.

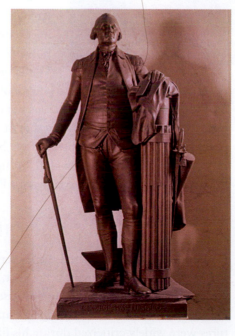

One of his more famous sculptures is that of *George Washington* (Fig. 2.14). Houdon's interpretation of sculpture reflects his belief in the Romanticism genre. The statue of *George Washington* strikes a classical pose. Washington's arm rests on a bundle of rods that symbolize the union of the thirteen states from colonization by Great Britain. Washington did not want to be portrayed as a hero typical of the Romantic style. Reluctantly he agreed to pose for the sculpture.

Fig. 2.14 *George Washington* by Houdon (Courtesy of Réunion des Musées Nationaux/ Art Resource, NY).

The statue is presently housed in the State Capital building in Richmond, Virginia, the state where Washington was born. Houdon received the commission to sculpt the statue as a result of an invitation by Benjamin Franklin, who spent considerable time in France. Houdon visited Mount Vernon where Washington modeled for the sculpture. Washington would sit while Houdon would sculpt with clay, in a similar fashion to someone posing for a portrait. Washington also allowed plaster life-masks to be made of his face to display his likeness throughout Virginia. This is the only statue for which Washington actually posed.

ANTONIO CANOVA (1757–1822)

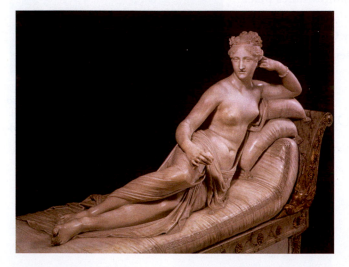

Fig. 2.15 *Pauline Borghese as Venus Triumphant,* c.1805–08 (marble) (see also 20019) by Antonio Canova (1757–1822) (Galleria Borghese, Rome, Italy/The Bridgeman Art Library).

During the Neo-Classical genre (to be studied in chapter four) Napoleon chose Canova as his favorite sculptor. Canova was reluctant at first to serve the Emperor. Napoleon's sister Pauline Borghese wanted Canova to sculpt her, as well, not as she truly was but as the reclining Venus, *Pauline Borghese as Venus* (Fig. 2.15). This sculpture is similar to ancient sculptures in that it was sculpted to be seen strictly from the front. Canova had conceived the idea as Borghese portraying Diana, the goddess of the hunt. Pauline however demanded that she sculptured as Venus, goddess of love. She is shown as a diva holding a golden apple, a symbol of the goddesses triumph in the judgment of Paris. The pose is sensuous but clearly is derived from Greek sculpture. The couch and the figure is that of a Greek work of art while the head is that of Pauline. Her insistence on being portrayed as a love goddess reflected her self-perception that brought into question her dignity and fidelity to her arranged marriage with Prince Camillo Borghese.

AUGUSTE RODIN (1840–1917)

Rodin is generally considered the leader of modern sculpture. Although he was not trying to rebel against the past, he simply took a new approach to current accepted standards. He possessed a new ability to model complex and deeply emotional works in clay and bronze. Most of Rodin's sculptures were widely criticized during his lifetime because his figure sculptures departed from traditional themes. He modeled the human body with realism and celebrated individual character and physicality. Rodin understood the controversy of his work but felt the change in his style was needed in the art world.

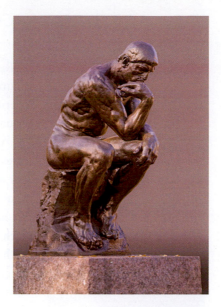

Fig. 2.16 *The Thinker* by Rodin (Courtesy of Vanni/Art Resource, NY).

Rodin's *The Thinker* (Fig. 2.16) was actually influenced by an early Christian Byzantine relief showing Adam in a similar pose. Over the years the question "who is *The Thinker?*" has surfaced. The logical answer might be Adam. Rodin never gave *The Thinker* a specific name because he was conceiving a new image of man where form and meaning come together.

Another of Rodin's more famous sculptures is *The Kiss* (Fig. 2.17). *The Kiss* depicts a 13th century Italian noble woman immortalized in Dante's *Inferno* who falls in love with her husband's younger brother. As they were reading the story of Lancelot and Guinevere, the couple are discovered and killed by the woman's husband. In the sculpture, Rodin includes the book which was in the younger brother's hand. Also in the sculpture, the lover's lips are not touching which suggests that they were caught and met their demise without ever having kissed. The consequent eroticism of the sculpture caused it to be controversial. When sent to the 1893 World's Columbian Exhibition in Chicago the sculpture was deemed unsuitable for public display.

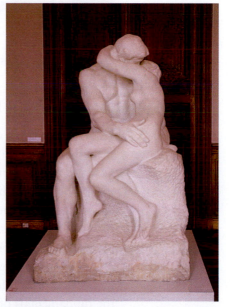

Fig. 2.17 *The Kiss* by Rodin (Courtesy of Vanni/Art Resource, NY).

Rodin has been considered one of the pre-eminent realist sculptors of the late 19th and early 20th centuries. His goal was to sculpt emotions through muscular movement. Due to his knowledge of anatomy, he paid special attention to the body's surfaces. Rodin's sculptures are not the smooth polished planes of a traditionally finished works, but are rough and appear to be unfinished. His love for the detailed modeling and energetic poses are striking and lifelike.

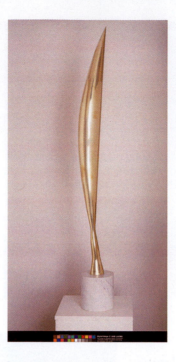

CONSTANTIN BRANCUSI
(1876–1957)

A Romanian sculptor, Brancusi was a key figure in the modern movement and pioneering **abstraction**. His work is noted for its visual elegance and sensitive use of materials. One of Brancusi's more graceful sculptures is ***The Bird*** (Fig. 2.18). Clearly this is not a literal depiction of a bird but it's the final result of a long process of elimination. He started with an image of a bird at rest with its wings folded at its side and ended with an abstract column form sharply tapered at one end. Abstraction means anything taken from nature and altered. During the 1920s through the 40s he was preoccupied with the Bird theme. Brancusi wasn't interested in wings, feathers etc., but attempted to focus on the swelling and elongation of a bird's body. His abstraction captures the essence of flight.

HENRY MOORE (1898–1986)

Henry Moore was a sculptor and artist. He is best known for his monumental abstract sculptures located around the world as public works of art. Many of his sculptures are abstractions of the human figure, usually depicting a mother and child or his famous reclining figures. Moore's sculptures are suggestive of the female form. Many interpreters liken the undulation of his reclining figures to the landscapes surrounding them. These reclining figures would be his signature form of art.

Moore shifted from carving in stone to modeling with clay, which he once despised. He wanted to experiment in abstraction in order to learn the fundamentals of the process. Through the process he moved from one method to another. Moore believed that modeling with clay helped the artist realize his concept and be more in touch with the process of achieving a finished work of art.

In the *Reclining Figure Series* (Fig. 2.19) the form is abstracted but is still recognizable as human. His sculptures are generally oversized with a combination of positive and negative space throughout the entire form. His figures indicate contours of hills and/or the surrounding environment in which they are placed. Moore was incorporating the human forms as abstracted landscapes and interplay of mass and void. In other words, his sculptures became one with the landscape.

DAVID SMITH (1906–1965)

Smith was an artist who was heavily influenced by Picasso and Cubism. He was interested in their pictorial revolution and their new concept of space. Smith began studying the history of sculpture from the ancient times and attempted to incorporate what he had learned into his own art with an entirely fresh approach.

David Smith's most famous works were a series of stainless steel sculptures which were comprised of cubes, rectangular solids and cylinders. The *Cubi Series* (Fig. 2.20) offers 28 different sculptures and was the last of the artistic outpourings of this American sculptor. By creating the *Cubi Series* Smith found that it gave him free access to abandon imagery completely and create predominately cubistic images in stainless steel. Several of his *Cubi Series* sculptures were inspired by events, foods, and memories of his teen years. Stainless steel, as a medium, allowed Smith to sand

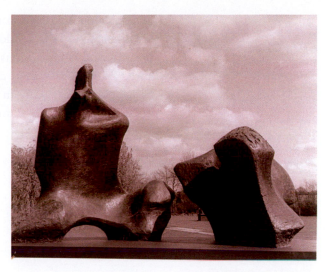

Fig. 2.19 *Reclining Figure, 1963* (bronze) by Henry Spencer Moore (1898-1986) / © Henry Moore Foundation, The Bridgeman Art Library. Courtesy of Henry Spencer Moore/Henry Moore Foundation.

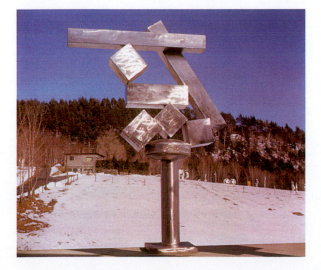

Fig. 2.20 The *Cubi Series* by Smith (Photo courtesy of Art Resource, NY. *Cubi XVIII* (1964) (Stainless Steel) © Estate of David Smith/Licensed by VAGA, New York, NY).

and/or create textures on the surfaces of his sculptures. These sculptures are intended to be in outdoor settings; stainless steel is a medium that does not rust and is impervious to weather. The *Cubi Series* was heavily influenced by Picasso and, of course Cubism, hence it being named The *Cubi Series*. Smith met with an untimely death in a car crash in 1965 leaving his work prematurely unfinished.

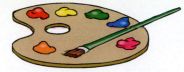

Name: _____

Class time: _____

Chapter 2 Homework
Sculpture
50 Points Possible

Complete **one** of the following three projects. **Staple** all additional sheets to this page. (**No bent corner-type attachments accepted**). Check which project you are completing.

Size restrictions: 8½ x 11 only. All work MUST be typed using complete sentences and correct punctuation to earn full credit.

Project 1: _____ Egyptian Style Sculpture

Depict you and a friend in the style of Egyptian sculpture, using their convention. (up to 15 points possible). Your depiction should include Egyptian dress but holding modern day items of interest to you (20 points possible). Figures must be in color and cover an entire sheet of paper (15 points possible).

Grid 15 points possible	
Sculpture Depiction 20 points possible	
Color & Size 15 points possible	
Total Points	

Project 2: _____ Greek OR Renaissance OR Baroque Sculpture

Find and attach an image of a statue from one of the three genres above that was not discussed in the book or in class (10 points possible). Give a summary of its location, original purpose, sculptor's name, and what qualities this statue has that makes it distinct to its genre (10 points possible for each element).

Image 10 points possible	
Location 10 points possible	
Original Purpose 10 points possible	
Sculptor 10 points possible	
Sculptural Qualities 10 points possible	
Total Points	

Chapter 7 Homework
Sculpture

50 Points Possible

Complete one of the following three projects. Staple on additional sheets to the page. Use your own materials at school or at home; prepare your own materials.

See Rubrics below. To earn ALL 50 points MUST be typed and complete a written statement to earn full credit.

Project 1.   Pop-can Style Sculpture

Depict you and a friend in the style of pop-can sculpture, using their convention. (up to 15 points possible.) Note: depictions should include Pop-can dress but leading modern-day items of interest (a total of points possible.) Figure must be in color and cover as entire sheet as large as possible.

Grid	
15 points possible	
Sculpture Depiction	
20 points possible	
Color & Size	
15 points possible	
Total Points	

**Project 2.   Greek OR Renaissance OR
Baroque Sculpture**

Find and attach an image of a statue from one of the three genres above that was discussed in the book or in class. (10 points possible.) Give a summary of the locale, original purpose, sculptor's name, and what qualities this statue has that makes it distinct to its genre. (5 points possible for each element.)

Image		
10 points possible		
Location		
10 points possible		
Original Purpose		
10 points possible		
Sculptor		
10 points possible		
Sculptural Qualities		
10 points possible		
Total Points		

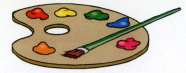

Chapter 2 Homework
Sculpture
50 Points Possible

Project 3: _____ **Modern Day Sculpture**

Sculpture has changed vastly over the last 100 years;
we now have a wide variety of genres. Find and attach
an image of a sculpture (10 points possible) created
within the last 100 years and describe the following:
Genre, media (material created from), sculptor's name
and year created, its present location (10 points possible
for each element).

Image 10 points possible	
Genre 10 points possible	
Media used 10 points possible	
Sculptor/year 10 points possible	
Location 10 points possible	
Total Points	

3

BASIC ELEMENTS
OF ART

A simple definition of art is: **a record of human experience**. Artists draw from their experiences to create works of art. Every artist uses and understands the basic elements of art and incorporates them into their images. Art, as in many creative fields, has its own language and meanings that belong strictly to its particular field. The elements of art are raw materials that allow the artist to create their art. In this chapter we will focus on the five elements of art: **Line**, **Shape**, **Value**, **Color** and **Texture**. We will be exploring various principles of design; for example, compositional styles and color theories. Artists through the centuries have been trying to figure out a simple way of utilizing the elements while creating an aesthetically interesting work of art based on the statement they are making. What is important in this chapter is how artists use each of these elements to create unique and different images. These basic elements of art are as valid today as they were thousands of years ago, and as they will be hundreds of years from now for one reason: they work! Even though aesthetics change from culture to culture, the basic elements remain the same.

Once one comprehends the elements of art, one can glean an understanding of an unfamiliar work of art. Color theory, composition and how space is organized in a systematic, orderly fashion are the key elements of any artwork. Learning to interpret an image involves some participation by the viewer through their own life experiences. Simply going to a museum or gallery and walking past works of art without realizing their meaning or content is the difference between looking at an image and gaining an insight from the image. Without this knowledge of the basic elements of art, no true meaning can be found in an image because the depths of possibilities are unlimited. Learning to interpret and attaining the meaning of works of art, particularly unfamiliar works of art, challenges the viewer and can create a whole new dimension to the viewer. Learning about the basic elements of art brings a new appreciation for delving deeper into more works of art. The process is contagious and allows the viewer a new way of experiencing art.

As you read through this chapter you will begin to notice certain trends and threads that are current in all works of art both historical and modern. Art makes a statement and is a reflection of the artist's life and/or culture. As music has something to say, the listener has to understand the meaning of the words and music to understand the musician, so is true in art. One who has little or no experience with art will not know how to interpret it. Art is something that can be understood and enjoyed from personal experience once the basic elements of art are learned.

Every work of art has basic elements that hold the image together. In composing an essay, the sentences within a paragraph create a thought; the grammar is the structural component that helps the reader understand the author's idea. Each paragraph, in turn, joins to create the composition. Works of art are structured in the same way, except the elements are all visual. There are five basic elements of art, and each work has to incorporate all the elements.

LINE—ELEMENT #1

The first element of art to explore is **line.** Line is the most commonly used basic element. The quality of the line is the most obvious element to the inherent style of any given artist. It is through line that an artist's personality comes forth and is presented each and every time. For example, when we write our name, we use a line that is expressive and represents our mark-making process. As children we learn to draw instinctively by using lines to complete thoughts that are visual more than verbal. The line in a drawing is different than a line drawn in a math problem. The line in a drawing is meant to be expressive and have character, which will describe the image being drawn, whereas in math it is simply moving from point A to point B. Line is used as a form of communication; one can draw an idea quicker than writing it out.

Lines have directions; they can describe spatial relationships between objects. Lines can be short or long, straight or curvy, thick or thin and, when combined with other lines, will complete an idea.

In regards to drawing, a line can be described several ways, **contour** (Fig. 3.1), **gesture** (Fig. 3.2) and **crosshatching** (Fig. 3.3).

A **contour line** is drawn slowly and done with much accuracy. It is an eye-hand coordination process that is taking place. The contour line is very descriptive. Contour has no emotion; it is simply recording.

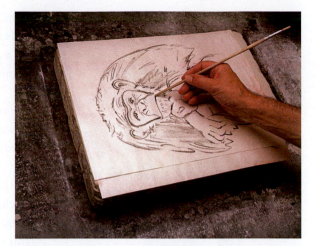

Fig. 3.1 Contour drawing (Andy Crawford © Dorling Kindersley).

When creating a contour drawing the artist keeps their eye on the subject while the pencil is on the surface of the paper. The artist imagines the point of the pencil is in actual contact with the subject they are about to draw. The artist's eyes move at the same steady pace as their drawing instrument moves along the paper creating the form from the beginning point to the end without lifting the pencil. The artist would begin tracing the outside edge of an object or subject and create an actual pathway that describes the form of the object. A beginning artist's contour drawing will most likely be distorted and inaccurate in its proportions; however, with time and dedication to the eye-hand coordination, each drawing will improve. Generally, a contour drawing takes anywhere from three to ten minutes to create, because the process is slow and deliberate.

Gesture lines, on the other hand, are expressive and not accurate. A gesture drawing uses lines in a quick sketchy hand movement attempting to capture the essence of the object being drawn. Gestural drawings are generally good warm-up exercises for artists preparing for longer more accurate studies of the subject. Rarely is a gestural drawing considered a work of art or even a finished product, it is merely an exercise of the hand and arm muscles to get the artist motivated.

When creating a gesture drawing the lines are exaggerated and expressive because they are quick non-descriptive lines drawn very rapidly without the intent to create an accurate reproduction of the object or

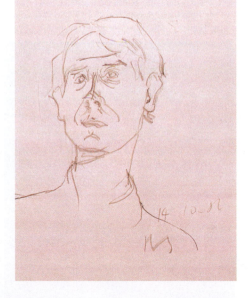

Fig. 3.2 Gesture drawing (Courtesy of Andy Crawford/ Dorling Kindersley. Copyright © Ray Smith).

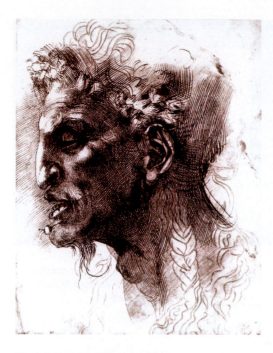

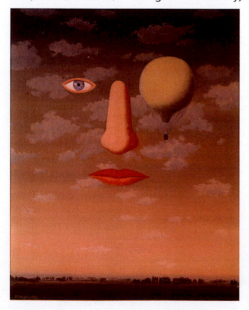

form. Most gesture drawings are from ten to thirty seconds in length. The objective in gesture drawing is to create a rapid drawing using the artists' emotions and not so much eye-hand coordination.

From the above contour and gesture descriptions, the reader quickly understands the vast differences between the slow and accurate versus the quick and emotional impact these two line drawings can create.

Lines placed parallel vertically then horizontally on top of the previously placed lines are called **crosshatching** (Fig. 3.3). The closer the crosshatched lines are to each other the darker the shape or shade will appear. You can create value through crosshatching, starting with light value lines and then moving to darker value lines to create the varying degrees of value within the shape. This is a way to fool the eye into thinking it is seeing shades of gray.

SHAPE—ELEMENT #2

Shape, by definition, is a flat, two-dimensional element without any interior detail. We might look at a seashell and see the shape and draw just the contour or outline of it. Shapes may be a realistic version of an object, a distorted or abstracted yet recognizable object, or a shape that is unrecognizable as a shape altogether or non-objective. When reading the word 'pyramid,' the mind automatically pictures a triangle, its shape. Shapes are used within compositions much like pieces in a puzzle. Piecing shapes together creates an image. Shapes help balance the composition, completing the artists' vision.

In our example (Fig. 3.4) we see a human head created by shapes. These are individual objects that the brain deciphers into a completely different image. The brain always tries to make sense out of chaos. The actual image is that of a landscape where the sky dominates the painting. We see a symbol of an eye, a nose, lips and a hot air balloon which create the basic features of the face. There is no face but we see one anyway because of the shapes arranged in a particular

Fig. 3.5 Gray Scale

manner. These images seemingly float in the sky. The one shape has nothing to do with the other shape but combined create a readable image.

VALUE—ELEMENT #3

Art would not be possible without light; we see with light. Without light we see dark shapes at best. Simply put, value is the measure of light to dark. In this chapter value is discussed here as one of the elements of art but it will also be discussed with its role in the description of color. Value has various meanings according to the element with which it is being used, black and white or color. Every work of art has a value scale within it. The value scale has some lighter and darker areas. In a value scale (Fig. 3.5) there are usually nine steps from pure white to pure black. This is called an **achromatic**; it is a scale of gray tones.

Value can be very confusing because it's not only associated with black and white or light to dark, but is integral in the element of color. Values can be very intense, such as bright reds, or they can be very dull, like pastel blue. Each color or hue has a value range from very intense and dark to very dull and light.

Artists use the values of colors to create the depth and spatial appearance in an image. Value creates volume and a three-dimensional feel to a piece. Value is of great importance to any work of art because it has the greatest potential for spatial definition within a work of art or composition.

COLOR—ELEMENT #4

There are three components of color: hue, chroma and value. Color stimulates the mind and the emotions. People are drawn to specific color according to their mind set. For example, the color red makes most people feel hungry. Many restaurants are painted red or use red overtones to stimulate the sensation of hunger. Other people see red as an expression of their anger. Blue reminds us of the water and the sky simulating a cool feeling or one of peace and serenity. Yellow is considered a happy color and creates a warm sensation, reminding us of the warmth of the sun.

Value is that measure of light to dark within a color. Any color can be lightened and/or darkened by changing its value with the addition of white or black. Adding white to a color is called a **tint**; it makes the color lighter. Adding black makes the color darker and is called a **shade**.

Hue is pure color itself. It is the characteristic by which we can distinguish the difference from one color to another; red, purple, blue, green.

Chroma is the brightness or intensity of a color. The color is at its strongest when it is fully saturated in its maximum strength and weakest in its de-saturated state or low intensity.

The **primary colors** are yellow, red, and blue. They are the basic colors found in the earth. They cannot be made by mixing other colors. Yellow is the weakest in mixing power with more dominant colors such as blue or red. On the other hand yellow can be seen from a farther distance than the other primaries. Have you ever thought about why school busses are yellow? The combination of yellow busses with black accents can be seen in severe weather conditions. The new trend in fire truck color is yellow because of its visual impact. They have traditionally been red which is associated with fire but visibility is obviously more important than symbolism.

Mixing two primary colors together creates a **secondary color**. The secondary colors are purple, green and orange. Mixing red and yellow together will make an orange if the percentage of red to yellow is correct. For example, red is a dominant color and mixing equal parts of red and yellow will only produce a weaker red. To create an orange, roughly 80% yellow and 20% red is needed. The same holds true for green; mixing equal amounts of blue and yellow won't make green, just a weaker version of blue. Once again, blue is a dominant color and the equation of 80%–20% is in effect. Purple is made by mixing red and blue together in approximately equal parts. When mixing colors, one color can dominate the other and must be mixed accordingly.

When mixing a primary with a secondary color, a **tertiary color** is produced. For example; mixing blue with green will create blue-green or red mixed with orange will produce red-orange.

So where do black and white fit in to the grand scheme of things? Rembrandt called black the queen of the colors. Black, is of course, one value, the darkest. Black is useful in taking any hue down to its darkest value. Black is also used to produce grays by either diluting it or by adding white to create lighter values and less intense grays.

Some artists will call white their "trump card" to be played dominantly but carefully. Areas of white in a work of art will attract the viewer's eye. It creates a sort of "mapping system" for the artist to help the viewer work their way through the overall image. White is the absorption of all colors. White creates contrasts between darker areas which, in turn, create more aesthetics within the work of art. In summary, darker tones will draw the view to the back of the image whereas lighter tones will bring the viewer forward in the image. These contrasts create an overall dramatic feel to the piece.

How is brown made and where does it fit in? Brown is an important color because it appears in nature. Brown is considered a neutral color that works well with the other colors and color schemes. Brown can be mixed several different ways. Red and yellow mixed together make orange, then when mixed with blue will create an interesting rich brown color. Artists will mix a concentration of orange and black together to produce a brown hue of varying tones.

The **Color Wheel** (Fig. 3.6) presents a universally arranged set of pure hues, those being the primary colors with secondary color and usually tertiary colors. Yellow is traditionally on top indicating its warmth as well as its lack of tinting power. Red being a dominant color falls on the lower left-hand side of the color wheel; while blue, an equally dominant color, falls on the lower right hand side. This arrangement engages the viewer into a sense of balance and order in the visual experience. To help artists understand color and to make the process easier to mix colors, the color wheel was invented. Thinking of color in terms of a wheel helps to organize and understand the principles of color schemes. Different combinations of colors will create various color schemes. The color wheel will help us to establish opposites and neighbors, an important factors in color schemes.

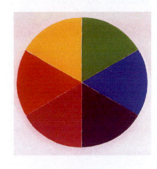

Fig. 3.6 Color Wheel (Copyright © Dave King / Dorling Kindersley).

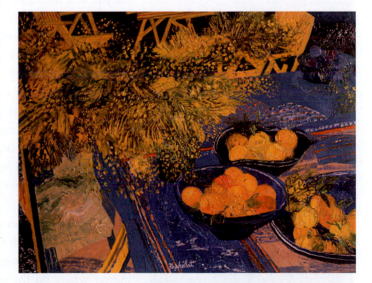

Fig. 3.7 Complementary color scheme
Dish of Oranges and a Blue Tablecloth (oil on canvas) by Pophillat, Jean-Pierre (b.1937) (Private Collection/ J.P. Zenobel/The Bridgeman Art Library).

COLOR SCHEMES (SUB ELEMENT OF COLOR)

A **complementary** color scheme (Fig. 3.7) is any two colors opposite each other on the color wheel. Complements complete each other. Opposites do attract and complete one another. If you marry your opposite you are likely to complete each other's traits and thinking patterns. On the color wheel the opposite of blue is orange, the opposite of yellow is

Fig. 3.8 Split-complimentary color scheme—VanGogh—*Bedroom at Arles*-(Blue/orange with red-green-yellow) (Réunion des Musées Nationaux/Art Resource, NY).

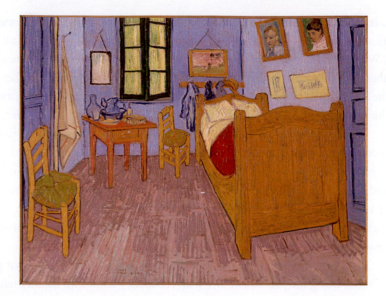

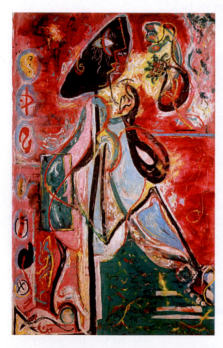

Fig. 3.9 Jackson Pollock—*Moon Woman*—Analogous color scheme Oil on canvas, 69 × 43⅛ inches (175.2 × 109.3 cm). The Solomon R. Guggenheim Foundation Peggy Guggenheim Collection, Venice, 76.2553.151. Jackson Pollock © 2007 The Pollock-Krasner Foundation/Artists Rights Society (ARS), New York.

purple and the opposite of red is green. Notice that this color scheme uses one primary color and one secondary color to make the complementary pair.

Another color scheme is **split-complimentary** (Fig. 3.8). It's similar to complementary but the colors on either side of the compliment are used as added colors to the overall color scheme. Think about the compliment of blue and orange. The split would then be colors on either side of the blue or orange such as red-orange or yellow-orange. These are colors found just to the right and left of the compliment. The colors next to blue can be used also. Those colors would be blue-purple and blue-green.

The **analogous color scheme** (Fig. 3.9) is created by using several colors next to each other on the color wheel. Analogous colors might be blue-green, green, and yellow-green. It doesn't matter where on the color wheel you begin as long as the colors are next to each other. The theory is that the colors are neighbors and therefore will get along or are in harmony with one another.

A **Monochromatic** color scheme (Fig. 3.10) uses primarily one color. Mono means one and chromatic means color. Images can have slight tones of other colors but one color will dominate the image.

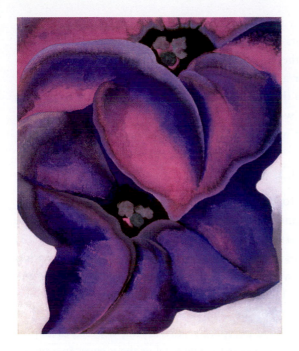

Fig. 3.10 Monochromatic color scheme—Georgia O'Keeffe—*Purple Petunias*
(Courtesy of The Newark Museum/Art Resource, NY. Copyright © ARS, NY.).

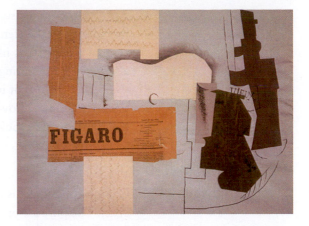

Fig. 3.11 Picasso—*Bottle of Vieux Marc glass, guitar, and newspaper*—Real texture
(Courtesy of Tate, London/Art Resource, NY. Copyright © ARS, NY.).

TEXTURE—ELEMENT #5

The rough or smooth surface of a stone, the touch of a tree, hair on a person's head or the fabric of clothing are just a few examples of the textures we experience in our daily lives. **Texture** is a tactile surface characteristic that may be real or visual. Many artists use texture in various ways to create the illusions needed in any given visual to suggest information about the surface of an object. In Picasso's *Bottle of Vieux Marc* example, the artist has created a work using **real texture** of overlapping surfaces (Fig.3.11). Dürer's *Self Portrait* uses **visual texture** (Fig.3.12), where the surface implies reality but is actually painted creating an illusion of texture. In the second example, the artist has simulated the texture in the work of art to make us, the viewers, feel as though it is a real surface.

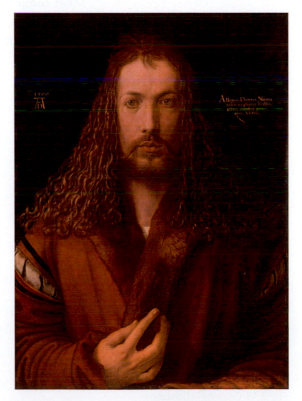

Fig. 3.12 Dürer—*Self-Portrait*—Visual texture
(Bildarchiv Preussischer Kulturbesitz/Art Resource, NY).

How do artists put the five elements into practice? They incorporate all five of the elements in each work of art to create a completed conceptual idea. Artists use the basic elements to create a work, whether it is a sculpture, a painting or a drawing. Knowing these basic elements gives the viewer an insight into the world of the artist and the ability to gain an understanding of how a work of art was created. The viewer is given a behind-the-scenes look at what rules apply when creating a work of art.

COMPOSITION

Composition in art is the formal arrangement of the shapes created by the artist. The purpose of composition is to visualize the work of art as a whole but also the individual parts within the whole. **Paul Cezanne** (Fig. 3.13) saw composition as a series of geometric shapes placed purposefully within an image directing the viewers' eyes from one place to another within the arrangement of the image. His goal was to direct the viewer's eye through the work of art by the means of the composition.

Most compositions have perspective in varying degrees of depth. The **horizon line** (Fig. 3.14) represents the eye level of the viewer. In a painting we can see depth by locating the **vanishing point** on the horizon line.

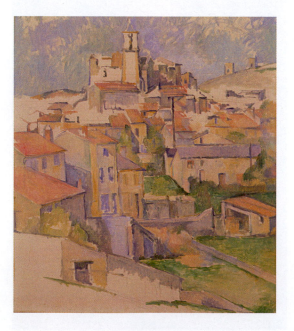

Fig. 3.13 Cezanne—*Gardanne*
(Image copyright © The Metropolitan Museum of Art/
Art Resource, NY).

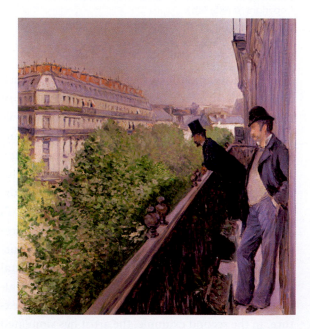

Fig. 3.14 Caillebotte—*On The Balcony*—Vanishing point
specific image
(Erich Lessing/Art Resource, NY).

A vanishing point refers to the farthest distance the artist wants you to see within a work of art. **Linear perspective** is when parallel lines converge, or come together as they recede in the image. Linear perspective is recreated everyday when you look into the distance.

When you look at an image locate the horizon line. If there is an obvious vanishing point within the image, there you will find the linear perspective at the point where everything converges.

There are numerous ways in which an artist can create a composition; however several compositional styles remain consistent throughout history. For the purposes of this book we will discuss the most commonly used compositions.

An **overlapping composition** is created with shapes placed in front of other shapes. For instance we may see an image with several objects in the foreground with other objects directly behind each other. Overlapping can also be as simple as laying down a series of dark shapes with a series of lighter shapes on top. Such is the case with Jackson Pollock's drip paintings (Fig. 3.15). What looks like random chaos is actually a series of lines creating the overlapping effect. Most overlapping compositions create a shallow environment rather than one that recedes into the distance.

Diminishing composition is commonly used to create deep shape within the work of art. Unlike overlapping, which creates a shallow space, diminishing is used to create an illusion of great distance; in nature, objects appear smaller the further away they are from the viewer. *The Gleaners* by Millet (Fig. 3.16) is a good example of diminishing composition with the women bending over picking wheat in the foreground. The farmer and his loaded wagons appear further back in the distance. This creates depth of space.

A **zigzag composition** is one that directs your eye from one object to another object using a zigzag pattern. This composition walks the viewer from the foreground into the background by a series of objects placed strategically through-

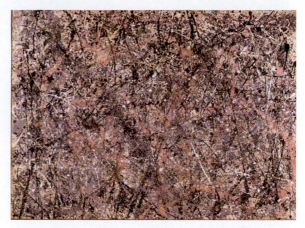

Fig. 3.15 Pollock—*Number 1*—Overlapping composition (Jackson Pollock (American 1912–1956), "Number 1, 1950 (Lavender Mist)," oil, enamel and aluminum paint on canvas, 221 × 299.7 cm/National Gallery of Art, Washington, D.C., USA/© 2003 The Pollock-Krasner Foundation/Artists Rights Society (ARS), New York/The Bridgeman Art Library, New York).

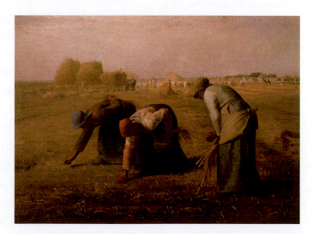

Fig. 3.16 Millet—*The Gleaners*—Diminishing composition (Erich Lessing/Art Resource, NY).

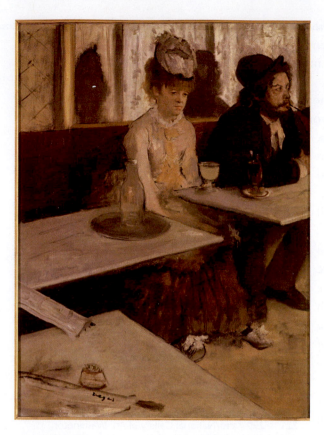

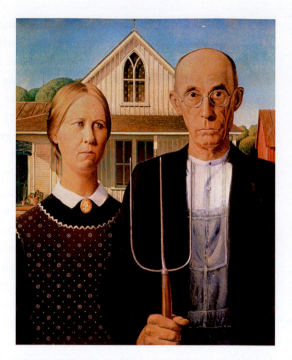

Fig. 3.18 Wood—*American Gothic*—Symmetrical composition. *American Gothic*, 1930 (oil on board) by Grant Wood (1892–1942) (The Art Institute of Chicago, IL, USA/The Bridgeman Art Library. © Figge Art Museum, successors to the Estate of Nan Wood Graham/Licensed by VAGA, New York, NY).

Fig. 3.17 Degas—*The Absinthe Drinkers*—Zig-zag composition (Réunion des Musées Nationaux/Art Resource, NY).

out the composition to achieve spatial depth. An example of a zigzag composition is that of Degas' *The Absinthe Drinkers* (Fig. 3.17), in which one table is placed at an angle that leads the viewer's eye to the next table where the two figures are sitting. Your eyes follow back to the seated figures, creating a zigzag movement from foreground to background.

Symmetrical composition is a balancing of both sides of the image around a central object. The human body is symmetrical, two eyes, two arms, two legs, one on each side of the body. In art, this balancing happens when an artist creates basically the same set of objects on each side of a central axis. There can be more objects on one side than the other but the overall composition still remains symmetrical. An example of symmetrical composition occurs in **American Gothic** by Wood (Fig. 3.18). Two figures are centered at the front of the image. The painting is bisected by an imaginary line starting at the lightning rod on the roof and ending just above the farmer's hand.

The **circular composition** draws the viewer in a circular manner starting at point A and moving around the image to end back at the beginning or point A. Mary Cassatt's famous work *The Bath* (Fig. 3.19) is an excellent example of a circular composition. In this image we see a mother bathing her daughter. The pitcher in the lower right corner is pointed towards the bowl in which the mother is washing the child's feet. From there we move up the mother's arm where the faces are placed next to each other and then notice the child's arm and its juxtaposition, which brings the viewer back down to the wash bowl to begin the process over again. This composition works well in guiding the viewer from the lower part of the composition to the upper part of the composition and then back around again.

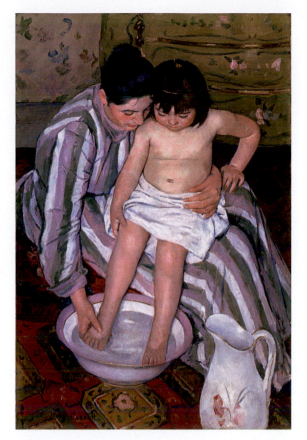

Fig. 3.19 Cassatt—*The Bath*—Circular composition (The Art Institute of Chicago, American, 1844–1926, *The Child's Bath*, 1893, oil on canvas, 100.3 × 66.1 cm).

The following chapters will use these basic elements to help the reader understand various works of art from different art genres. More importantly, knowledge of the basic elements covered will increase the reader's awareness and comprehension of unfamiliar works of art. As you walk through museums and galleries be aware of how line, shape, value, color and texture were used to create and recreate images over the last millennium. As you become familiar with the various compositions, color schemes and the overall theme of the piece, more enjoyment will be gained from looking at unfamiliar works of art. It is important to learn and understand the basic elements of art and the roles they play in the art world to appreciate the everyday things we see and come in contact with in our lives.

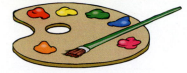

Chapter 3
Basic Elements of Art
50 Points Possible

Complete **one** of the following three projects. **Staple** all additional sheets to this page. (**No bent corner-type attachments accepted**). Check which project you are completing.

Size restrictions: Minimum 8 × 10—Maximum 8 ½ × 11. All work MUST be *typed using complete sentences and correct punctuation to earn full credit*.

Project 1: _____ **Analyze the basic elements**

Find and attach a work of art (not seen in class or illustrated in text) and analyze all five basic elements. Justify your statements. This should include all five elements that make your work of art. Your image must fill an entire sheet of 8½ × 11 paper. Hint: Black/White and neutral are not considered color schemes.

Line 10 points possible	
Shape 10 points possible	
Value 10 points possible	
Color 10 points possible	
Texture 10 points possible	
Total Points	

Project 2: _____ **Advertisement Analysis**

Find and attach an advertisement from a magazine. The ad must be a **minimum of 5 × 7 inches (images smaller than 5 × 7 will earn "0" points)**. Scan the ad to your computer, then change the color scheme to create a totally different feel to the advertisement. Both images must be attached. Explain the following: Original color scheme, new color scheme, type of composition. Justify all your answers. Hint: Black/White and neutral are not considered color schemes.

Image 10 points possible	
Original Color Scheme 10 points possible	
New Color Scheme 20 points possible	
Composition 10 points possible	
Total Points	

4

HIGH RENAISSANCE TO POST IMPRESSIONISM (1495–1920)

Have you ever thumbed through a magazine, saw a work of art and simply stared at it, not really investigating or exploring its meaning any deeper? Have you ever been to a museum or art gallery and were curious about what inspired the artist to create the image? The good news is you're not alone; too many people today do not understand or even know how to begin to interpret the meaning behind art. The next two chapters will discuss art from High Renaissance through Post Modernism so the viewer can begin to understand an unfamiliar work of art. Art today poses many challenges and much confusion as to why it is even considered art and who considers it art. These chapters will clarify the meaning behind the image. For example, if you were to come across a Madonna and Child scene (Fig. 4.1), it would be safe to say the original image came from the Italian Renaissance. On the other hand, if one sees a painting of a Campbell's Soup Can it would be a modern work of art, most likely done in the 1960's (Fig. 4.2).

Chapter 4 explores art from High Renaissance to Post Impressionism that has influenced art over the decades. It explores the highlights and

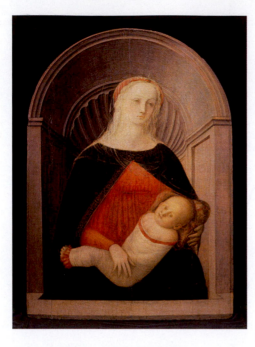

Fig. 4.1 Fra Lippi—*Madonna and Child* (Scala/Art Resource, NY).

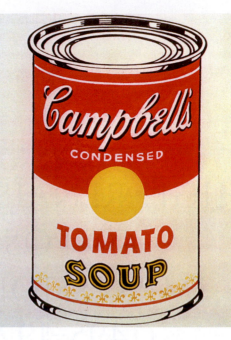

Fig. 4.2 Warhol—*Soup Can* (Copyright © The Andy Warhol Foundation for the Visual Arts/ARS, NY. Photograph courtesy of The Andy Warhol Foundation, Inc./Art Resource, NY.).

characteristics that are associated with them. Once the characteristics of major art genres are learned, going to a museum or art gallery can be more rewarding. If the viewer understands how to interpret the image and its characteristics, simple conclusions can be made about works of art. Each style in history is different from the previous style but most likely influenced by it. Take clothing styles for example. Fashions considered hip in the 1970's went out of fashion. However, years later those same fashions came back in style. What was hip went out of style but influenced future generations. The same is true with the visual arts.

HIGH RENAISSANCE (1495–1525)

Italy produced a handful of artists that would change the course of art history, so much so that we are influenced by their style even today. The main patron of the Renaissance was the church, and most images from the Renaissance are religious in nature. A commonly repeated image was the Madonna and Child (Fig. 4.3). Even more characteristically, one would expect to find the Madonna holding her Son who is staring back at the viewer. There are always exceptions to these characteristics but typically, the Madonna and Child is the traditional image Renaissance artists would portray.

In Renaissance art, the colors are cool and aloof. Renaissance images are meant to be viewed as an outsider, just watching the scene. One stares at the image and the image stares back. Very little emotion, interpretation or reaction is asked of the viewer. Renaissance images are **static**, meaning there is very little movement shown in the image. The figures are arranged in a triangular composition. There are always exceptions to the rule, but this is a typical characteristic of the time period. Most Renaissance images are symmetrical to some degree. The Renaissance artists felt that since the human body was symmetrical, images needed to be the same. This historical time period produced some of the world's most famous artists—Leonardo Da Vinci, Michelangelo and Raphael to name a few.

Leonardo Da Vinci (1452–1519) is considered a genius, an artist and a scientist. His curiosity led him to observe, experiment and invent. He studied many fields including art, anatomy, engineering and physics; yet his life was filled with contradictions. Leonardo saw patterns in nature, believed in the power of human endeavor and sought to fly during his life time. He went on to question everything and distrusted human nature. Leonardo's images are typical of the Renaissance in that his figures are static, his images are symmetrical and his colors are very cool to the eye. Leonardo produced very few paintings, *the Last Supper* (Fig. 4.4),

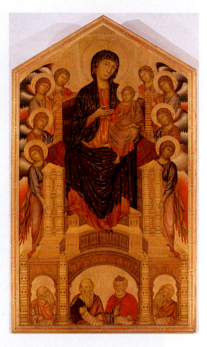

Fig. 4.3 *Madonna of the Holy Trinity* (Scala/Ministero per i Beni e le Attivitá culturali/Art Resource, NY).

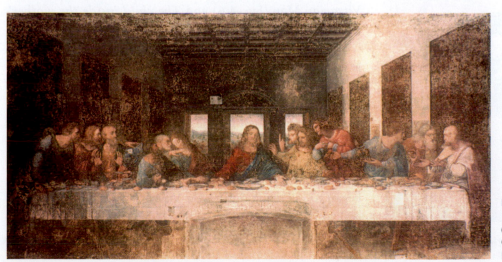

Fig. 4.4 Da Vinci— *The Last Supper* (Courtesy of The Granger Collection, New York.).

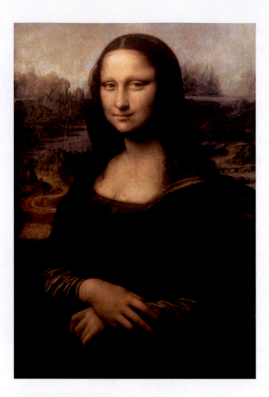

Fig. 4.5 Da Vinci—*Mona Lisa*
(Courtesy of The Granger Collection, New York).

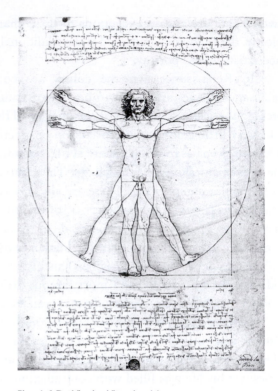

Fig. 4.6 Da Vinci—*Vitruvian Man*
(Courtesy of The Granger Collection, New York).

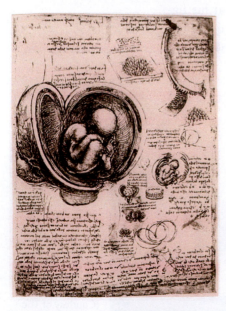

Fig. 4.7 Da Vinci—*The child inside the
mother's womb*
(HIP/Art Resource, NY).

and the most famous portrait of all time, ***The Mona Lisa*** (Fig. 4.5). Beyond these two, most people cannot name another Da Vinci painting. His scientific drawings include ***The Vitruvian Man*** (Fig. 4.6) and ***The child inside the mother's womb*** (Fig. 4.7).

Da Vinci's *Last Supper* was painted for a refectory in Milan, Italy. Leonardo began experimenting with a **fresco** base but using a recently invented new medium, oil paint. **Fresco** paintings are created by applying a thin coat of plaster over an area large enough for the artist to paint before the plaster dries. Typically artists would use tempera paint, which blends with the wet plaster. This was a disastrous experiment because as everyone knows, water and oil don't mix. The painting began to fall apart during Da Vinci's lifetime. He made several corrections but to no avail. Over the centuries the fresco has been repaired many times, and today, experts are trying to save what remains of this masterpiece.

The *Last Supper* has several interesting characteristics. The entire painting is based on the number seven, a Christian symbol that is repeated throughout the New Testament. We see four side windows and three rear windows equaling the number seven. Upon studying the figures one notices four groups with three figures in each group. Supposedly Jesus has just informed disciples that one of them would betray him. Each individual is asking "Is it I?" and Jesus sits very calmly with His hands spread on the table. This was a recurring theme in Leonardo's style, to capture the individual revealing the intension of their soul. The one person distancing himself from Jesus, on His left side, is Judas. Judas is holding his blood money loot in his hand while realizing he has just been exposed. The overall composition is symmetrical, static, and does not invite the viewer into the scene.

Leonardo's most famous painting is the *Mona Lisa*. He began the painting in 1503 and probably finished four years later. It is without doubt the most famous work of art worldwide. This painting draws somewhere around six million visitors to the Louvre every year. This is not the first portrait of Mona Lisa Leonardo painted. He also painted her when she was about 16 years old at the request of her family. In the famous *Mona Lisa* she is now 24 years old, married to a wealthy banker and is the mother of five children. Over the centuries people have wondered about the mysterious smile. But is she smiling or being smug? Could it be that she is fickle? If you stare at the painting long enough you'll notice that she smiles but then her smile disappears. X-rays have shown that there are three versions of *Mona Lisa* under the present one indicating that Leonardo painted this portrait more than once.

The Vitruvian Man was created sometime around 1490 and illustrates how Leonardo would apply physical and mathematical principles to the human body. This particular drawing stems from the ancient Roman, Vitruvius, who was a first century B.C. architect. Vitruvius believed that proportions of a temple had to correspond to the proportions of man, fitting into both a square and a circle. Leonardo studied anatomy for over 20 years, dissecting humans and animals illegally. Leonardo came to many conclusions, some of which were correct and some of which were not, based on theories and ideas he felt were ground breaking during his time.

Da Vinci's embryological drawings of the fetus in *The child inside the mother's womb* are found in the third volume of his notebooks. These drawings were produced between 1510 and 1512. His method of cross-sectional depictions of the fetus revealed an understanding of the birthing process. Leonardo began dissecting with the purpose of understanding the human form more accurately in order to draw and paint more realistically. These endeavors inspired an entirely new form of science.

Michelangelo Buonarroti (1475–1564) was a contemporary of Da Vinci. He was an artistic genius who understood the nature of color, form, composition and how to unify the elements into a whole composition. Michelangelo is renowned as a sculptor, but is famous for his ceiling painting in the Sistine Chapel, just outside Saint Peter's Basilica in Rome. The Sistine ceiling (Fig 4.8) was painted over the course of four years from 1508–1512. The ceiling's theme is that of the nine scenes from Genesis, beginning with the creation of man to the fall of man. This painting was commissioned by Pope Julius II. A commission is a contractual agreement between an artist and a patron. Michelangelo saw himself as a sculptor, a three dimensional artist, but the Pope persuaded him to paint either willingly or by force. In the end the painting became an act of love, not only for the Renaissance period but for all of mankind.

The Pope asked him to paint twelve disciples and appropriate decoration to the small Sistine chapel. Michelangelo felt the Pope's request was uninspired and he began work to create something that would not only inspire the Pope but also the human race. During the next several years Michelangelo created a vision that would have over 300 figures on the ceil-

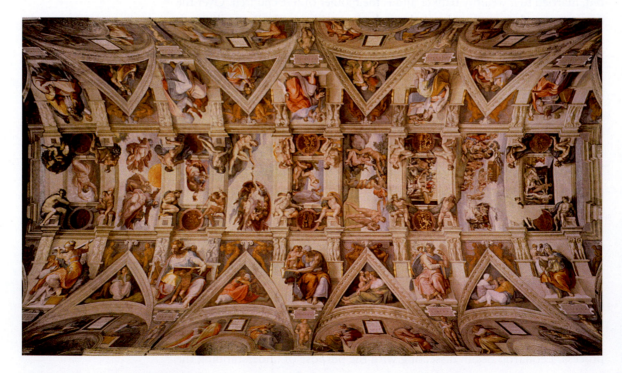

Fig. 4.8 Michelangelo—*Sistine Ceiling*
(Erich Lessing/Art Resource, NY).

ing. Along the sides of the ceiling, Michelangelo painted Prophets and Sybils. The human beings are not suffering their Earthly pain but rather they rise to a higher understanding of God's will for their lives. Each figure is totally enraptured in a spiritual act of contemplation.

One of Michelangelo's Genesis scenes is the figure of God creating Adam in His own image. Michelangelo struggled with the concept of "God's own image." So what did God look like? After reading and rereading the Bible Michelangelo came up the concept of intelligence. In the creation of Adam, Michelangelo has God floating in a cloud-like shape. Upon closer inspection that shape reveals itself to be a profile of a human brain. Michelangelo's image of God is reaching to His fullest to impart His intelligence to man. Adam, on the other hand, is in a position of rest totally uninspired and indifferent to God.

Raphael Sanzio (1483–1520) studied with both Leonardo and Michelangelo for brief periods of time and attempted to copy the best artistic qualities of each. The Renaissance period is characterized by the paintings of Raphael. Most people agree that he is the synthesis of the Renaissance by combining the very best the older masters had to offer. The most famous painting by Raphael, *The School of Athens* (Fig. 4.9), is a fresco painting located in Pope Julius' personal library. This painting has all the classic characteristics summed up by the Renaissance such as colors that are aloof, symmetrical composition and figures all in a precise pose.

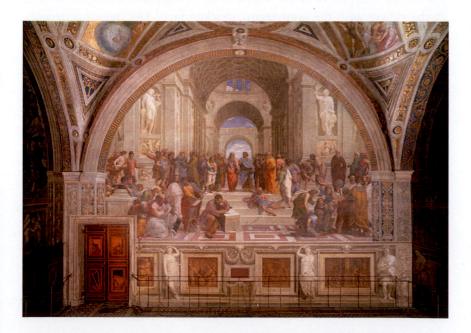

Fig. 4.9 Raphael—*School of Athens*
(Scala/Art Resource, NY).

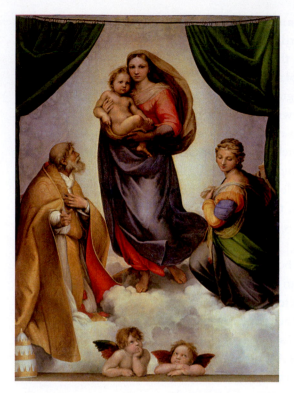

Fig. 4.10 Raphael—*Sistine Madonna*
The Sistine Madonna, 1513 (oil on canvas) by Raphael (Raffaello Sanzio of Urbino) (1483–1520) Gemaeldegalerie Alte Meister, Dresden, Germany/© Staatliche Kunstsammlungen Dresden/The Bridgeman Art Library.

The two central figures are Aristotle and Plato. Aristotle is on the right and is holding a book in his hand. His hand is indicating down to Earth which means he is putting his faith into science and beliefs of this world. Plato on the other hand is barefoot and points up to the heavens indicating his faith in a higher being. Raphael, like many artist throughout history used his friends as models for particular figures in his paintings. Plato is most likely Leonardo Da Vinci. Heraclitus in the lower left front of the painting is most probably Michelangelo. Archimedes, the figure on the far right bending over is assuredly Bramante, the architect who designed the Vatican. Raphael even painted himself into the fresco on the far right hand side. We can just barely see his face peeking around the corner of the arch.

The Sistine Madonna (Fig. 4.10) is probably one of Raphael's best oil paintings illustrating an extreme example of Renaissance art. Many consider this painting equally as good as Da Vinci's *Mona Lisa*. What has baffled people over the years is the look on the face of Jesus and that of his Mother as well. A close-up reveals the Child's teeth are clenched with a shocked expression. Mary is looking at the viewer with the same terror stricken face. The question over the centuries has been, why the troubled look on Mary and the Child's faces as they appear to be looking at us? If you follow the pointing finger of the Holy Father who is gesturing outward towards the viewer, you would have found on the opposite wall an altar piece of a crucifixion. The faces of the Mother and Child are a reaction to what He sees in His future.

BAROQUE (1600–1700)

Artists of the 1600's were attempting to create a new style that would later be called Baroque due to its religious nature and dark images. By definition Baroque art is dramatic, bold, theatrical, and filled with emotion, unlike the static art of the Renaissance. The characteristics are best summed up by a darkened image with no apparent light source. The viewer has no idea what is causing the light or where it's coming from, be it a window, a doorway or simply a divine moment in time. The artists of this genre would use common everyday scenes to portray a religious message. Their images look secular but are biblical scenes. People of the Baroque genre would recognize the common scene but could read its religious overtones. The Baroque genre occurred during the time of the reformation and counter-reformation, a time of much confusion within the church structure. It was an era of **absolutism**, meaning that what the government and the church set forth as rules, the people would not challenge. It was a time of re-evaluating humanity and trying to understand its relationship to the universe. The leading Baroque artist was Caravaggio.

Caravaggio (1571–1610) was not a typical artist. He was a man given to fighting and corruption. He was on his way to see the pope to be pardoned for a murder he had committed when he was killed by several men he had cheated. It is Caravaggio who is considered the most important Baroque painter and inventor of the period. His paintings are typical of the Baroque style, using everyday settings to portray biblical stories. In *The Calling of St. Matthew* (Fig. 4.11) we see a drunken Matthew in a bar being called by Christ to be an apostle. At first glance, one could misinterpret the meaning of the painting, but knowing the characteristics it becomes obvious that it is of the Baroque style with its light coming from above Christ with no visible source. This painting influenced artists for the next several generations.

In the painting *Martha and Mary Magdalene* (Fig. 4.12) Caravaggio gives a biblical view of two sisters in conversation. Martha is attempting to persuade her sister Mary to convert from her old ways to a life in Christ. Martha, whose face is in shadow, is trying to influence Mary. Mary is holding a flower in one hand and caressing a mirror with the other, thus symbolizing the earthly pleasures she would have

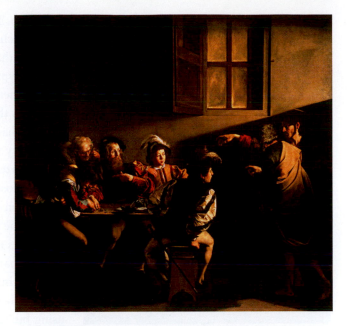

Fig. 4.11 Caravaggio—*The Calling of St. Matthew* (Courtesy of Scala/Art Resource, NY.).

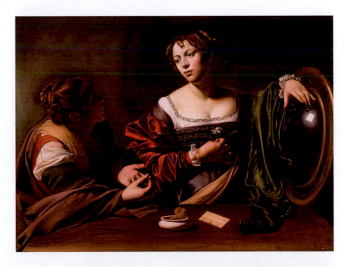

Fig. 4.12 Caravaggio—*Martha and Mary Magdalene* Martha and Mary Magdalene, c.1598 (oil & tempera on canvas) by Michelangelo Merisi da Caravaggio (1571–1610) Detroit Institute of Arts, USA/Gift of the Kresge Foundation and Mrs. Edsel B. Ford/The Bridgeman Art Library.

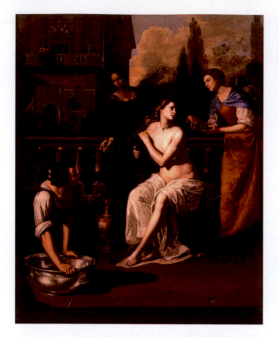

Fig. 4.13 Gentileschi—*Bathsheba and David* (Courtesy of Columbus Museum of Art).

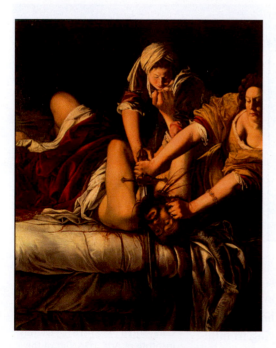

Fig. 4.14 Gentileschi—*Judith and Holofernes* (Courtesy of Scala/Art Resource, NY.).

to give up. The main focus of the painting is that of Mary's face, which is in bright light. It appears to be at the very moment that she decides to convert and give her life to Christ. Typical of the Baroque genre, this is a painting of two women in a tense conversation and yet if one does not know the story it would not appear to be biblical. The painting has the mysterious dramatic lighting from above and a very theoretical play of emotions.

Artemisia Gentileschi (1593–1656) was a female artist whose father had her trained to be a painter at a time when painting was considered a man's profession. During the Renaissance, women artists began to emerge, but it was not until the Baroque genre that they became predominant. Artemisia was not just a follower of Caravaggio, but was an excellent painter in her own right. Most of her work is based on the lack of female rights using biblical scenes to produce her socially motivated themes, namely "men and the evils they do." Her two main subjects were *Bathsheba and David* (Fig. 4.13), who was the object of King David's lust. The other subject being the biblical figure of Judith, whose book is now in the Apocrypha, the 39 books King James removed from the protestant bible believing they were not divinely inspired. *Judith and Holofernes* (Fig. 4.14) illustrates a typical Baroque scene. It is an image of two women in a darkened room, presumably the bedroom where Judith is beheading her fiancée Holofernes. The mysterious light in the image creates an atmosphere of intrigue across the faces of Judith and her maidservant. The overall effect is theatrical with a unique blend of drama. Artemisia cuts off the head while her maidservant assists by holding Holofernes down. Artemisia paints with rich colors of passion that have a lasting impression.

Baroque art had a tendency to be both theatrical and dramatic by posing the figures in the composition as opposed to the static figures of the Renaissance artists. It is clear that the Baroque art was a new style distinct from, but emerging out of, the Renaissance. It would be the lessons learned from the Baroque artists that would create the next period, Neo-Classical/Romantic.

NEO-CLASSICAL/ROMANTIC (1750–1850)

After the reformation and counter-reformation the artistic genre that followed refers not so much to a specific style but rather an attitude. The concepts of the Neo-Classical and Romantic are harder to define because the artists favored several styles instead of one particular style.

"I think therefore I am."

Descartes (1596–1650)

"I feel therefore I can."

Romantic artists

This illustrates how the Romantic artists would put emotion over intellect in choosing their subject matter. This radical change came about due to the church, which had long been the largest patron of the Arts, but was no longer in charge. Responsibility shifted to the public, and Neo-Classical/Romantic artists were representing their generation. This period corresponds with the American Revolution of 1776 and the French Revolution of 1779. It allowed a new mindset of standards that believed human feelings were determined by reason rather than an established authority, unlike the state of absolutism that existed during the Baroque genre. The church and the government no longer dictated to artists.

The following summarizes the Neo-Classical and Romantic artist's perceptions:

The genre is called "Romantic" because of the medieval tales of adventure, written in Romance languages such as French, Spanish and Italian.

Return to nature, real events, and contemporary themes

Nature is wild and unbounded, ever changing, like man.

Artists use emotion over intellect through color and subject matter.

The heart has reasons that reason itself does not know.

Romantics favored many styles in their artwork.

Painted large "history" paintings to tell the world also known as documentation paintings.

A leading artist of the time was **Jacques-Louis David** (1748–1825), who developed the Neo-Classical genre and created compositions that were influenced by Renaissance compositions in their symmetrical and static imagery. He also borrowed from the Baroque with dramatic lighting and theatrics.

Fig. 4.15 David—*The Death
of Socrates*
(Copyright © The
Metropolitan Museum of
Art/Art Resource, NY.).

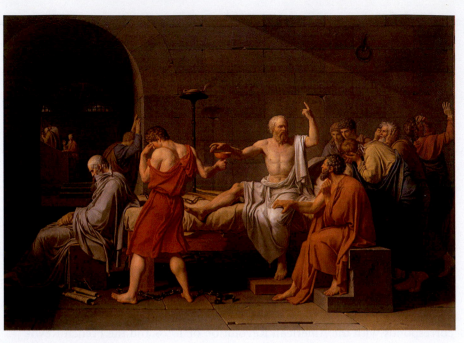

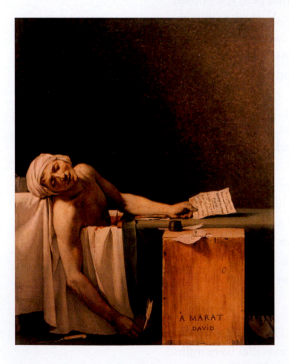

Fig. 4.16 David—*The Death
of Marat*
(Scala/Art Resource, NY).

His painting *The Death of Socrates* (Fig. 4.15) he creates dramatic imagery as Socrates is about to take hemlock and give up his own life. He is presented in a way that suggests Christ with his twelve disciples around him. Socrates is pointing upwards, signifying his belief in a creator, while his subjects are dramatically displaying strong emotional feelings towards his resolution to sacrifice his life. David paints strong lighting and yet the viewer is not privileged to its source.

Another painting with passionate overtones is *The Death of Marat* (Fig. 4.16), where we see the political writer Marat. Marat, a friend of David, is lying in a bathtub with a letter in one hand and his quill pen in the other. The scene has characteristics of a Baroque image that look dramatic and theoretical; light is streaming in with no indication of the source. What makes this image Neo-Classical/Romantic is the fact that it's documenting an actual event in much the same way as a news reporter of today documents important events. The death of the popular political writer was big news. Marat was very influential with the political leaders in Paris. Charlotte Corday,

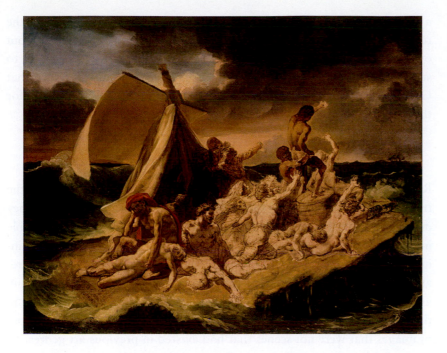

Fig. 4.17 Gericault—*The Raft of Medusa* (Réunion des Musées Nationaux/Art Resource, NY).

who disagreed with the leaders of the French Revolution, believed she was doing her part to stop a civil war in France. She stabbed Marat in the chest, piercing his lung, aorta and left ventricle. In the lower left corner of the painting the knife is lying on the ground. At her trial she stated "*I killed one man to save 100,000.*" Four days after Marat's death, Corday was beheaded by guillotine.

Another prominent artist of this genre was **Theodore Gericault** (1791–1824). His painting *The Raft of Medusa* (Fig. 4.17) which is almost life size (16' × 24') is based on the story of a naval ship which sank while traveling to West Africa in 1816. The captain and crew abandoned ship using the longboats, leaving 146 men and one woman passengers to survive on a very unstable make-shift raft. The raft was towed behind the long-boat but was dragging them down. To save themselves, the captain and crew cut the raft loose. The passengers spent 13 days on the raft, and only 15 survived. There were few provisions and fights broke out. During the first night, 20 men were killed or committed suicide. Dozens more died fighting to get to the most stable part of the raft, the center. By the fourth day, only 67 of the 147 passengers were alive, and some had resorted to cannibalism. On the eighth day, the strongest threw the weakest and wounded overboard until only the 15 strongest passengers survived. Gericault chose to paint the image at the very moment when all hope was lost but miraculously a ship appeared on the horizon saving their lives. This painting depicts the reality of human suffering and the horrible conditions that were drawn out over a period of days. The image represents man's steadfast resolution to survive in nature at all costs. What makes this work a stunning feat was that Gericault used the actual survivors and the make-shift raft as the models for the painting where the scene was recreated in his studio.

REALISM (1850–1880)

Realism was a reaction to the **French Academies**, who were steeped in the traditional style of the past. The Academies, or art schools, were rigid. They dictated what artists could and could not paint and what was acceptable in the **salons,** or art galleries. The Realist painters struggled with remaining in the structured format of the Academies. They looked for ways to create new images concerning what they saw without idolizing the subject in any way. Their subjects would be common, everyday scenes and people in their familiar environment. The artists were experimenting with new types of images that were not scenes that had existed in previous art genres.

Realism artists felt that the Romantic artists' faith in emotion over reason was an escape from the "reality" of the times. The Realists were convinced that they must use direct experiences from life to be a Realist. Realism means naturalism, or objective observation of facts. Realist art portrays the subject in a straight-forward manner. The Realist artists were becoming very anxious about the influence the Academies had and were struggling with how to satisfy their own desires and still meet the demands of the Academies.

Gustave Courbet (1819–1877) created art that exemplifies heroism in modern life and lead the Realist painters to their pursuit of naturalism. In his work *The Stone Breakers* (Fig. 4.18), destroyed in 1945 by the Nazis, one sees full Realism as felt by Courbet. We see two men working alongside the road. Courbet saw the

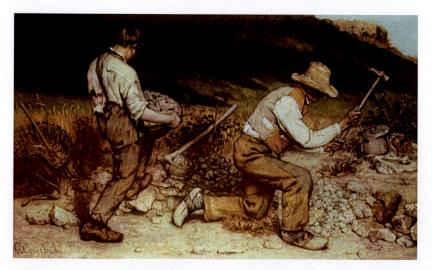

Fig. 4.18 Courbet—*The Stone Breakers*
(© Staatliche Kunstsammlungen Dresden/The Bridgeman Art Library).

two men working and asked them if they would pose for him in his studio. *The Stone Breakers* was a life-size matter-of-factly painted image with no sentiment. The young man's face is not seen because the young man is too young to be doing hard labor, the back-breaking task of breaking large stones into smaller ones. By this same token the old man, whose face is half-hidden, is too old for the back-breaking labor. What is important in this painting is the contrast in age, one man too young, other too old for the task at hand.

The *Interior of My Studio: A Real Allegory of my Life as an Artist* (Fig. 4.19) is a completely different type of Realism that when first exhibited shocked the public. There are two groups purposefully posed within the image. The group on the left is individuals, peasants, and common laborers which symbolize poverty. On the right are people of wealth, artists, clients and intellectuals. All are there by invitation of the artist, some are talking, some are quiet, and some are hovering in the background. They are not his audience because no one is really paying attention to the main subject, that of Courbet at a canvas. Only the little boy watches the painter,

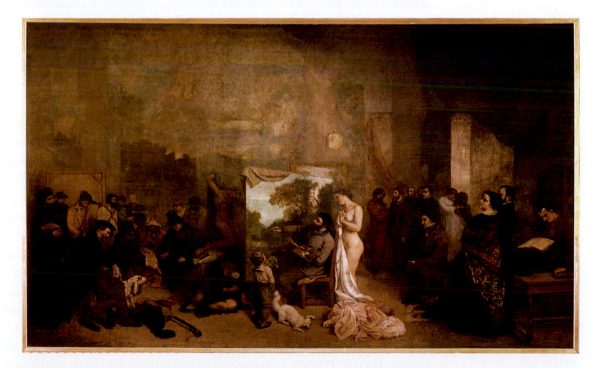

Fig. 4.19 Courbet—*Interior of My Studio: A Real Allegory of My Life as an Artist*
(Gustave Courbet (1819–1877), "The Studio." 1855. Oil on canvas, 361 × 598 cm. Inc. RF2257. Musee d'Orsay, Paris, France. RMN Reunion des Musees Nationaux, France. Erich Lessing/Art Resource, NY).

Fig. 4.20 Manet—*Luncheon on the Grass* (Courtesy of Réunion des Musées Nationaux/Art Resource, NY.).

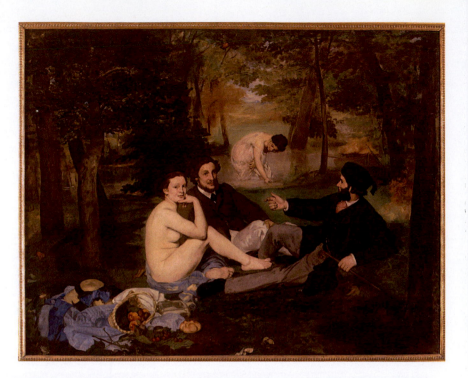

which symbolizes an innocent eye. The nude model may be a symbol of inspiration and/or a muse. What are their roles? The model may be nature or even truth, which was the main principle to Realism. The overall painting reveals layers of the artist's life.

Another Realist painter, who would eventually be more known for his Impressionist paintings, is **Edouard Manet** (1832–1883). He would shock the public even more than Courbet's *Allegory* painting by creating a nude woman with clothed men in an outdoor setting. Manet was the first to utilize Courbet's ideals and incorporate them in his paintings. ***Luncheon on the Grass*** (Fig. 4.20) was offensive to the contemporary audience. Moral issues rose from a nude woman posing with fully dressed men for all to see. This was not an actual event but rather this painting is about artistic freedom. This scene was a very revolutionary concept which combines elements that pleased the artist's aesthetics. This broke from the traditional French Academic schools and was rejected by the Academies and the public alike. They saw it as a picture of pictures, where the model doesn't fit into the scene; neither does the woman in the background bathing herself. The whole image is a combination of a Greek statue and a Raphael sketch that Manet had seen on one of his travels. The overall composition is a typical triangular Renaissance pose incorporating the three figures in the front up to the bathing woman in the background. The painting is flat and lacks the artistic style of the time. Manet purposefully placed three separate planes in the composition, knowing they were not proportionate to one another. From the still-life to the woman bathing he has stacked his subjects, making the overall effect a flat composition. The woman bathing is too large to be in the background and the still-life in the foreground is too small for the central figures. Manet painted this image to create a stir and to protest the Academies' harsh rules. Even though Manet accomplished what he wanted to in this painting, he was greatly disturbed that so many people took a negative view towards his work and other Realist artists because of his work.

Jean Francois Millet (1814–1875) was a French landscape painter who mainly painted melancholy scenes of peasant workers at their labor. *The Gleaners* (Fig. 4.21) is an excellent example of Millet's Realism in which he recreated rural life in the 19th century. We see three female figures gleaning leftovers of a wheat harvest. The farmer has reaped a huge harvest and now allows the old women to go in and pick the leftovers. Millet was making a social statement of the time regarding the poor remaining poor and the rich getting richer. The painting was met with mixed reviews because the public attacked the depiction of the poor women. The wealthy did not want to see the poor struggling for their very survival. There's a correlation between the Old Testament Book of Ruth and *The Gleaners*. Millet would use that story to defend his painting.

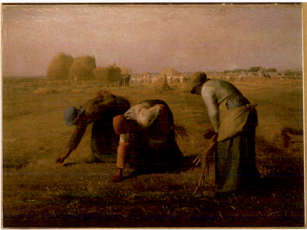

Fig. 4.21 Millet—*The Gleaners* (Erich Lessing/Art Resource, NY).

Realism gave way to Impressionism. Impressionists thought they were the final phase of Realism. In fact their early paintings were from the Realist genre. The Impressionists would move rapidly into their own genre of Parisian life and everyday scenes of modern man living in the industrialized new city of Paris.

IMPRESSIONISM (1870–1890)

The Impressionist painters were primarily a group of French friends and artistic rebels that determined that they wanted to redefine art; they wanted their images to represent their generation in their own instinctive way. They were the first group who would solely rely on the wealthy to buy their work for support. They painted images people wanted, such as people boating, at parties, and enjoying leisure time. This was the first generation to have extra time on their hands and not have to work most of their waking hours. They enjoyed new inventions like the steam train that could take them further from home than they had ever been at what they felt was incredible speed. Before the invention of the steam train, transportation remained the same since the days of Jesus.

The Impressionist artists set up their canvas out-of-doors and painted nature as they saw it. They began experimenting with light, and the effects of the sun as it traveled across the sky. They would incorporate the moving of the sun into their work as **atmosphere.** Atmosphere can be described as something you could see but cannot touch; for example, sun filtering through the trees casting shadows on the ground; how the object would change color through the day and shift patterns as the shadow moved from one hour to the next in the course of a day. Atmosphere was key to the Impressionists' goal of creating images that reflected the affects of light on objects.

The Impressionists never really won over the art world. They were able to sell a few paintings during their lifetime, but it wasn't until 1975 that Impressionism was truly realized. In a retrospective exhibit in New York, the public fell in love with Impressionistic works, and today it is the most sought-after art. Impressionists were rejected from the Academies and the galleries for producing art that was considered ugly and out-of-focus. The Impressionist artists were ahead of their time.

Claude Monet (1840–1926) painted *Impression Sunrise* (Fig. 4.22), which is an image of a harbor. The viewer can make out images but must rely on their own experiences to create the 'whole' of the image. A boat is seen in the foreground and the sun is rising in the sky; beyond that are other boats and industrial buildings. The paint was applied in a thin layer affect

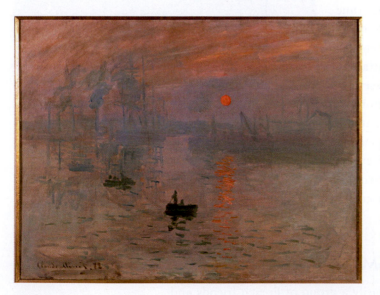

Fig. 4.22 Monet—*Impression Sunrise* (Erich Lessing/Art Resource, NY).

rather than using the typical thick heavy color over the canvas. A critic writing about its first exhibition in 1874 said he couldn't quite make out the image because it was blurred, but got the impression of a sunrise, hence the name *Impression Sunrise*. This is also the origin of the name of this artistic genre, Impressionism. Monet would paint images that reflected his life and places he would travel.

Another Impressionist artist was **Auguste Renoir** (1841–1919) who produced colorful scenes of people enjoying themselves at parties or doing leisurely activities. His painting **Luncheon of the Boating Party** (Fig. 4.23) illustrates atmosphere and the affects of light on objects. Its panoramic view is a feast for the eyes. People are talking, enjoying lunch, and one woman plays with her dog. The complementary colors of blue and orange harmonize the entire painting to produce a cooling effect. Notice the composition as Renoir guides us through the image using a zig-zag of people front to back then back to front. The Impressionists wanted to guide the viewer through their works of art, and they controlled how the viewer saw the paintings.

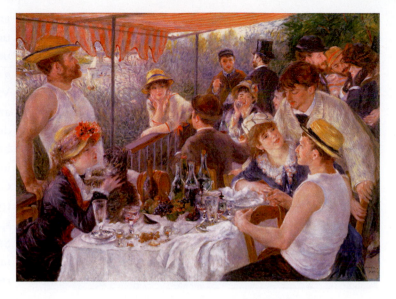

Fig. 4.23 Renoir—*Luncheon of the Boating Party* (Courtesy of The Bridgeman Art Library).

The Impressionists, as a group, were always on the verge of collapsing. The impressionist artists were constantly moving in different directions, creating a variety of images from landscape, urban realism, rural life, to everyday scenes. It would come as no surprise that following the final Impressionist exhibition of 1886 the group would disband and work independently for the rest of their lives.

POST IMPRESSIONISM (1886–1892)

The Post Impressionists, meaning "after Impressionism" followed in the footsteps of the Impressionists but were liberated completely from the academic tradition of the past. The Post Impressionists created works that have less to do with reality and more to do with color relationships and complex compositions.

The most famous Post Impressionist artists was **Vincent van Gogh** (1853–1890). Van Gogh's life was one of searching for personal meaning. He led a tragic life while creating many works of art that are considered masterpieces today. Van Gogh did not think Impressionism gave the artist

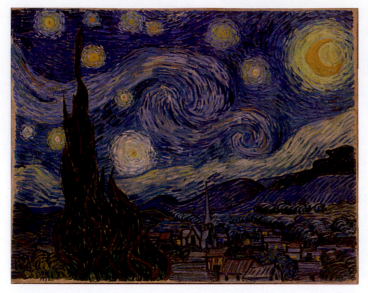

Fig. 4.24 Van Gogh—*Starry Night* (Digital Image © The Museum of Modern Art/ Licensed by SCALA/Art Resource, NY).

enough freedom to express their emotions. He was dissatisfied with the values of the industrial society and began a mission to paint as he interpreted life. Van Gogh's paintings come alive to anyone who sees them in person; the deeply spiritual side of the artist becomes real. The paintings seem intensely personal and full of van Gogh's own emotions. His work stands today as a testament to his beliefs and spiritual reality. Most people recognize *Starry Night* as van Gogh's most famous masterpiece but few people realize that he painted an earlier version. The first version painted in September of 1888 was called *Starry Night Over Rhone*. The famous version of *Starry Night* (Fig. 4.24) is a scene he painted while committed to an insane asylum at Saint-Remy in June 1889. He was unable to see the night sky, and painted it from memory. Van Gogh's painting is remarkable for its color, texture and personal style created in the night sky.

He became an artist at 27 and died ten years later of a self-inflicted gunshot wound. In those ten years van Gogh created more works of art than most artists create in a lifetime. This is a testament to his drive and character.

Another Post Impressionist artist was **Paul Gauguin** (1848–1903). Of utmost importance to Gauguin was his manipulation of composition and color placement in a way seldom seen in other works of this genre. Being liberated from the academic past, Gauguin began translating photographs, creating interesting changes that would allow the subject to become the most important part of the conceived painting. Gauguin would execute a number of paintings with this pictorial editing of photographs depicting particular elements within the image to recreate the composition. Gauguin's intent was very deliberate, preferring to be mysterious at times and always avoiding simple pictorial imagery for more complex universal symbolism.

In the painting *Vision after the Sermon* (Fig. 4.25) of 1888, Gauguin created a landscape scene where we see people praying after a sermon. To Gauguin, the fight between Jacob and the angel exists only in the minds of the praying women. The entire image is out of proportion, and the Christian subject matter is in reality symbolism. The distinction between Gauguin and other artists is that of observation and vision as he combines two pictorial planes into one composition. His use of an intense red for the ground and the deep blues, yellows and oranges for the imaginary figures separates the spiritual world from the lifeless dull reality of the women. The tree bisecting the composition is another visual symbol that divided the two factions. Its trunk is painted in brown and highlighted in orange on the imaginary side to reinforce the division between the natural world and the spiritual world.

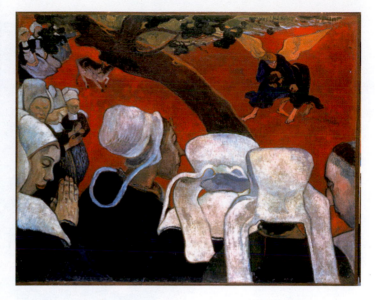

Fig. 4.25 Gauguin—*Vision after the Sermon* (Courtesy of Art Resource, NY.).

Convinced that Impressionism would not last, **Paul Cezanne** (1839–1906) began searching for a way to capture intense color in timeless landscapes and still-lifes. This artist studied how light affected color but was not interested in the illusion of light, as in Baroque, or atmosphere, as in Impressionism. He was most interested in how light changed the tone of the color in a shape or a form within the composition. His affect was a heightened emphasis on the structure using multiple values of a single color, like a puzzle, to create a complex grid of horizontal, vertical and diagonal lines resulting in a sense of volume infused with vitality. Cezanne would analyze every brush stroke and contemplate it's meaning in the composition taking many days to complete a work of art, versus one sitting by van Gogh. One can only imagine him standing at his easel, applying a single brush stroke and then sitting down and thinking about it for the next 30–50 minutes, and then walking back to the painting to make another mark only to sit down and contemplate again. For obvious reasons this imposed self-isolation for many years. He had his first one-man exhibition very late in his life. Today he is considered the **Father of Abstraction**, a title he could definitely find displeasing. What Cezanne did was to create a path for modern artists, especially Picasso to create abstract images.

In the painting *Mount St. Victoire* (Fig. 4.26) we see a series of individual color planes that are typical of Cezanne's later style. The imagery has been abstracted down to color shapes that will indicate houses, trees and of course the mountain in the background. Even the sky has the same

Fig. 4.26 Cezanne—*Mount St. Victoire* (Erich Lessing/Art Resource, NY).

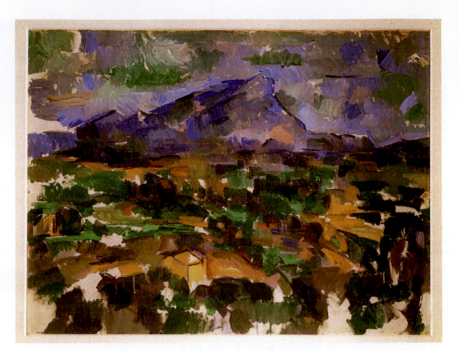

coloring as the foreground. This was his style, harmonizing the color and creating the visual map to direct the viewer's eye. Note the limited color palette of blues to greens to yellow-browns. Cezanne's main goal was to unify the images within his paintings. Every mark and every placement of color has a purposeful meaning to Cezanne.

Over the course of 400 years, the artists' mindset changed from being dictated by religion to free-thinking artists that painted whatever they felt. The works of art discussed in this chapter have influenced modern day art and sets the stage for art movements to come, such as Abstraction, Cubism, and Abstract Expressionism. There was a major shift in the art world that took place during the time periods discussed in this chapter from artists being dependent on the church for patronage to paintings that were for documentation purposes to a generation of artists trying to paint everyday life as they saw it. The invention of the steam train and the beginning of industrialization influenced the cultures and the artists living during this time.

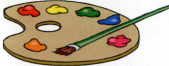

Chapter 4 Homework
Renaissance to Post Impressionist Art

50 Points Possible

Complete the following project. **Staple** all additional sheets to this page. (**No bent corner-type attachments accepted**).

Size restrictions: Minimum 8 × 10 – Maximum 8½ × 11. All work MUST be _typed using complete sentences and correct punctuation to earn full credit._

Painting Analysis

Find and attach **one** image from any genre discussed in this chapter. The painting must have been completed during the time frame discussed in this chapter. The image **MUST NOT** have been discussed in class or in the text and must be a minimum of 5 × 7 inches. You can use the internet to search for the image. Justify **ALL** of your answers.

Answer the following questions concerning your chosen genre. Hint: Black/White and neutral are not considered color schemes.

What genre is being used?
     (10 points possible)
What is the title of the image and year painted?
     (5 points possible)
Who is the artist?
     (5 points possible)
What color scheme is being used?
     (10 points possible)
What compositional style is being used?
     (10 points possible)
What are the characteristics of this genre?
     (5 points possible)
Site your resource.
     (5 points possible)

Genre 10 points possible	
Title/Year Painted 5 points possible	
Artist 5 points possible	
Color scheme 10 points possible	
Composition 10 points possible	
Genre characteristics 5 points possible	
Resource 5 points possible	
Total Points	

Chapter 4 Homework

Renaissance to Post-Impressionist Art

50 Points Possible

Complete the following project. Staple all additional sheets to this page with least information on a separate sheet.

Note restrictions: Minimum 5 – 10 – Maximum MLS. All same MLS for total once complete sentences and correct information to earn full credit.

Painting Analysis

Find and attach one image from any genre discussed in this chapter. The column must have been completed discussed since the time we studied this chapter. The image MLS 1–60 F Five (each discussed in class item discussed) must be a minimum of 5 – 7 inches. You can use the Internet to search for the image. Justify ALL of your answers.

Answer the following questions concerning your chosen genre. Think Black/White and answer and use connected color scheme.

What genre is being used?
(10 points possible)

What is the title of the image and year painted?
(5 points possible)

Who is the artist?
(5 points possible)

What color scheme is being used?
(10 points possible)

What compositional style is being used?
(10 points possible)

What are the characteristics of the genre?
(10 points possible)

Site your resource.
(5 points possible)

Genre	
10 points possible	
Title/Year Painted	
5 points possible	
Artist	
5 points possible	
Color scheme	
10 points possible	
Composition	
10 points possible	
Genre Characteristics	
5 points possible	
Resource	
5 point possible	
Total Point	

5

ART OF THE 20TH CENTURY (1900–PRESENT)

MODERN ART (1860–1970)

Modern art falls under a large umbrella of genres that were produced in an experimental way with new ideas about the functions of art. The early forerunners to Modern art were the Romantics, Realists and Impressionists. Post-Impressionism ultimately influenced the new style of modern art. Modern art leans towards abstractions that would be produced in the United States. Another example of how rapidly the world was changed from the mid-1800s to the mid-1900s can be seen in the way that man went from horse and buggy to landing on the moon in 1969; the United States went from slavery to civil rights; from farming as the main source of food for your family to industrialization and factory work as the main means of income. During this period, art also changed so much that the public found it hard to understand and appreciate. Artists are now creating images that appear chaotic, often it is difficult to read and find meaning within them. By the 1970s the many different genres began to disappear, but the damage on the public's opinion regarding art was already done. Works of art consisting of urinals, broken glass and ready-made objects caused people to question the art world.

Modern art is a general movement that contains many smaller genres or developments. In this chapter, a few of the main genres and influential artists of the past one hundred years will be explored.

Among the different genres that flourished during the first half of the 20th century were Fauvism, Cubism, Surrealism, and Abstract Expressionism. Some artists didn't fit into any "ism" but were completely independent with genres all their own. Modern art came to America by way of the Armory Show of 1913 when European artists moved to the United States during World War I. Ever since this time the United States has been the leader of the artistic world.

During the second half of the century several genres emerged: Pop Art, Neo-Expressionism and Post Modernism.

THE FAUVES (1903–1908)

An art critic, Louis Vauxcelles, coined the term "Fauves," meaning wild beasts, which he meant as a derogatory manner. He described a small Donatello sculpture in an art gallery side-by-side with art of modern artists as, "a Donatello in a cage of wild beasts (Fauves)." Ever since, the name has been associated with works of art that looked violent as opposed to images of harmony and intimate subject matter of the Impressionists. Characteristics of Fauvist art are violent colors used directly from the tube, an influence of Post Impressionist painters, along with distortions and alterations for expressive purposes. The Fauvist genre was very short lived but produced several noteworthy artists. After a few years the painters began working on different concepts and moved completed away from the Fauve genre.

One of the leading artists of the Fauves was **Henri Matisse (1869–1954)**. Matisse was out there on his own not relying on any artist from the past for his compositions. There was no previous genre of art for him to be influenced by; therefore Matisse relied solely on his own theories. His images were flat and the challenges imposed on him did not allow for expansion and development beyond the main sense of liberation and experimentation in color and image. Matisse developed images that stir our imaginations even today.

The Red Studio (Fig. 5.1) is a good example of the Fauvism genre with its flattened image and exaggerated color. Following the lines in the composition, the image has a two dimensional look. The dimensions of the room are outlined and the brain translates that it is a three-dimensional room even though everything is flat. What Matisse does so well is omit everything that is not needed, including various shades of color, to indicate the dimensional space of the room itself. Notice that the tablecloth, the clock, and the chair in the right hand corner are all the same flat red color. He harmonizes the composition by way of repeating some basic shapes throughout. These appear random but are, in fact, very calculated. Matisse understood exactly what he was doing in creating very bold images.

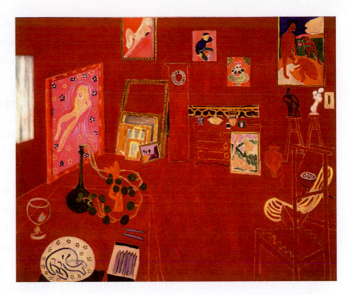

Fig. 5.1 Matisse—*The Red Studio*
(Copyright © Succession H. Matisse, Paris/ARS, NY. Photograph copyright © The Museum of Modern Art/ Licensed by SCALA/Art Resource, NY.).

The Fauve genre held together for just a few years because the individual personalities of the artist were too independent to maintain their common goals. **Andre Derain** (1880–1954) was one such artist. Derain was much younger than Matisse but was excited to join the experimentation of color adopted by the Fauves. He had an appetite for fresh independent ideas of color arrangement that all but matched Matisse. By 1906 Derain was attempting to "tame" the wild beast genre. His color theories became cooler as he began turning away from the Fauve genre.

The Westminster Bridge (Fig. 5.2) painted in 1905 is a good example of Derain's new color theories. The sky is bluish/green with orange mixed to make it a complementary color scheme. The smoke in the foreground is

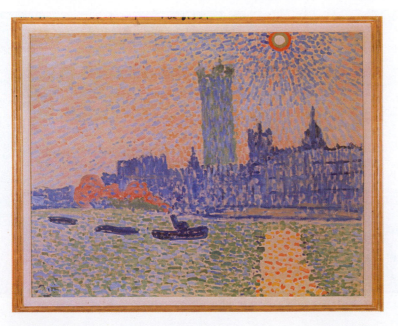

Fig. 5.2 Derain—*The Westminster Bridge*
(Courtesy of Bridgeman Giraudon/Art Resource, NY. © 2010 Artists Rights Society (ARS), New York/ADAGP, Paris).

red while the water reflections is yellow with dots of orange mixed throughout. Details are evident as Derain is looking for a renewal of expression while using the Fauves' liberated colors.

NON-REPRESENTATIONAL ART

The artist who became the most original and completely expressive in his inner reality of creating a work of art was **Wassily Kandinsky (1866–1944)**. Kandinsky would be the first to eliminate the image altogether by 1913. He wanted to create an art form that was spiritual in nature. The viewer would have to draw upon their own life experiences to interpret the image and the meaning within the image. In looking at his painting the eye of the viewer attempts to make sense of the chaos and tries to find imagery where there is none—it is devoid of objects. In his painting *Composition 7* (Fig. 5.3) Kandinsky clearly and freely splashes paint in a spontaneous manner, as if free to scribble across a canvas with paint. This was Kandinsky's attempt to create a piece that elevated art to a new level of spiritual reality. Kandinsky thought his images represented staccato rhythms within a musical form; short and unconnected shapes. He wanted the viewer's mind to create purely from its subconscious. Whether the viewer sees an image or not all takes place within the viewer's brain because the brain attempts to make sense of chaos.

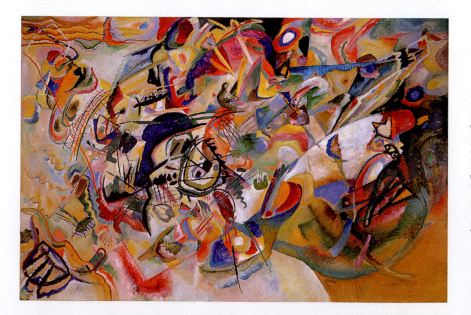

Fig. 5.3 Kandinsky—
Composition 7
(Erich Lessing/Art Resource, NY).

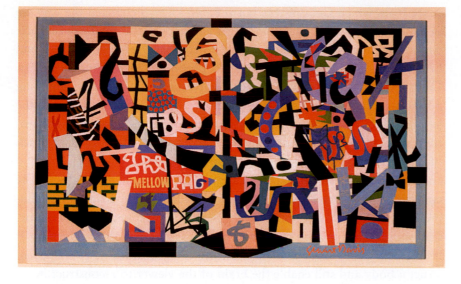

Fig. 5.4 Davis—*The Mellow Pad* (Brooklyn Museum of Art).

Stuart Davis (1894–1964) was committed to modern art in America with his use of contemporary subject matter inspired by American jazz music. His images helped set the stage for what Picasso would create in the years ahead. His work is a model for abstraction as well as a model of integrity for American artists. He believed in the right to free expression and he used many styles and forms in his own work over the years. Even though he was somewhat of a revolutionary, his work represents his time. It's vibrant, jazzy, volatile and always lively, as evident in his image *The Mellow Pad*. (Fig. 5.4)

Stuart Davis would simplify his forms and eliminate all but the descriptive content reducing it to a system of flat plains and geometric shapes. An avid lover of jazz and other popular art forms, his images reflect the new rhythms of the "roaring '20s" in his abstract painting. Davis' work was influenced by modern American life with its irregular silhouettes and brightly-colored city lights.

CUBISM

Pablo Picasso (1881–1973) was attempting to destroy the realistic image in art to create a new form of reality through distortions and even dislocated facial features to create a new three-dimensionality. He methodically and systematically broke images into angular shapes that would become flat at times and yet shaded in such a way that created a certain modified space from which **Cubism** was born. Pablo Picasso changed the way we saw the human figure. A nose no longer had to be in the middle of the face. An ear might be dropped down or left off completely. Many people found his images disturbing because he had produced an unfamiliar reality. Cubism can be broken down into the simplest form of a cube. Comparing a head to a cube; the front of the cube represents the front of a head; the left side of the cube, the left profile; the right side of the cube, the right profile; the top of the cube, the top of the head; the back of the cube, the back of the head. Picasso would combine the front view and a side profile of a cube together in a single image, creating what he would call Cubism. The contrasts of color and texture along with reducing the images into minimum shapes produced images that were complex and yet systematic. Cubism is a form of abstraction and was Picasso's own observed reality. It is as if he was playing a game with nature to see how far he could deconstruct a body and still enable the brain of the viewer to reconstruct it.

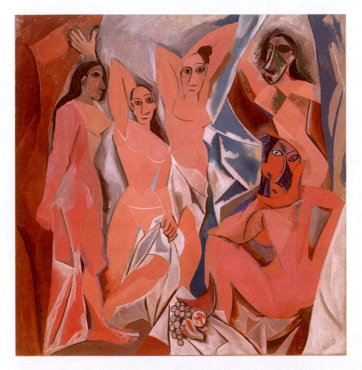

Fig. 5.5 Picasso—*Les Demoiselles d'Avignon*
(Pablo Picasso, "Les Demoiselles d'Avignon." Paris (June–July 1907). Oil on canvas, 8' × 7'8" (43.9 × 233.7 cm). The Museum of Modern Art/Licensed by Scala-Art Resource, NY. Acquired through the Lillie P. Bliss Bequest. Photography © 1995 The Museum of Modern Art. © 2010 Estate of Pablo Picasso/ARS Artists Rights Society, NY).

Picasso's work, *Les Demoiselles d'Avignon* (Fig. 5.5), is an extraordinarily powerful portrait of five nude women. It portrays his idea of each woman rather than representing them exactly as his subjects. This painting reflects the influence of African and Egyptian art on Picasso, which liberated the artist from any previous conventions in art. The painting is an emotionally charged image about ambiguity of space and form. The shapes in the painting appear to be shards of glass. Two women are wearing African masks. The woman in the lower right hand corner is sitting with her back to us with a frontal view of her head, while the woman on the left has the Egyptian profile with the frontal eye. The women seem to have twisted torsos. All of these elements are very purposeful in the lavish representation of the five female figures.

Another of Picasso's works, *Girl Before a Mirror* (Fig. 5.6), is an excellent example of cubism. The woman's face can be seen in profile and frontal view in typical Cubistic fashion. The viewer can see the woman is actually standing in front of a mirror with the reflection being darker than the woman herself. The reflection looking back at her is how the woman perceives herself rather than how she actually looks. Picasso creates a psychological drama common to everyday human emotion. He understood from life experience that one's self-perception of appearance often differs drastically from how one actually appears. Looking further there are other abnormalities within the figure, as Picasso has taken liberty to break up space and abstract parts and rearrange what once was thought to be the classical ideal of the human figure. No longer is the human form harmonious or beautiful as the Greeks might have related; Picasso has liberated the imagery into a new form of reality. Picasso's features move back and forth at will instead of the typical classical works created by Polykleitos. Picasso rebels against the classical ideal and turns to African and Egyptian art for inspiration for his own western liberation.

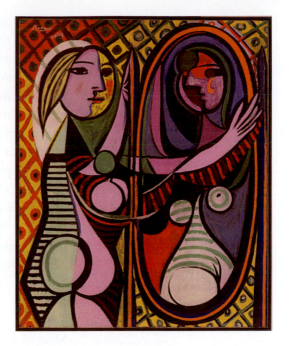

Fig. 5.6 Picasso—*Girl Before a Mirror* (Pablo Picasso (1881–1973) Spanish, "Girl Before a Mirror" Juene Fille Devant un Miroir. (Copyright © ARS, NY. Photograph copyright © The Museum of Modern Art/Licensed by SCALA/Art Resource, NY.).

Guernica (Fig. 5.7) was a work Picasso created during the very early days of WWII. On the afternoon of April 26, 1937, the German air force attacked the small Basque village of Guernica with three thousand pounds of bombs for over three hours. When the fires cleared three days later, the main part of town had been totally destroyed.

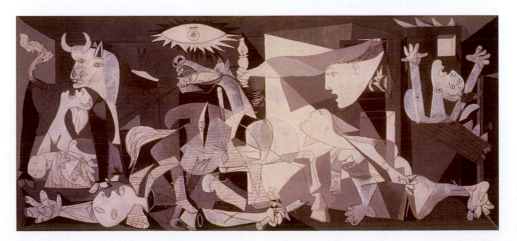

Fig. 5.7 Picasso— *Guernica* (John Bigelow Taylor/Art Resource, NY/ © ARS, NY).

Nearly 1,000 people lay dead. Picasso, who was never politically minded nor involved in the war, was outraged by the event and painted *Guernica* for the republican government of Spain as a mural for the entrance hall of the Spanish Pavilion in the World's Fair of 1937 in Paris. He began sketches for the mural on May 1; the work was finished by June 4. The painting, which measures 11 feet 5½ inches by 25 feet 5½ inches, represents the heroism and tragedy of the Spanish people with his own symbols depicting the horrible events, in this black, white and gray painting. The man/bull represents bullfights. The electric light bulb at the top of the painting and the oil lamp held by a woman coming out of a window represent the old and new ways of seeing, as well as seeing the light of God in the face of war. The slain soldier at the bottom holds a broken sword and a flower representing the absurdity of war and the hope of peace. The screaming woman on the left holds a dead baby, representative of the *Pietà*, the Virgin holding her dead son. Each element in the painting stands for the irrational forces of the human psyche in the atrocities of war.

Most of what's been discussed thus far has been analytical cubism. **Analytical Cubism** is intellectual; it was the first phase of cubism and, at times, hard to read. The second phase of Cubism was **Synthetic Cubism**. Synthetic Cubism was not as serious as Analytical Cubism but was easier to interpret. Picasso saw posters and advertisements being overlapped on public walls in Paris. This inspired him to begin constructing collaged images by pasting and gluing images from newspapers and poster together. This form of creative outlet is called Synthetic Cubism. Instead of analyzing a work of art as he created it, he began constructing the work of art through pasting images together.

SURREALISM

Another form of art that came along in the 1920s was **Surrealism**, sometimes called Fantasy Art. Surrealism attempted to define itself as the pure process of thought, free of any aesthetic or moral purpose. Ideas were borrowed from psychoanalysis. Surrealism was not necessarily to be taken as seriously as other forms of traditional art. These artists believed that dreams, having an unconscious reality of being in one place while being physically in another, free humans from the logical means of everyday reality. For example, in dreams people can fly or a person may sense that a particular house is in a different location. The subconscious creates a conscious awareness through dreams and surrealism arose by exploiting those chance images. The surrealist artists created works rich in imagery and false reality, thus freeing them from logical thinking. **Salvador Dali (1904–1989)** is considered one of the leaders of the surrealist genre. Dali would use realism to render paranoid images distorted in a very convincing composition. One of his most memorable works of art is titled *The Persistence of Memory* (Fig. 5.8). It is a small painting that illustrates how time has died and insects are devouring it. The illusion of space and time is muted through this extraordinary set of images. The barren landscape shows a self portrait of Dali in the lower middle section where the viewer can

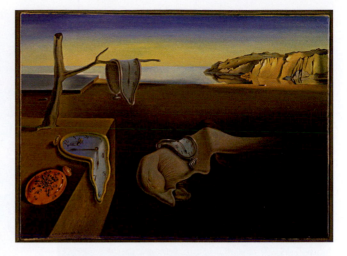

Fig. 5.8 Dali—*The Persistence of Memory* (Copyright © ARS, NY. Photograph copyright © The Museum of Modern Art/Licensed by SCALA/Art Resource, NY.).

see Dali's face in profile with a dead timepiece laying over his form. This was Dali's way of creating distorted imagery in a paranoid state of subconsciousness.

Another famous surrealist was **Rene Magritte (1898–1967)**. He employed a completely different type of realism with an altogether different type of reality. Magritte could create pictures and give them totally different meanings through scale, juxtaposition and pictorial device within his composition. Clearly his images are a fantasy. His visual images become a puzzle-like presentation that is simple yet abstract. The viewer may feel the image is actually plausible. Two examples of Magritte images are *Train from Fireplace* (Fig. 5.9) and *Studio Easel* (Fig. 5.10)

The surrealists felt that modern man was out of touch with his own reality and surrealism was a vain attempt to realign man and recapture the ideal within society. Their attempts were grandiose, if not absurd, since art no longer contained the power to control society or any cultural group in the 20th century. The surrealists were visionaries with paranoid schizophrenia. Their technique created a new reality that was outrageous and irrational using systems that are perversely real. It was a trick of the eye causing the viewer

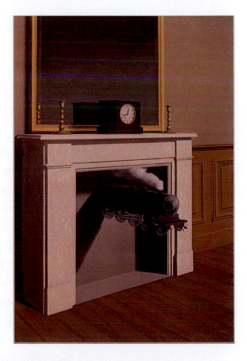

Fig. 5.9 Magritte—*Train from Fireplace* "Time Transfixed," 1938, oil on canvas, 147 × 97 cm. (Courtesy of The Bridgeman Art Library. Copyright © ARS, NY.).

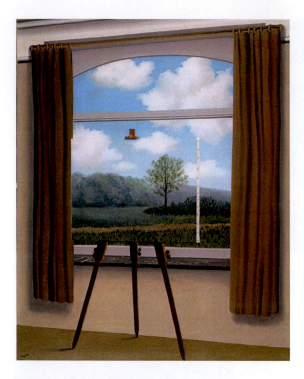

Fig. 5.10 Magritte—*Studio Easel*
"La condition humaine," 1933. (Copyright © 2000 Board
of Trustees, National Gallery of Art, Washington, Gift of the
Collectors Committee. Copyright © 2004 C. Herscovici,
Brussels/Artists Rights Society (ARS), New York.).

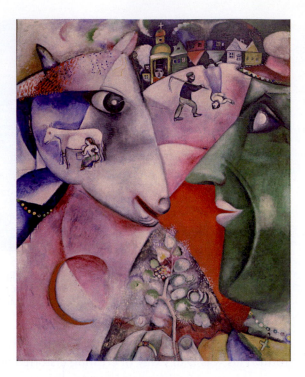

Fig. 5.11 Chagall—*I and the Village*
1911. Oil on canvas, 6 ft. 3⅝ in 3 59⅝ in.
(192.1 × 151.4 cm). (Copyright © ARS, NY. Photograph
copyright © The Museum of Modern Art/Licensed by
SCALA/Art Resource, NY.).

to do a double-take. The content was almost too weird and required some
sense of abnormality to read the image painted by these artists. Today, the
art world is shock worn, and we no longer find these images alarming.
However, in the 1920s surrealist images were quite shocking, and the public had difficulty digesting any type of explicit imagery that dealt with the
non-reality of the subconscious.

The Russian artist **Marc Chagall** (1887–1985) had his own vision.
The power of dream and fantasy dominated Chagall's work, a Russian Jewish artist who went to Paris to explore the realm of fantasy. *I and the Village* (Fig. 5.11) is a fairy tale of Russian folklore with Jewish symbols and
a Russian countryside all in one vision. Chagall weaves childhood memories into his images in a dreamlike fashion. He would relive important
moments which reshaped his imagination for years. Most of Chagall's paintings fit neatly into several modern styles which would include cubism, Fauvism, the Paris school, as well as surrealism.

Chagall's colors communicate happiness and even optimism in a world
of turmoil where he grew up. He saw himself as an observer of the world.

ABSTRACT EXPRESSIONISM

The events of WWII had a serious impact on art. In the years following WWII, after the nuclear holocaust, there was uneasiness and tension between America and Russia called the Cold War. People had the feeling that this might be the last generation to live on the planet, the end of the world as they knew it. American culture had changed and they no longer felt safe to live the American dream. A new style in painting emerged at this time known as **Abstract Expressionism.** It would last for approximately 15 years past the end of WWII. The style was born from a number of New York artists who were influenced by Fauvism, Cubism and Surrealism. They developed a new approach to their own art.

The Abstract Expressionist, AB EX for short, would take up the challenge of reacting to the fears of society and the effects of WWII. Their images were exaggerated forms of consciousness based on the fear that the world now had the ability to destroy itself. Abstract Expressionism can be defined as altering nature while creating images purely from one's own emotions. Artists simply painted however they felt. Art became a counterpoint to life. It was the process and not the end product that the artist most desired. Some images would be nothing more than shapes of color, no form, no sense of an image. The public was forced to take these images at face value.

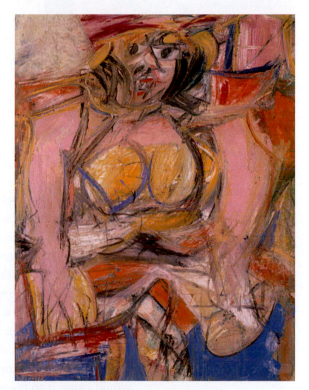

Fig. 5.12 de Kooning—*Woman IV*
Nelson-Atkins Museum of Art. Willem de Kooning, American, 1904–1997, b. The Netherlands. Woman IV, 1952–1953. Oil, enamel, and charcoal on canvas. 4 feet 11 inches × 46¼ inches (149.86 × 117.48 cm). Gift of William Inge, 56-128. © The Nelson-Atkins Museum of Art, Kansas City, Missouri.

The leader of the AB EX group was **Williem de Kooning** (1904–1997). Between 1950 and 1952 he created a series of paintings based on women, most notably Marilyn Monroe, which he titled *Woman IV* (Fig. 5.12). Although the person was sometimes unrecognizable, de Kooning always used recognizable imagery. His images emerged from large brush strokes as if painted by a madman. His work became an outpouring of energy, and when his energy was spent, the image was finished. In his painting *Woman IV* the figure is completely distorted. There is no resemblance to Marilyn Monroe, however the image appears more of an anxious nightmare than a beautiful movie star. His women were not seductive and were said to represent a primitive side of the viewers psyche.

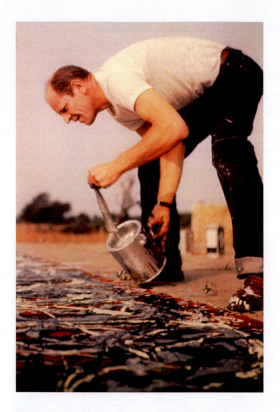

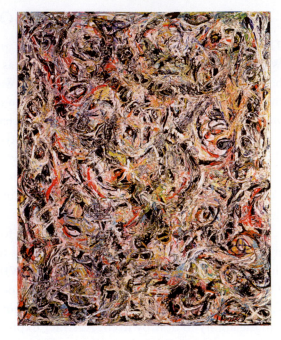

Fig. 5.14 Pollock—*Eyes in the Heat*
(The Bridgeman Art Library, NY. © 2004 The Pollock-Krasner Foundation/Artists Rights Society (ARS), New York.).

Fig. 5.13 Pollock at work making drip paintings (Hans Namuth/Photo Researchers, Inc.).

Jackson Pollock (1912–1956) was another AB EX artist who gave up the image for his now famous "drip paintings." In the late 1940s Pollock began the process of losing the image completely by doing what he called "all-over" painting. He began the drip painting purely by accident, but it was a process that affected the entire art world. He began to make ritual images by pouring and dripping color onto a canvas (Fig. 5.13). At first, his images had a labored look about them, but he quickly mastered the painting technique through the movement of his wrist. He would grab paint from a bucket, sling in onto the canvas, and then go back for more paint. The paint's short flight to the canvas and the laws of fluid motion would cause it to lay in arches and loops. This process was repeated over and over until the painting was complete. His images did not have depth, and often there were bits of canvas left exposed.

After Pollock moved from New York City to Long Island in 1945 his palette became lighter because of the influence of his rural environment. In the summer of 1946 he started a series of images for an exhibition sponsored by Peggy Guggenheim to open in January of 1947. *Eyes in the Heat* (Fig. 5.14) has figurative reference to eyes that are totally submerged in the layers of built up paint on the surface. By this time Pollock no longer applied the paint with a brush but squeezes the paint directly on the canvas from the tube, pushing and smearing the paint with blunt instruments to create a textured surface. As one looks at the image, watchful eyes appear throughout concealed in the swirling layers of paint, creating an overall movement to the composition.

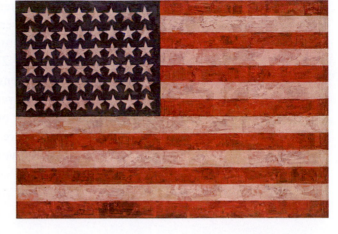

Jasper Johns (1930–) is best known for his earlier work described as not quite Pop Art even though he uses pop iconography. He is considered an Abstract Expressionist but some historians will cross reference him with the Pop Art genre. His painting *Flag* (Fig. 5.15) was inspired by a dream. He would continue to paint with simple images of American symbols such as maps, targets and numbers, while treating the surface with a fine art finish to them. Johns work is about popular images reflecting symbols of American culture associated with recognizable icons. *Flag* is such an image. It's devoid of any references and yet he created an American icon in a new fine arts manner.

Fig. 5.15 Johns—*Flag* (Copyright © Jasper Johns/ Licensed by VAGA, New York, NY. Photograph copyright © The Museum of Modern Art/Licensed by SCALA/Art Resource, NY.).

Robert Rauschenberg (1925–2008) was an American artist with German and Cherokee descent. It has been said "that Rauschenberg breathed in as Johns breathed out" by Robert Hughes in his PBS series *Shock of the New* aired in the 1980s. This statement is a testimony to how close one artist reacted to another artist. Rauschenberg rejected abstract expressionism for something new, something he could embrace in painting. He began covering the canvas with house paint or applying ink to a car tire and running over the canvas to begin his painting process. He believed that coloring the canvas was a means to an end. He also began creating what he would call "combines," which was a process of finding an object(s) and forming it (them) into a painting in a three-dimensional collage or combine.

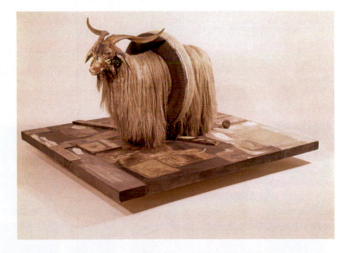

Fig. 5.16 Rauschenberg— *Monogram*, (mixed media) by Robert Rauschenberg (1925–2008) Private Collection/The Bridgeman Art Library. Art © Estate of Robert Rauschenberg/ Licensed by VAGA, New York, NY.

His most famous combine is *Monogram* (Fig. 5.16). He had a house rule of each morning walking one square block to find enough litter to use for that day's creation. In *Monogram* he had found a stuffed angora goat, an old tire, a police barrier, the heel of a shoe, a tennis ball and some paint. Rauschenberg created a new course in modern art with his combines that caused the viewer to notice the objects in a new, mostly different way than in their natural forms. Later he would move from 3-D combines to creating only 2-D combine paintings using magazines, photos, rubbings and silk screens of current events. He would paint on or over the collaged images whatever he felt that day. The paintings were abstractions with a commentary on contemporary society using cultural symbols and images that created the American culture. Rauschenberg continued to experiment with various media and art forms until his death in May of 2008.

POP ART

Starting in 1959 and into the 1960s was the beginning of what we call the **Pop Art** genre. It was essentially popular culture images that were original works of art but looked mass produced. The Pop artists wanted to create an image that was instantly read, with no deep hidden meaning. The image was to look as mechanical as possible. This was a genre that never matured. It was in the hands of a half dozen artists for roughly a ten year period. Their images have had a profound impact on our culture today. Commercial art was their source of inspiration, recreating magazine illustrations, advertisements and even comic strips. Most of the Pop Art artists were commercial artists attempting to ignore the traditions in art by creating a simple instantly read image. The leading member of this group was **Andy Warhol** (1928–1987).

Warhol was a commercial artist turned fine art artist. Any commercial image could become his obsession. He created images using mass media techniques learned from commercial art. He became a master of manipulating the media to create an image the general public would recognize instantly. A good example of his work is the *Campbell Soup Can* (Fig. 5.17). Warhol's imagery shows his uncanny under-

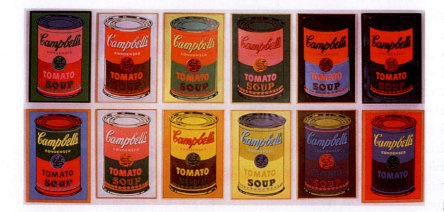

Fig. 5.17 Warhol—*Campbell Soup Can*
(Courtesy of Private Collection/The Bridgeman Art Library. Copyright © The Andy Warhol Foundation for the Visual Arts/ARS, NY.).

standing of popular culture, which has translated through the decades to our modern culture today.

Roy Lichtenstein (1923–1927) began his first series of Pop Art paintings using comic book images as inspiration (Fig. 5.18). He derived his technique from his experiences in commercial printing. This series of work continued through 1965 and suggested common everyday social statements on love and war. Most of his paintings are very close to real comic book panels. This was his trademark and his way of treating the image as "life" where there are no two people the same, no two images would be the same.

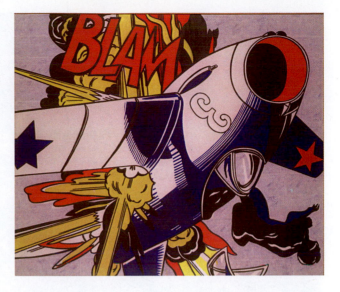

Fig. 5.18 Lichtenstein—*Blam* (Courtesy of Yale University Art Gallery/Art Resource, NY. Courtesy of The Estate of Roy Lichtenstein.).

NEO-EXPRESSIONISM TO POST-MODERNISM

By the late 1970's the art world redefined itself through AB EX, Pop and an ever changing culture to create what is now known as **Neo-Expressionism**. A new genre of modern art was becoming popular around the world. Neo-Expressionism created precedents in art with developing reactions against Pop Art and the art of the 1970s. Neo-Expressionism illustrates recognizable images such as humans; however, they are now portrayed in a more violently emotional style. Abstraction had become boring and virtually dead when artists reinvestigated cultural foundations created out of the post-war world. They recreated a modern perspective. The tradition of abstraction, which had affected art over the last 50 years, now took on a new appearance, capturing the emotional state of modern artists.

The most notable is **Anselm Kiefer** (1945–). Kiefer is a German born artist. His family experienced the war firsthand with the bombing of his homeland by the Allied Forces during WWII. Kiefer confronted his personal memories and the moral issues imposed by the Nazis and used them to create major themes relating to WWII.

Kiefer's images are large, for example *To the Unknown Painter* (Fig. 5.19) which measures 9'2'' × 9'2,'' is a powerful statement of how WWII expressed tragedy to the German people. The painting is a depressive image showing a bombed out shelter where Kiefer uses not only paint but tar, earth, straw, rope, and various kinds of tangible elements left behind by the destruction of the war. Through the years images from

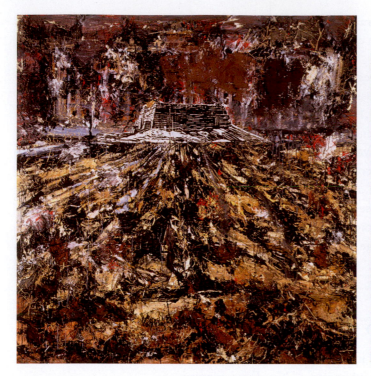

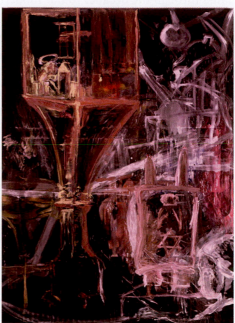

Fig. 5.19 Kiefer—*To the Unknown Painter*
(Courtesy of the Gagosian Gallery. Copyright © Anselm Kiefer).

Fig. 5.20 Schnabel—*Cabalistic Painting*
1983 (oil on velvet) by Julian Schnabel (b.1951)
Detroit Institute of Arts, USA/Founders Society
purchase, W. Hawkins Ferry fund/The Bridgeman
Art Library. (Courtesy of Julian Schnabel Studios).

Kiefer's childhood have haunted him and today he creates works that convey epic tragedies from his past. His images are conceptually well built and influence young artists today.

One of the most critically argued artists of the early 1980s is **Julian Schnabel** (1951–). Schnabel came on to the scene with a new and powerful set of images that are now his famous "plate painting." These are large scale canvases covered with broken pieces of ceramic plates glued onto the surface. Schnabel then paints his images on canvas over the crockery. This new style combined influences from Schnabel's childhood and was reminiscent of mosaic art, the "combines" created by Rauschenberg, and "*Les Demoiselles d'Avignon*" by Picasso to create a three-dimensional fusion of ideas (Fig. 5.20). Schnabel's works contain brutality, structural imagery and are about the emotional state of everyday people that he encountered.

An artist closely associated with Schnabel is **David Salle** (1952–) whose images appear to be random or painted on top of each other but are done purposefully. Critics have debated that Salle's work is a modern take on Synthetic Cubism whereby he is juxtaposing images that seemingly have nothing in common (Fig. 5.21). Salle's work is preoccupied with the tragic and sublime romantic allegories of a late modern world. Salle, like Schnabel, is a talented painter who would not allow himself to paint well. His art was originally for his artist friends and small audiences. The work centers on the lack of friendship, depression over lost relationships, outcasts from society and the downtrodden in general. People noticed that his imagery was emotionally charged with negative overtones. The Realists of the middle 1800s were about the rich getting richer and the poor getting poorer but the aristocrats didn't want to see that type of imagery. Salle's work comes full circle to where this is now the popular trend of the culture.

Creating public attention with his chalk drawings in New York City **Keith Haring** (1958–1990) was influenced by graffiti art that he saw on the streets. Haring's images (Fig. 5.22) have become cultural symbols that have established him as one of the leading artists of his time. Haring's use of nontraditional materials to **tag** subways became an aesthetic form

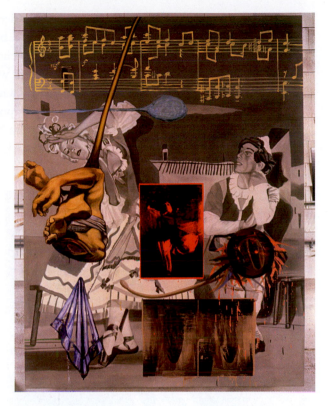

Fig. 5.21 Salle—*False Queen* (Art © David Salle/Licensed by VAGA, New York, NY).

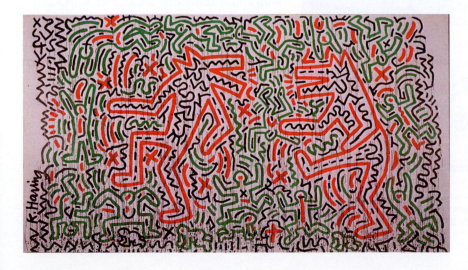

Fig. 5.22 Haring—*Untitled* 1981 (oil and acrylic on canvas) by Keith Haring (1958–90) Deichtorhallen, Hamburg, Germany/ Wolfgang Neeb/The Bridgeman Art Library. (Courtesy of Keith Haring, Inc.)

of expression to the underground world that exploded onto the art scene. Tagging is the term used by graffiti artists to describe the method of application of paint to their chosen surface. People were taken by his animated cartoon-like images that were no more than glorified stick-figures. He was branded immediately as a modern graffiti Neo-Expressionist. He singlehandedly changed the contemporary art world. By 1983 Haring's Graffiti Art had become acknowledge by New York City's finest galleries. He successfully brought his outside work to the inside, transforming galleries into totally new environments. His iconic style was created out of fear of arrest in the subway systems where he had to create quick but recognizable images. He became famous as the anonymous master of subway art and moved into respectable arenas of New York City and galleries the world over.

Barbara Kruger (1945–) is an American graphic/conceptual artist. Much of her work is in the form of black and white images with overlaid words such as *You Substantiate Our Horror* (Fig. 5.23). Her images are powerful with meanings of a contemporary world of declarative juxtaposition of imagery and text. Much of her work is about the kindnesses and brutalities in our social structure. She reflects on how our culture treats one another with and without prejudices. Her works direct and evoke a response by the viewer. It's a form of Pop Art and Contemporary Art mixed with multi-media presentations that suspend the viewer between fascination of the image and the accusation of the text. Her work is about a visual art that borrows from or recycles images to create a new work for a Post Modernist culture. Her technique as an artist borrows images from others to create a new work that focuses on the culture but doesn't destroy the value of the original image. One example

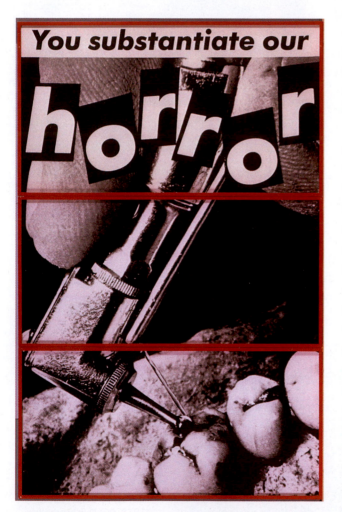

Fig. 5.23 Kruger—*You Substantiate Our Horror*
CNAC/MNAM/Dist. Réunion des Musées Nationaux/Art Resource, NY. Courtesy of Mary Boone Gallery, New York.

of her work uses Michelangelo's *Creation* from the Sistine ceiling showing the hands of God and Adam with an over lay of text that states "You Invest in the Divinity of the Masterpiece." Another example of her work is a billboard piece which shows a man with a telescope staring at us with the text overlaid "Surveillance is your busy work." This indicates the Post Modernist voyeuristic culture that we live in. Kruger's art was influenced by spying taking place during the Cold War of the '60s, the Vietnam war presented in our homes each evening on the nightly news during the 60s and 70s and "Big Brother is Watching" from George Orwell's book *1984*. Today's plethora of TV reality shows are a prime example of how far these voyeuristic tendencies have come since Kruger created them in the early to mid '80s.

In the last 100 years more changes have occurred in art and culture than did in the previous 500 years. This a record of how we live in a post modern changing culture which redefines itself more often than it understands itself. Today we live at breakneck speed using the internet, cell phones, and 24/7 news in an effort to keep abreast of what is going on in the world. With modern technologies come modern problems. The world is not the same world of the previous generation, and moral values are declining by the day. It is no wonder that art is ever changing and increasingly difficult to comprehend. The viewer, however, should not look at works of art as being rubbish or unworthy of appreciation. In the future, people will look back and admire the art being created today with the same admiration we have for the masterpieces of the past. It seems as though it takes about 100 years for art to be fully appreciated for what the artist or genre was trying to represent.

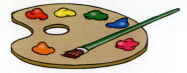

Chapter 5 Homework
Art of the 20th Century

50 Points Possible

Complete the following project. *Staple* all additional sheets to this page. (*No bent corner-type attachments accepted*).

Size restrictions: Minimum 8 × 10 – Maximum 8½ × 11. All work **MUST** be *typed using complete sentences and correct punctuation to earn full credit.*

Painting Analysis

Find and attach **one** image from any genre discussed in this chapter. The painting must have been completed during the time frame discussed in this chapter. The image **MUST NOT** have been discussed in class or in the text and must be a minimum of 5 × 7 inches. You can use the internet to search for the image. Justify *ALL* of your answers.

Answer the following questions concerning your chosen genre. Hint: Black/White and neutral are not considered color schemes.

What genre is being used?
        (10 points possible)
What is the title of the image and year painted?
        (5 points possible)
Who is the artist?
        (5 points possible)
What color scheme is being used?
        (10 points possible)
What compositional style is being used?
        (10 points possible)
What are the characteristics of this genre?
        (5 points possible)
Site your resource.
        (5 points possible)

Genre 10 points possible	
Title/Year Painted 5 points possible	
Artist 5 points possible	
Color scheme 10 points possible	
Composition 10 points possible	
Genre characteristics 5 points possible	
Resource 5 points possible	
Total Points	

MUSIC

6

WHY MUSIC?

Let us consider Music in the human experience. It is a rare day that goes by when one does not hear any music. We walk into a restaurant and music is playing. We step into an elevator and there is music. We hear music as we shop in stores, both large and small. We turn on the television. We go to a movie. We go to church. We attend a concert. We buy a CD. We play a video game. Music is everywhere. It cannot be avoided in life. It has a wide variety of functions in our society and in the human experience throughout the world. Some of these functions are routine for all of us. Some may seem quite strange. How exactly does music function in our lives?

Everyone likes some kind of music. Some people listen to Country Music but not Jazz. Some people enjoy Classical Music and but not Popular Music. Some do not even consider Rap as music. Others do not consider Pop as music. Some people enjoy certain Popular songs, certain Classical pieces, and some Country songs. As music goes, our tastes are as different as each individual.

Music appears to be a natural expression of humans. In every part of the world, music of some sort occurs. In Japan, music accompanies Shinto worship. In Australia, the sound of the didgeridoo is heard in Aboriginal ceremonies. In Africa, the sound of the drums is used to imitate tones of language in a way that actual "speech" can be understood. Although some form of music happens throughout the world, different cultures view music differently. In some African cultures, anyone who speaks naturally sings. They do not consider music to be the exclusive domain of the "trained" musician. Singing and dancing are as normal to the average person as talking and walking.

We have considered art of the world. We have looked at its uses and ways artists have expressed themselves through color, form, and even architecture. This section of the book will focus on how musicians have taken the tools of music to express many of the same feelings and values but through an entirely different medium. As color is to art and word is to literature, so sounds are to the music. We must first understand the elements that make up music before we can understand how composers use those elements to express ideas.

WHY THAT MUSIC?

Music is everywhere but why is so much time, effort, and money spent on music? How does music affect us? Consider the background music you hear when you dine out. Why is there music in the restaurant? Research at Fairfield University found that restaurant patrons took 3.23 bites per minute when there was no music in the background, 3.83 bites per minute when slow music was played, and 4.44 bites per minute when up tempo music was being played. The restaurant management can pick music to cause you to eat faster and leave sooner, making room for other patrons. Then there is the research that showed a 32% increase in supermarket sales when slow, soothing music was played in the background. And how uncomfortable is a long elevator ride that is totally silent?

> Music as Medicine from
> The Seattle Times
>
> http://seattletimes.nwsource.com/html/
> health/2002286998_healthmusic25.html

Does music really change us? Recent research has indicated that listening to music can be beneficial. One research project found that listening to Mozart's *Sonata for Two Pianos in D Major*, (K. 448) caused a subsequent enhancement of reasoning, the so-called Mozart Effect. This resulted in a huge market for Classical music recordings to help one become smarter! Another study published in *Neurological Research* announced that six months of piano keyboard training caused enhancement of spatial-temporal reasoning in preschool children. They scored 34% higher on problem solving. Even physical health is affected by music. A study of patients with Alzheimer's disease found that levels of serum melatonin increased significantly after four weeks of music therapy sessions. The conclusion stated that this increase may have contributed to the patients' relaxed and calm mood.

The psychological and neurological effects of music are just now being discovered. For centuries, it has been used to set moods and influence the emotions and thoughts of people in church, in social functions, even in wars. For centuries, military bands have marched before the soldiers to frighten the enemy. One branch of our military even uses all types of music as a psychological weapon on enemy positions!

Beyond the psychological, physiological, and neurological effects on humans, music moves us. It brings out emotions that cannot be expressed in any other way. Music can comfort an infant or rally troops into battle. Music can bring out emotional responses from tears to terror. It can express our deepest devotion to God.

Music is a remarkable part of culture and it requires a closer look. Let us first consider some of the physical properties of music and sound.

DOES THAT TREE IN THE WOODS MAKE A SOUND?

First, we must consider how we hear music. Hearing music can be considered from the viewpoint of physics and from the perspective of psychology. For a physicist, music is the complex combination of pressure waves in the atmosphere. We have all heard the question, "If a tree falls in the woods and there is no one there to hear it fall, does it make a sound?" If you are a physicist, the answer is "yes" because you define sound as the vibrations in the air that are *capable* of being heard. The sound is simply a physical action in nature in the same fashion as waves on the ocean.

Sounds are quite complex and the spectrum of sounds is incredibly large. You may have heard the term "A 440." That refers to the frequency of the sound or the *pitch*. The note we have labeled as "A" vibrates at 440 cycles per second. As a reference, consider the pitches of the piano. A 440 is near the center of the piano keyboard. If we double the frequency, that is, if the sound vibrates at twice the speed, the resulting sound is another note we label as "A" that is an *octave*, or eight notes, higher. As we move up the keyboard, we find that the highest note on the piano keyboard is a C that vibrates at 4186 *hertz*, or cycles per second. In the same manner, we can divide the frequency by 2 to determine the frequency of the same note an octave lower. For example, an octave below A440 is A220. If we continue this, we find that the lowest note on the piano keyboard is an "A" which vibrates at 27.5 hertz.

Interestingly, our ears are capable of perceiving sounds as low as 20 hertz and as high as 20,000 hertz, although this range varies greatly from individual to individual. In a later chapter, we will learn how this extended range of hearing helps analyze specific qualities of sounds entering our ear. So the lowest sound of the piano is approaching our lowest threshold of hearing, but the upper end of the piano is far below our upper threshold of hearing.

As complex as music is, the waves produced are rather simple. The vibrations in the air are simply the back-and-forth motion of air molecules at various speeds and various degrees of distance traveled. From that, it seems almost astounding that we can tell the difference between a rustle of leaves and a baby breathing. Both produce similar motion of the air, but with different combinations of amplitude and frequency. The subtle differences are very small, but we are able to comprehend those differences.

That takes us to the realm of psychology. Every person processes sounds in the same way, but everyone also "hears," or perceives things differently, even though they are hearing the exact same sounds. One person hears ecstasy while another is bored. One person hears excitement while another "hears" monotony.

If we return to our "tree in the woods" question, the psychologist would have a different answer to the question. A psychologist would say that the tree did not make a sound because there was no one nearby to actually perceive the sound. To a psychologist, the sound exists *because* it is heard. As we consider our hearing, the brain takes on a huge role. If the brain was not capable of sorting out and analyzing the sounds that entered the ear, the whole process would be worthless.

The miracle of hearing is this processing of the sounds. If we consider the size of the actual hearing receptors in the ear and the vast complexity of sound waves, the analysis of this sound is nothing short of

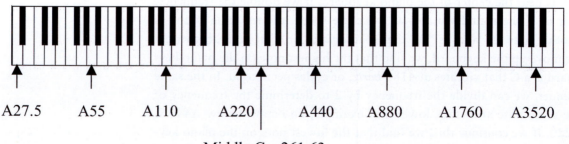

A27.5   A55   A110   A220   A440   A880   A1760   A3520

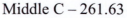

Middle C – 261.63

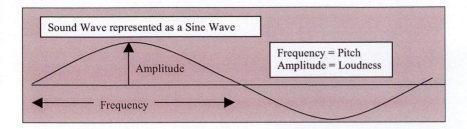

miraculous. It is not totally understood how sound is processed in the inner ear. The sensitivity of various hair cells and the speed at which they move all contribute to the analysis of sound. So much activity happens at this minute level. One of the interesting aspects is that the inner ear masks out the sound of breathing, the heartbeat, and other sounds occurring naturally in the body. How often have you actually heard your heartbeat without the use of a stethoscope?

As we consider hearing and perception, we must not only consider the sound of a single frequency vibrating the eardrum and transferring the vibrations to the inner ear, we must also consider multiple frequencies arriving simultaneously through complex sound waves. We must also consider the fact that different frequencies arrive at different amplitudes, that is, loudness. Some sounds are louder—they have greater amplitude of physical waves. These sounds are perceived differently than those with less amplitude, or softer sounds.

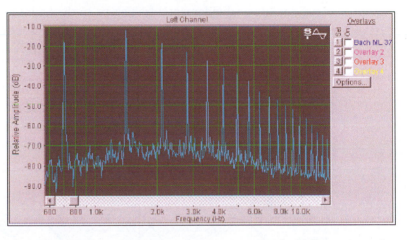

Graph of a Trumpet sound.

Finally, we must sort out sounds of different complexity. For example, we can easily identify the sound of a trumpet as being different from the sound of a clarinet, even when they are playing the same frequency. This is due to the fact that each instrument or voice is made up of many frequencies, not just one. Because of the arrangement of frequencies above a particular pitch, our brain is able to analyze the various frequencies and determine the instrument or voice being sounded. Beyond that, the trained musician can even analyze a sound in so much detail as to be able to determine if the sound of the trumpet is a "good" tone or a "bad" tone.

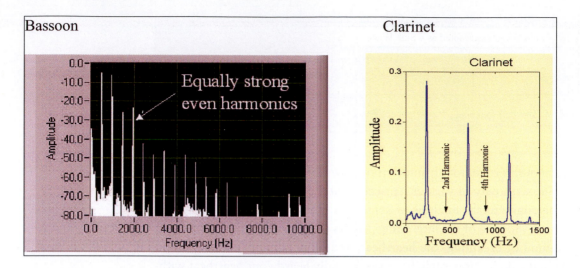

As the sound moves through the air, all of the harmonics affect the fundamental frequency. In the figure below, the sine waves for the fundamental and each of the harmonics is seen in the first graph. The second graph shows the wave as it actually occurs. You can see that each of the overtones causes a slightly different shape of the fundamental tone. As the brain analyzes the incoming sound, the fundamental and these slight differences are analyzed as the sound of a particular instrument based on the strength of the harmonics. It does seem quite complex, but hopefully you can see just how marvelous our sense of hearing truly is!

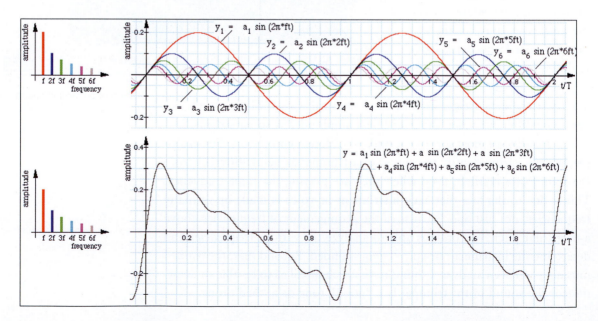

Taken together, the analysis of this myriad of information by the brain is almost mind boggling. As with other senses, the more we understand about our capabilities, the more miraculous our bodies seem.

MUSIC, "THE UNIVERSAL LANGUAGE"

Music has often been referred to as the "universal language." Ideas and feelings are not expressed in music as they are in language. In language, ideas are expressed through words. All words have specific meanings, although some may have multiple meanings. Notes in music are simply sounds and do not carry specific "meanings" as words do. Indeed, it is said that if language could express all that music does, we would not need music!

The analogy of music as a language can be made in another aspect of music, however. Everyone hears the exact same sounds in music, but each person reacts differently to those sounds. When a person says, "I love you" in English, that is understood by someone who speaks English; but those words may be meaningless to someone who speaks Spanish. By the same token, when a Spanish-speaking person says, "Te amo," it may mean nothing to the English-speaker, even though it means "I love you." If a person takes the time to learn Spanish, the phrase "Te amo" is clear. The individual's understanding of meanings through the perception of different sounds is increased. The more languages one learns, the more one understands a variety of expressions.

The same idea happens in music. If a person listens to Country Music all the time, they become familiar with the texts, devices, and various sounds that express ideas in Country Music. If these same people listen to the music of Mozart, they may not understand any of the expression because they are not familiar with the texts, devices, and various sounds of Mozart. If one takes the time to become familiar with Mozart or Classic Rock or Jazz, a greater understanding of music in its various forms naturally follows.

Let's again consider Love. To one person, the expression of love may be best heard in Tchaikovsky's "Romeo and Juliet." However, another person may hear the same expression of love through "You're the Inspiration" by Chicago. The expression is equally valid to each individual but it is perceived through different "languages," that is, different styles of music. As one broadens the understanding of different styles of music, the world of music in all its variety becomes more clearly understood.

WHAT DID I JUST HEAR?

Everyone experiences the vast array of sensations in the world differently. The mind is bombarded with sights, sounds, touches, tastes, and smells. Each individual makes decisions regarding where to focus attention. Have you ever driven or walked somewhere and, upon arrival, been unable to remember anything about the trip? During the trip, we might focus on the CD player, a cell phone call, a beautiful sunset, or some other sensation. However, if a police bulletin was heard that mentioned a dangerous suspect in a red car with a certain license plate, you would most likely remember every red car and license plate seen during the whole trip. We focus our attention on specific things.

Consider this—have you ever sat down to a meal and really focused on how the food tastes? So often, we eat without really tasting what we are eating. We may remember the first bite or two, but after that we often let our focus move to a conversation, a television program, or something else. Try this experiment—the next time you eat a meal, concentrate on every bite you eat. Chew very slowly and taste each bite completely. You will probably find that your eating experience is totally different. With all of the sensations around, it is so easy to completely ignore information that is gathered by our minds.

The same thing happens when we listen to music. In our society, there are so many musical stimuli, it becomes very easy to just let the music "wash over" our minds while we focus on other sensations. Often, retailers count on this use of music to influence your buying decisions. Some composers even wrote music specifically as "background" music and insisted that no one listen to it!

To truly experience music, one must focus on the sounds. In the next chapter, we will discuss the elements of music and determine what to listen for. By learning more about musical sensations, one can begin to gain understanding of the composer's intent.

WHO IS RESPONSIBLE FOR THIS?

In music, there is another consideration for each performance. The great majority of performances are given by someone other than the composer. The actual creation of the music is done by the composer. In popular music, this person is identified as the "song writer." These are the real "artists" in the same sense that the creator of a painting or sculpture is the artist. In music performances, we often give credit (or express criticism) to the performer rather than the true creator of the work, the composer. The function of the performer is to give an accurate presentation of the composer's intent. The composer does expect the performer to emphasize different aspects and to interpret the work to a certain extent. Some of the individual changes a performer gives may include the tempo (speed of the music), the dynamics (loudness), or the phrasing. The performer brings the music to life in the same fashion that an actor brings a character to life in a movie. We begin to relate more to the actor in a movie than we do a screenwriter who actually created the script for the movie. The same thing happens in music.

It is important that we consider the contributions of the performer. Two people may play or sing the same work. One may move us to great joy while the other never moves us beyond boredom. A fine performer will spend years and years perfecting the craft of performance in order to bring music to life rather than just play or sing notes in sequence. Also, the performer takes a great chance on stage. Besides the months of work required to play or sing a work correctly, the performer is always concerned with the actual circumstances on stage at the time of the performance. Sometimes a warm, humid evening will cause a clarinet reed to react differently causing great anxiety in the mind of the performer. A performer may have been sick within the last week and might have problems breathing deeply, thus affecting the presentation of the music. Even something as seemingly unimportant as a flash picture taken during performance may cause a performer to lose concentration and have great trouble finishing a performance.

In the art of Jazz, the performer often moves into the realm of the composer. This activity is called *improvisation*. A composer of a jazz piece will write the melody and harmony for the piece but the performer will use these to actually compose sections of music live on stage. As the piece moves forward, the jazz musician will actually compose unique melodies and rhythms based on the composition. Every time a piece is performed, the improvisation will probably be different.

Some people believe that the musician who improvises is making everything up on the spot, but that is not entirely true. First, the musician bases everything on the melody and chords that the composer wrote. Secondly, musicians practice improvisation by repeating patterns and melodic fragments over and over in different sequences. The actual performance is "put together," or created, on stage at the moment of performance. However, the improvisation usually consists of fragments that the musician has used before. Some jazz musicians have favorite musical fragments that occur in almost every improvised performance.

All of this does not minimize the creative work of the composer, for without the creative genius of the composer, the performer would have the task of creating and performing. The work of the composer is done individually, often in isolation. If you have ever tried to create something that no one else has ever created, you know the difficulty of inspiration. Artists, writers, and composers take the tools of their art and spend months, even years, creating something that is totally unique. This act of creation is the genius behind any art. As you listen to music or observe art of any kind, always consider the great effort and genius that went into the creation of that art work.

Chapter 6—Why Music?

1. Research journal articles on the psychological or physical effect of music, other than the ones mentioned in the chapter. Summarize the findings of one article.

2. From a single location, focus on all of the sounds heard. Give the location and list 5 sounds that you hear at that location.

3. Often, music is present in situations that we do not notice, such as in a restaurant, in a movie, at a store, or in an elevator. Make a list of music that you experience during a typical day that you normally do not notice.

4. List 3 of your favorite songs and give the composer of each (not the performer!).

5. List your favorite style of music (Classical, Country, Rock, Rap, etc.) and your least favorite style of music.

7

ELEMENTARY,
MY DEAR WATSON

Sherlock Holmes often used this rather sarcastic statement with his friend and colleague, Dr. Watson. No matter how unrelated or disjoint the facts of the case seemed, his explanation did seem to be just that, elementary. As we consider the elements of music, they may seem extremely complicated at first, but in actuality, the basic concepts are "elementary."

When we begin our first class in chemistry, one of the first things we must do is learn the periodic table of the elements. As we learn these elements, we find that they have different properties and act differently when combined with other elements. We find that each element has an individual structure. The more we learn of these elements, the more knowledge and understanding we have of the physical world.

The same is true of the elements of music. The focus of this book is on the basic principles of musical elements. The more one studies these elements, the more one understands the complexity and subtlety of this unique discipline. The elements of music include *melody, rhythm, harmony, dynamics, timbre, texture*, and *form*. As we look at each one of these elements, we will begin to understand how composers and other musicians work with physical sounds to bring forth expression.

MELODY

Melody can be conceived as a "musical sentence." Before we consider the "sentence structure" involved in a melody, let's first consider the nature of a melody. A melody can bring great joy and excitement or it can be very boring.

Not long ago, Paul McCartney wanted to purchase the rights to many of the songs he and John Lennon wrote when they performed with the Beatles. However, another celebrity bought the rights of a large catalog of music, including many of the Beatles songs. Michael Jackson owned the songs that made many other musicians famous. You may wonder why he spent $47 million to own the rights to these melodies. The reason is that music has a copyright just as printed material and movies do. As a result, every time a song is played, in an elevator or restaurant or on the concert stage, 50% or the royalties must be paid to the owner of the copyright and the other 50% goes to the song writer. You can imagine how much money can be made by owning the copyright to the most popular songs. Now that Michael Jackson has passed away, his estate would still own the copyrights to this large catalog of songs that included so many McCartney/Lennon songs.

Interestingly, melodies can be copyrighted. Rhythms and harmonic progressions cannot. It is the melody of a song that is recognizable as unique. Some melodies are short and simple. Some are very complex. There is something about a well constructed melody that moves us. There is also something about a bad melody that makes us uncomfortable.

A melody is made up of individual notes or *pitches*. A pitch is a single sound frequency. Western musical tradition has labeled these notes with the letters A, B, C, D, E, F, and G. During the Medieval times, the notes had different labels, that is *do, re, mi, fa, sol, la,* and *ti,* syllables made famous in the musical "The Sound of Music." A similar set of syllables have developed in India. They are *sa, re, ma, ga, pa, dha,* and *ni.* The names of the notes are not important but there must be some way to label them. The names are just used as a reference for composers to communicate with performers. Notice that there are only seven different labels, even though there are multitudes of different frequencies. The reason for this is based on the physics of the sound itself.

Once seven letter names have been used, the cycle of letters begins again. If the note names begin with "A," what happens after we reach a "G?" As already discussed, there is a unique property that happens with frequency called an *octave*. This was discovered by Pythagoras while experimenting with a fixed string. He found that the string vibrated at a particular pitch, that is, a particular frequency. He also found that stopping the string in the middle caused it to vibrate twice as fast. This sound was so similar to the original that it sounded the same. If both frequencies were played, they would be lost in one another. Because of this similarity, the higher note was labeled with the same letter as the lower. Using the letters of the alphabet, an octave above "A" was also labeled as "A;" the octave above "B" was also labeled "B," and so forth.

Beyond this, Pythagoras began to try stopping the string in different mathematical proportions. If the string were stopped two-thirds down the string, a completely different note sounded, the "fifth" of the scale. For example, if the string were tuned to an A, the note sounded when stopped at two-thirds was an E. ("A" is the first letter of the alphabet; "E" is the fifth letter of the alphabet.) When the string was stopped at a point three-fourths down the string, a "C" (third letter) was produced. As he continued, he slowly constructed a *scale* of notes which consisted of seven letter names. From this initial experiment, a series of notes, called a *scale*, was developed and the basic notes used in our music today were established.

> Pythagorus: Music and Space
>
> http://www.aboutscotland.com/
> harmony/prop.html

When the notes were played in succession beginning at C, that is, C, D, E, F, G, A, B, and C (white keys on a piano), it was observed that each of these notes were not the same distance, or *interval*, apart. The distance between "E" and "F" was half the distance between "F" and "G." This same interval occurred between "B" and "C." By adding these *half steps* between all of the other intervals, a scale of twelve notes came about. This can be seen clearly on a piano keyboard. The white keys represent the letter named notes. The black keys represent half steps between the white keys. Observe that there is no black key between "E" and "F" or between "B" and C."

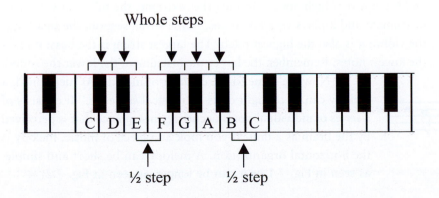

The interval, or distance between notes, is important to the organization of the melody and in the harmony, which we will discuss in a later section. Consider the white keys on the piano keyboard on the previous page, specifically the notes C, D, E, F, G, A, B, and C. The interval from C to D is called a *second*, the interval between a D and an E is also a second, and so forth. So the interval between any two consecutive notes is a second. The interval between a C and an E is a *third*. By the same fashion, the interval between a C and an F is a *fourth*, C to G is a *fifth*, and so on. One way of analyzing a particular melody is to determine the intervals between each note. Often, music theorists who analyze music in great detail will use this method to gain insight on the characteristics of different melodies.

We have already seen that a pitch is determined by a particular frequency—the faster the vibrations per second, the *higher* the pitch. We label notes as relatively *higher* or *lower* in relation to other notes. Again, consider a piano keyboard. The higher the note, the faster the frequency and the farther right the note is on the piano keyboard. By the same token, the lower the note, the slower the frequency and the farther left it is. When notes are placed on a musical *staff*, the higher notes are higher on the staff and the lower notes are lower on the staff.

Lower Pitches

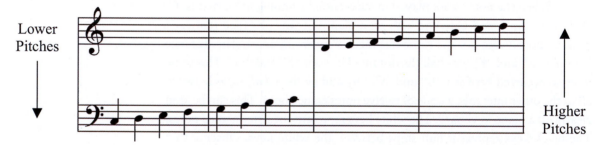

Higher Pitches

One principle needs to be mentioned here. Musical instruments come in many different sizes. Consider the piccolo. It is a very small instrument and it plays very high notes. On the other extreme, the tuba is a very large instrument and it plays very low notes. In the string section, the smallest is the violin; it is also the highest pitch. The largest string is the bass; it plays the lowest notes. Remember, the larger the instrument the lower the sound.

Now we come to the concept of melody. As mentioned, a melody can be thought of as a "musical sentence." It consists of a series of individual notes occurring in sequence that is perceived by the brain as a unit. If you look at a piece of music, melody is the horizontal organization. A melody can be short and simple, as seen in Fig. 7.1 or it can be longer, as seen in Fig. 7.2.

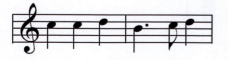

Fig. 7.1 Melodic Fragment from "America"

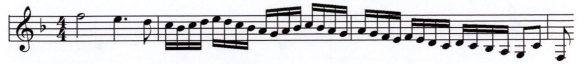

Fig. 7.2 Melodic Fragment from Tchaikovsky's Symphony No. 4, movement 4

When listening for melodies, one may also note a *theme* or a *motif*. A theme is a longer melody with a brief sense of finality. This can be thought of as a complete sentence that ends in a punctuation mark, just as in spoken language. The composer often uses the theme, in part or complete, in different places of the composition to express different ideas. A motif, on the other hand, is a very short melodic fragment that is used throughout a piece. This can be thought of as a short phrase or clause. It does not have the same feeling of completeness as a theme. Probably the most famous motif in Western music is the four-note motif from the Beethoven Fifth Symphony. Beethoven used this fragment to compose all four movements of the symphony. (The term *movement* will be discussed later.) Each longer theme uses the motif.

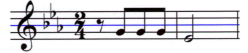

When listening to music, there are definite points of rest. All music is the ebb and flow of tension and relaxation. These points of rest are called *cadences*. A cadence occurs melodically at the "end of a sentence." A cadence can also occur harmonically as we will see later in this book. When trying to hear cadences in melodies, it is often helpful to think of them as "musical punctuation marks." Some of them sound complete, as does a period at the end of a sentence. Some are very strong, as with the exclamation point. Some have a momentary rest and move on to complete the thought, as with the comma.

One unique aspect to Western music is that strong, final cadences often occur on the same relative musical pitch. The more you listen to a piece of music, the more you will be aware of a specific pitch that seems to be the center of attention. That pitch is called the *tonic*. As the music of our culture has developed, the concept of a tonic pitch has been established. Although it may seem subtle to you, you will soon find that it is easy for you to find this pitch. Also, if the composer purposely strays from this pitch, it will create an uncomfortable feeling in you, adding to the tension of a piece of music. If you have trouble finding the tonic pitch, do not worry. You can learn to find it over time.

When listening for melodies in music, there are two terms to be considered, *conjunct* and *disjunct*. A conjunct melody is one that flows in a

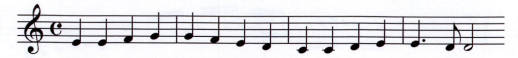

Fig. 7.3 Conjunct Melody from Beethoven's 9th Symphony

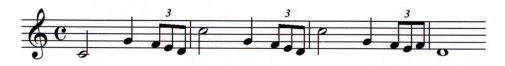

Fig. 7.4 Disjunct Melody the Main Title from the Movie *Star Wars*

step-wise fashion, that is, it moves smoothly with a minimum of large leaps. (See Fig. 7.3) A disjunct melody is more angular and uses many more leaps. (See Fig. 7.4) These terms are relative to each other. Rarely does one find a melody that is totally conjunct or totally disjunct. A melody is usually described as "more conjunct" or "more disjunct."

Melody gives us one sense of organization of the music. However, performing a series of notes in a certain order would make little sense if we did not organize those notes in a specific way in time. This organization is called *rhythm*.

I'VE GOT RHYTHM, WHO COULD ASK FOR ANYTHING MORE?

The second basic element of music is *rhythm*. Rhythm is defined as organized music in time. Music is one of several arts, including dance and theater, which is wholly dependent on time. Once an artistic work occurs, it ceases to exist. When considering a painting or sculpture, one can sit for hours and study the techniques used by the artist. In music, one can focus on the artwork for a limited period of time. Besides that, the work is constantly being revealed so it becomes difficult to dwell on any single aspect of the work.

We experience a rhythm of life everyday. We wake up at a certain time in the morning. We prepare for work or class in a certain sequence, spending a similar amount of time on each activity each morning. We plan trips based on how long the driving, walking, or flying will take. We wear a watch to make sure we are not giving too much time to certain activities. At night (or in the early morning), we go to bed and spend a certain amount of time sleeping. If the timing of our routine is upset, we can become disoriented or confused. Everything in our life is based on time.

The aspect of time is one characteristic that makes the study of music, dance, and theater a bit more challenging. When considering painting, sculpture, or architecture, it is possible to observe the actual work for hours, days, or even years. Some aspects of European cathedrals have been studied for hundreds of years. However, once music has been performed, it no longer exists. We must focus all of our energy on the sounds that occur, their order, their combinations, and on every aspect of organization. The only way we can study a musical work is to hear it repeatedly. Even then, unless one is listening to a recording, the work may be slightly different each time.

All elements of music are organized in time. For example, within a melody, the notes may occur in quick succession or they may sound very slowly. The duration of each note is very specific. Within the chord progressions, the chords may change very slowly or they may change quickly. Rhythm helps the composer create logical, expressive music.

We Got the Beat!

Within rhythm, there are several concepts that need to be understood. When listening to music, it is important to be aware of the **beat** of the music, that is, the pulse of the music. There are many examples of the regular, recurring pulse. The human heart has a beat. Events such as the passing of a day or the regular changing of the seasons also have a "pulse-like" recurrence.

In music, this pulse can be very strong in some music and very subtle in other music. For example, marches have a very strong beat that is easy to hear. Also, rock and roll music often has a very strong beat. Soft music often has a very subtle beat that is difficult to hear. Anytime you tap your foot or move in some rhythmic fashion to music, that is the beat of the music.

Beats are often organized in patterns in much the same way as poetry is organized. You have probably heard the terms "iambic" or "trochaic." These terms specify a particular pattern of emphasis in poetry, as illustrated in Fig. 7.5. The same concept occurs in music and is called **meter**. The meter of a piece of music is the organized pattern of emphasis on certain beats.

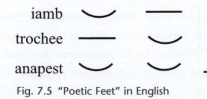

Fig. 7.5 "Poetic Feet" in English

The organization of patterns of emphasis in music is best understood by listening to popular music that has a strong beat. Often this music has a "backbeat" that is easily recognized. This backbeat can be described as "iambic" because it has recurring patterns of a weak beat followed by a strong beat. In most cases, beats "2" and "4" have a heavier accent than beats "1" and "3." Set drummers will often bring this pattern out by striking the snare drum loudly on beats 2 and 4.

As we consider the metrical organization, we will focus mainly on two beat patterns, *duple meter* and *triple meter*. Duple meter will have beats organized in groups of 2 or 4. Triple meter will organize beats in groups of 3. One way to discover if the music has duple or triple meter is to count along with the music. If the music is duple, one can count "1, 2, 1, 2. . ." and it will fit with the beat pattern. If the music is triple, counting "1, 2, 3, 1, 2, 3. . ." will fit the beat pattern.

Take Note of This!

Musical sounds last for a certain period of time that is relative to the other sounds. When assigning a certain amount of time to a sound, the composer will use different types of note values. You have probably heard of whole notes, half notes, quarter notes, etc. Based on the rhythmic organization of the music, a *whole note* may receive 4 beats. By dividing a whole note in half, we get two half notes. By dividing each half note in half, we get two quarter notes. Just as in mathematics, this process could go on infinitely. However, in practice, note values smaller than 32nd notes are fairly rare and note values smaller than 64th notes, though not unheard of, are extremely rare. Fig. 7.6 shows the relative note values of the most commonly used types of notes.

OK, Where's the Fire!

Music occurs at different speeds. Some music is very fast. Some is very slow. The speed of the music is called *tempo*. The tempo of a piece may remain constant or it may vary greatly. The composer will use tempo to add expression to the piece. When you listen to a CD, you will notice that the pieces are in different tempos. Often, the producers will alternate slow and fast pieces on a single CD.

One final concept to be considered is called *syncopation*. Syncopation occurs when the composer emphasizes beats that are weak. Extreme syncopation occurs "off the beat," that is, the strong accent does not coincide with any beat. This is easier to identify if there are repeated accents that occur off the beat.

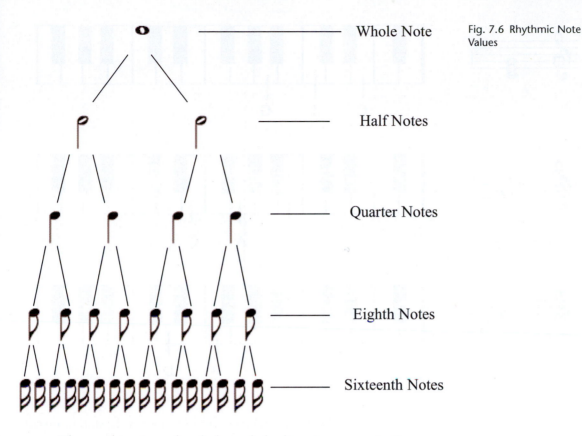

Whole Note

Half Notes

Quarter Notes

Eighth Notes

Sixteenth Notes

Fig. 7.6 Rhythmic Note Values

The combination of melody and rhythm give us music. In many parts of the world, these two elements are the foundation for all of the music of certain cultures. In Western music, a third element gives us a different kind of sound along with a different opportunity for expression. That element is *harmony*.

HARMONY

Harmony occurs when two or more notes are sounded at the same time. If one looks at a sheet of music, this is the vertical organization of the music. Harmony can be very simple or it may be very dense and complex.

Western music has developed over the centuries into a highly organized system of harmony that uses *chords* and *chord progressions*. Basic chords are built with 3 notes that are intervals of a "third" apart. These chords are called *triads*. Consider the piano keyboard again. If we begin with the note C, we can build a triad by using C – E – G, each note is the interval of a third above the previous note. Another example of a chord played on the white keys would be G – B – D. In the examples in Fig. 7.7,

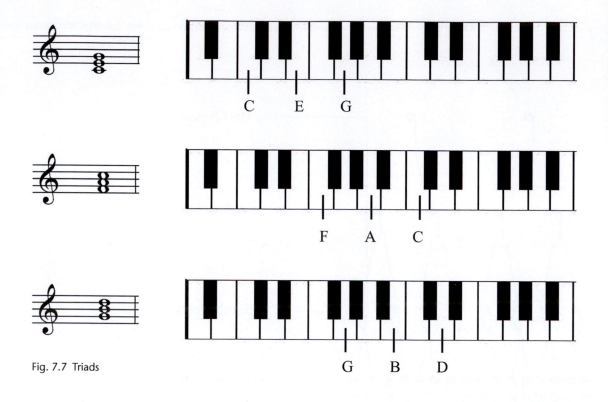

Fig. 7.7 Triads

notice that a triad always occurs on consecutive lines of the staff or on consecutive spaces on the staff.

Music in the Western world did not always use harmony. In the Medieval era, the church did not allow the use of harmony in worship music, although harmony did occur in secular music. Over the centuries, harmony was added to all music and a specific system of *functional harmony* was developed. Functional harmony establishes a priority to different chords. An entire piece is centered on a specific chord. As we have already learned, pieces are built around a specific pitch called tonic. The triad built on this pitch is called the *tonic chord*. The chord progression of a piece, that is, the order that the chords occur, is designed to begin on tonic, move away from tonic, and ultimately return to the tonic chord. This type of progression aids in the build up of tension in a piece and the ultimate release of tension at the end of the piece.

Our system of harmony utilizes cadences in the same fashion as discussed before. With a melody, the cadence is a point of rest or musical "punctuation mark." A *harmonic cadence* will have the same feeling of completeness as the melodic cadence. The harmonic cadence typically uses specific types of chord progressions. Music theorists study the progressions of composers to determine technical ways that composers can express different ideas.

As mentioned before, harmony is not used in all musical systems around the world. It is characteristic to music of Western culture and other cultures strongly influenced by Western music. Music devices and expectations are brought about in a culture by the process of inculcation. As we grow up, we hear music in our culture. We hear similar musical devices repeatedly throughout our life. Eventually, we come to expect these devices and music sounds strange to us if these devices are not used. This becomes our basis of understanding as we expand our knowledge. When we hear music of different cultures, we often find ourselves confused.

Think of it this way. If you learn to drive in the United States, there are certain conventions that are patterned. For example, in the United States, cars drive on the right side of the road. As we gain experience with driving, those patterns become stronger and stronger. If we take a trip to Great Britain, we are suddenly confronted with a similar set of rules but with some major differences. For example, we find driving on the left side of the road unnerving. We do not understand all of the signs. Many of the road markings are unfamiliar.

The same thing happens as we learn different styles of music and music from different cultures. If we listen to Country Music all of the time, we are comfortable with the conventions used in Country Music. As we branch out to Popular Music, Classical Music, or even Music from India, we can become disoriented and confused. If this happens, be determined and press on. As you gain experience, you will become more comfortable with the new "musical environment" and you will soon experience a whole new world of expression.

This happens with harmony. We have certain expectations in harmony which may not be understood. We have heard music in a particular way all of our lives. We have certain expectations. As we learn new sounds, we should expand our experiences to embrace new types of expression.

These elements give the basic parameters for music. In the next section, we will consider how these elements are used to begin to put sounds together.

WEAVING A TEXTURE

In music, the term *texture* is used to describe how different melodies and harmonies are put together to create "depth" or "thickness." In art, texture refers to the way something "feels" or the way one perceives that it

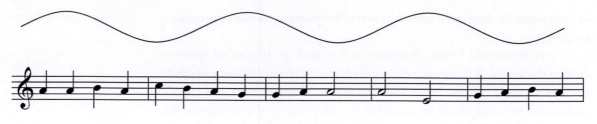

Fig. 7.8 One single melody
= Monophonic Texture

feels. Sometimes this is done by placing many layers of different materials one on top of another to create thickness. At other times, the artist may create a two-dimensional object that gives the *impression* of thickness.

In music, this layering occurs with the various melodies. There are three main types of musical texture, **monophonic**, **homophonic**, and **polyphonic**. These words are understood from their original roots. "Mono," meaning one, put with "phonic," meaning sound, is "one sound." By the same process, "homophonic" means "same sound" and "polyphonic" means "many sounds."

First, let's consider monophonic music. This music is made up of one single melody and nothing else. There is no harmony. It may be performed by more than one person, but if that is the case, everyone is performing the same melody on the same notes. If men and women are singing music monophonically, they may be singing in different octaves, that is, women higher than the men, but they will be singing the same notes an octave apart. (See Fig. 7.8)

When harmony is added that is secondary to the main melody, the texture that results is homophonic. There are actually two different forms of homophonic music. One form is probably very familiar to many because it is the type used in most popular music. This type is one melody that is accompanied by harmony, whether the harmony be guitar chords and a bass line, a piano accompaniment, or some other type of supporting harmony. (See Fig. 7.9)

As we have seen, a homophonic texture occurs when there is one melody with accompaniment. Another type of homophonic texture occurs when the melody is sung or played in one voice and all other voices sing or play harmony notes at the same time. This type sounds when a hymn is sung in church. Everyone changes notes at the same time as the melody but many parts are singing harmony. (See Fig. 7.10)

In the late Medieval era and in the following musical eras, composers would write polyphonic music, that is, two or more equally impor-

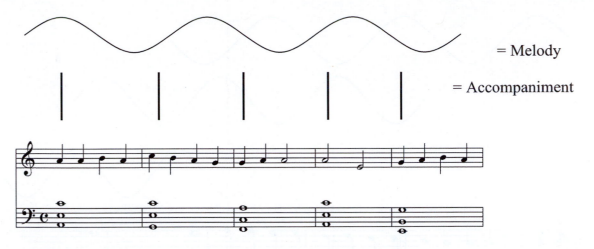

Fig. 7.9 A single melody with supporting accompaniment = Homophonic Texture

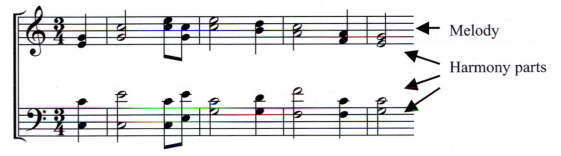

Fig. 7.10 All voices move at the same time = Homophonic Texture

tant melodies played or sung at the same time. Listening to this type of music requires great concentration. The mind must be aware of what is happening on two or more different levels. (See Fig. 7.11)

So, as you can see, the texture of a piece can be very thin, as in monophony, or very thick, as in multilayered polyphony. Just as in the visual arts, the composer can create layer upon layer of sound just as the painter would put layer upon layer of paint to create a kind of depth, a *texture*!

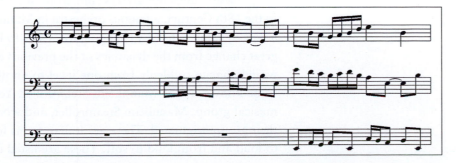

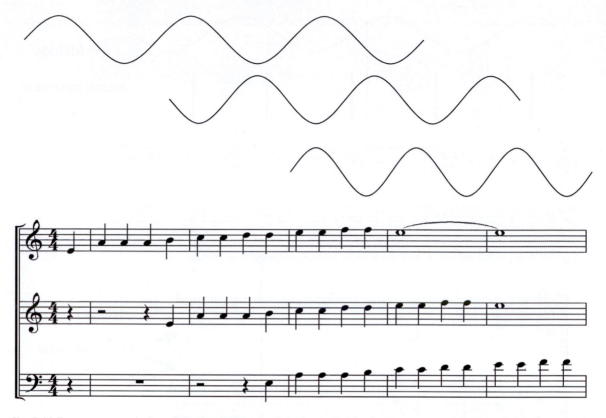

Fig. 7.11 Two or more melodies of equal importance = Polyphonic Texture

WHAT'S THE MATTER WITH YOU KIDS!? TURN IT DOWN! IT IS TOO LOUD!

The fourth element of music is *dynamics*. Dynamics determine how loud or how soft the music is. There are various levels of loudness which are designated by Italian terms. (See Fig. 7.12)

Music does not always shift from one level of loudness to another. In the 18th Century, a famous orchestra in Mannheim, Germany developed a new dynamic effect by changing from soft to loud gradually. This was a great change from the dynamics of the previous era. Prior to this, the music would change suddenly from one level to another. This new effect came to be known as the Mannheim Steamroller. You may have heard of the musical group, Mannheim Steamroller, and wondered where the name of their group originated. There are Italian terms for these changes from soft to loud and from loud to soft. These are listed in Fig. 7.13.

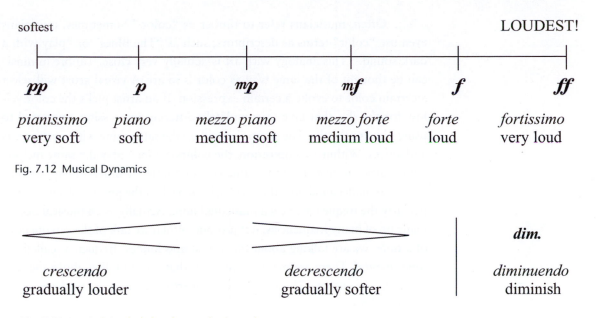

softest   LOUDEST!

pp	*p*	*mp*	*mf*	*f*	*ff*
pianissimo	piano	mezzo piano	mezzo forte	forte	fortissimo
very soft	soft	medium soft	medium loud	loud	very loud

Fig. 7.12 Musical Dynamics

crescendo   *decrescendo*   *dim.*
gradually louder   gradually softer   *diminuendo*
                                            diminish

Fig. 7.13 Musical Symbols for changes in dynamics

When a composer writes a piece, relative loudness is very important to the expression of a piece. Often soft, reflective music will calm the listener. On the other end of the spectrum, loud music often generates feelings of excitement or patriotism. The composer may use fewer instruments to achieve softness and many more to achieve loudness. Finally, the composer may make instrument choices based on how loudly or softly each instrument can play. Woodwinds and strings simply cannot play as loudly as brass instruments. Certain percussion instruments are very soft and some are very loud. The composer makes choices of instrumentation to bring about certain dynamic levels. However, this is only one reason certain instruments are chosen by the composer. More importantly, instruments and voices are chosen because of their characteristic sound; they are the colors that composers use to "paint" sounds.

WHY ISN'T IT SPELLED "TAMBER"?

The next element is **timbre** (pronounced "TAM-ber"). Timbre is easy to determine but hard to explain. It is the quality that distinguishes one instrument or voice from another. For example, when an oboe and a trumpet play the same note, we can tell one from the other.

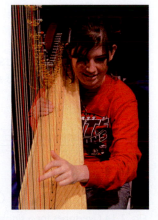

Photo by Lisa Pesavento

Often, musicians refer to timber as "color." Sometimes, musicians even use "color" terms as descriptors, such as "The Blues" or "play with a dark sound." This analogy with art is actually very close. Timbre in music can be thought of the same way as color is in art. A visual artist will select a certain color to evoke a certain expression. If an artist picks the color yellow for the sky, that gives a completely different impression compared to using blue for the sky. The composer will do the same thing with instruments and voices. Within a composition, the composer may play the same melody with a different instrument to bring out a completely different expression.

To understand how this works, look back at the physics of sound, particularly the frequency of each individual note. Actually, each musical note is made up of many frequencies, not just one. When we talk of the "frequency" of a note, we are talking about the lowest and loudest frequency, called the *fundamental*. There are many frequencies that are sounding above the fundamental frequency. These are called **overtones, partials,** or **harmonics.** (See Fig. 7.14)

Interestingly, Pythagoras developed the musical scale from these overtones. By touching a string at a certain place, an overtone is emphasized. If all of the overtones are put together, our musical scale will be built (with a few minor changes). If you ever wondered why our notes occur

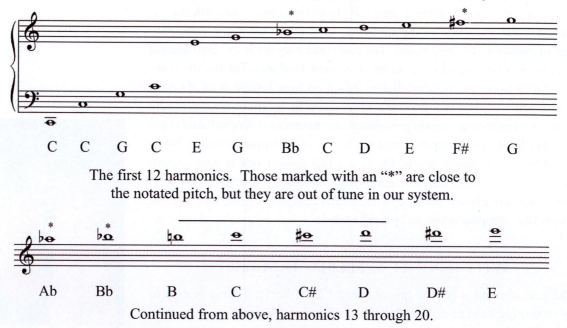

The first 12 harmonics. Those marked with an "*" are close to the notated pitch, but they are out of tune in our system.

Continued from above, harmonics 13 through 20.

Fig. 7.14 Overtones for a single musical note

as they do, it is because of physics. We simply use what is naturally occurring in nature.

It is important to understand that the main purpose of a musical instrument, after the initial production of the tone, is to filter out certain overtones. This gives each instrument a characteristic sound. Notice that the overtones for a trumpet are all present but as the overtone gets higher, it is slightly softer. The overtones of the bassoon are quite different. Notice how the even harmonics are equal in volume to the preceding odd harmonics. Compare these to the graph of the clarinet. In that graph, we see that the clarinet filters out the even number harmonics. Those tiny differences are perceived by the ear and classified by the brain as different timbres.

It's All in How It Sounds.   Different timbres or tone colors are classified in five categories based on how sound is produced by the instrument. *Aerophones* are instruments that require air to create a sound. These would include woodwinds and brass instruments, pipe organs, whistles, and any other instrument that is blown. *Chordophones* are instruments that produce sound by setting a string vibrating. These would include guitars, banjos, violins, violas, cellos, basses, mandolins, etc. *Membranophones* are instruments that have a "head" or some sort of "membrane." These instruments include snare drums, bass drums, timpani, bongos, congas, timbales, each drum on a drum set, and many more. The head of these instruments is usually struck by a stick of some sort. Another classification of percussion instruments is the *idiophones*. These instruments are struck and the sound is created by the vibration of the body of the instrument itself. Idiophones include all types of cymbals, gongs, xylophones, chimes, bells, marimbas, etc. The last classification is called *electrophones*. These instruments create a sound by using an oscillating electrical circuit rather than the vibration of a physical object. This category includes synthesizers, MIDI guitars, MIDI drums, and electronic organs.

There are some instruments that create confusion as to the proper classification. For example, the electric guitar is actually a chordophone rather than an electrophone. The sound of the electric guitar is created by a vibrating string. This sound is then amplified electronically so it will be louder. This electronic amplification does not change the guitar's classification. However, if we consider a MIDI guitar, we find that to be an electrophone. The strings of a MIDI guitar do not vibrate to create the sound. Electronic impulses in the instrument create the vibration of the air.

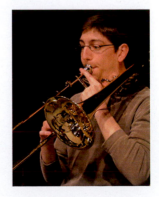

Photo by Lisa Pesavento

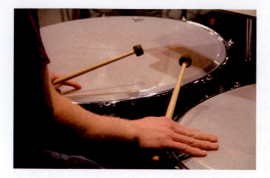

Photo by Lisa Pesavento

Another instrument that can be confused is the piano. Inside the piano, there are a large number of strings. When playing the piano, these strings are struck by a small hammer. So, is the piano a chordophone, because it has strings, or an idiophone, because the strings are struck by a hammer? Most consider the piano to be a stringed instrument and, thus, a chordophone.

In a discussion of musical instruments, many tend to overlook one of the most flexible and fascinating instruments of them all, the voice. The voice is very unique. It is capable of great variation of pitch and timbre. One can actually change the timbre of the voice by simply manipulating certain muscles of the throat and neck. A singer will practice for years to develop the best tone color for their particular voice type.

Voices can be broken down into four major categories. There are two voice types for women, *soprano* (high) and *alto* (low), and two voice types for men, *tenor* (high) and *bass* (low). Advanced study in vocal music reveals that within each of these four voice types, there are many sub-types. For example, a soprano can be a mezzo soprano, a lyric soprano, a coloratura, a dramatic soprano, or a spinto soprano. An alto may be an alto or a contralto, a very low and dark woman's voice. The male voice may be a tenor, a countertenor, a lyric tenor, a spinto tenor, a dramatic tenor, a baritone, a bass-baritone, a bass, a basso cantante, or even a basso profundo, a very low, dark male voice. For the scope of this text, the voice classifications will be soprano, alto, tenor, and bass.

We can actually use these voice types to help us further classify musical instruments. For example, there are a number of different types of saxophones. They are classified by the relative highness of the notes they produce. Of the most common, the highest saxophone is called a *soprano sax*. This is the straight type that Kenny G uses in performance. As the instruments get larger, and thus, lower, the voice names are used to distinguish one from another. The other common saxophones include the *alto sax, tenor sax,* and *baritone sax.* There is a *bass sax* but it is rarely used today.

This same principle also applies to the clarinet family. The most common clarinet is classified as the *soprano clarinet.* The larger clarinets are called the *alto clarinet, bass clarinet, contra alto clarinet* ("contra" meaning "beneath"), and the *contrabass clarinet.*

Sometimes, instruments are referred to as "B flat clarinet" or "F horn." This classification is based on the key of the instrument. Instruments are in different keys to make them easier for the players. This subject can be very confusing to the novice.

All Together Now! When considering musical instruments, it is important to know what instruments are typically used for certain types of music groups, called *ensembles*. In the Medieval era, ensembles were not designated. People would bring instruments together and the group would include whatever instruments were present. In the late Renaissance era, composers began to specify exactly what instruments they wanted to play the music. That was the beginning of our modern ensembles.

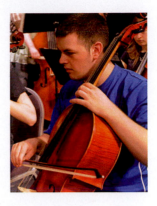

Photo by Lisa Pesavento

The most important ensemble is the *orchestra*. The exact instrumentation of the orchestra has developed over centuries and it can vary from piece to piece. There is a "standard" orchestra with instrumentation that we expect to hear in a piece. (See Fig. 7.15) Part of the fascinating experience of hearing a live orchestra is to see how a composer has added to or subtracted from a standard instrumentation to achieve a particular sound.

As the orchestra developed, the number of instruments increased. Part of this is due to the principle performance space used. In the 1600s, for example, many concerts were given in small theaters built on the estates of nobility. As a result, a smaller group of instruments could fill the space. As the main activity of music moved to larger concert halls for the general public in the Nineteenth Century, the size of the orchestra needed to be larger to fill the often enormous theaters.

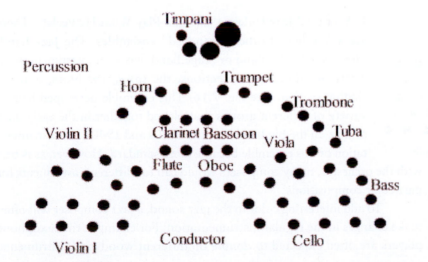

Fig. 7.15 Instrumentation for a "Standard" Orchestra

The size and make up of the orchestra was also influenced by the improvements on old instruments and the development of new instruments. As instruments were perfected, composers had more options in expressing themselves. As a result, a greater number of instruments were needed for newer compositions. Today, the orchestra has developed to become one of the most varied and interesting ensembles, capable of producing a wide range of notes and timbres.

From the earliest compositions, vocal ensembles have played an important role in music. Because of the unique capabilities of the human voice, the blend and tone created by vocal ensembles is extremely beautiful. In the Medieval times, much of the sacred music was sung. As a matter of fact, instruments were not used for sacred music at all in the early church. As the art of vocal music developed during this period, different voice parts were combined to create new sounds. By the middle of the Renaissance period, vocal ensembles were extremely active and complex. Also, by this time, instruments were used primarily as a support for the voices.

From these beginnings, the modern choir has developed. In general, a mixed choral ensemble consists of equal numbers of sopranos, altos, tenors, and basses, usually referred to as SATB (soprano, alto, tenor, bass). Of course, compositions have been written for many different combinations of voices, including SSAA (soprano I, soprano II, alto I, alto II), SSA, SAB, TTBB, and even some pieces for SSAATTBB. By combining a choir with the orchestra, an ensemble of great force and nuance is possible. This combination, used by Beethoven in his Ninth Symphony, for example, allowed for extremely expressive and moving music.

It Ain't Real Jazz Unless a Cat Can Play What He Feels! There are a number of other "standard" ensembles. The Jazz Band, often called a Big Band or Stage Band, has a set instrumentation. There are three major sections, the saxes, the brass, and the rhythm section. (See Fig. 7.16) This ensemble developed from a variety of different groups that played together in the early days of Jazz. In the Big Band Era, the 1930s and 1940s, the instrumentation of this ensemble became more standard. However, as is true with the orchestra, many composers would call for different instruments for particular compositions.

To add interesting color to the jazz sound, a jazz composer will often make changes in the regular instrumentation. For example, the saxophone players are often expected to *double* on different woodwind instruments.

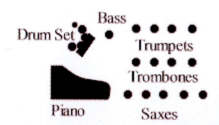

Fig. 7.16 A Typical Jazz Band Set Up

Those playing alto sax may also be asked to play flute, clarinet, or even oboe. The baritone sax player may be asked to double on bass clarinet or even bassoon. This adds new colors to the standard ensemble.

To change the color or timbre of the brass instruments, the players will sometimes use several special devices called **mutes**, which trumpet or trombone players will put into the bell of the instrument. (See Fig. 7.17) The term "mute" seems to refer to making the instrument softer, but although it does soften the instrument, that is the least important function of the mute.

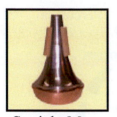
Straight Mute

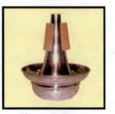
Cup Mute

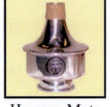
Harmon Mute

Fig. 7.17 Standard Trumpet Mutes

The main reason for using a mute in a brass instrument is to change the timbre. A "straight mute" will give a certain sound that is different from the sound of a "cup mute," which has a different sound than the "harmon mute," and so forth. When watching a jazz band perform, it is easy to tell when a mute is used. The player will push the mute into the bell of the instrument. The next time you listen to a Jazz Band, watch for this and take note of the difference in the sound produced by the instruments.

Strike Up the Band!   During the Twentieth Century, another standard musical organization developed. The Band or Wind Band actually developed from a military tradition. Military bands were used far back in history. Even the Romans used groups of brass instruments in their armies. This tradition continued through the centuries and included groups such as the fife and drums of our Revolutionary War, the bagpipes of the Scottish military tradition, and bands of our own military, most notably the Marine Band under the direction of John Philip Sousa.

A unique circumstance led to the growth of school bands in America that was a result of world politics. At the end of World War II, there were a number of veterans returning from the war who played in military bands. Many of them got teaching jobs in the public schools and taught students to play various instruments, often the instruments from their experience. As a result, band programs began to grow throughout the country.

Over the decades, two distinct, but similar groups emerged, the Concert Band and the Marching Band. (For "standard" instrumentation for these groups, see Fig. 7.18) The Marching Band was used in parades, as they are used in the military. One bright band director had an idea. While watching a football game, he wondered if there was a way the band could provide entertainment during the halftime. Using military maneuvers,

Fig. 7.18 Concert Band Set Up and Marching Band Instrumentation

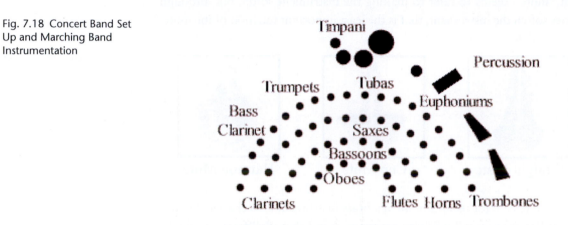

Typical Concert Band Set Up

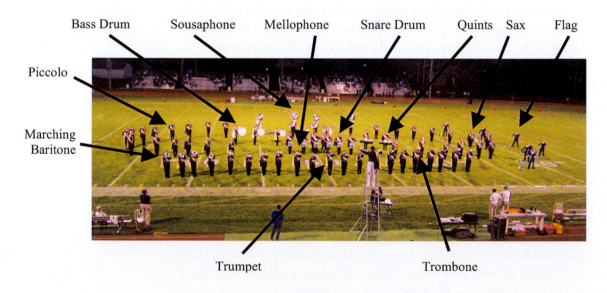

Marching Band on the Field

school bands began marching during the halftime of football games and the modern marching band was born. Many of those military traditions are still used today. For example, the marching band commands of "attention," "dress right," "parade rest," and "at ease" are all military commands. Originally, all bands used a 30 inch stride just as in the military. This worked well on the field because the individual would take six 30 inch steps from one yard line to the next (that is, five yards). Directors found that this was difficult for younger members and members who were shorter in stature. As a result, the step size was shortened to 22½ inches or eight steps to five yards.

The modern marching band today has undergone many innovations. The art form of the competitive band presents both a difficult musical performance and a complex and interesting visual performance. With the addition of flags, rifles, sabers, and all sorts of props, the visual aspect of the band has emerged to become a wonderful addition to the music.

The Concert Band originally played two types of works. One was marches written by the great march composers of the late 1800s and early 1900s. The other main type of music performed was *transcriptions*. These were works written for the orchestra that had been rewritten, or *transcribed*, for the instrumentation of the Concert Band. As composers began to realize the potential for expression in the Concert Band, compositions written specifically for the band were created. The *repertoire*, or the standard literature, for the Concert Band has grown significantly. There is even a move underway to add a Grammy Award for Wind Band recordings and compositions.

Small Is Good, Too! A number of small instrumental ensembles have developed throughout the history of music. These are called *chamber ensembles*. Originally, royalty would hire musicians to provide entertainment for their guests on their estates. These chamber ensembles would play background music, accompany dance, or even present their own recital. Although there are a wide variety of chamber ensembles, the most common include the String Quartet, the Woodwind Quintet, and the Brass Quintet. (See Fig. 7.19 for instrumentation) Some composers were drawn to particular chamber groups. For example, Joseph Haydn, a composer from the Classical era, wrote sixty-eight string quartets!

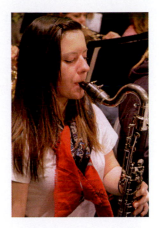

Photo by Lisa Pesavento

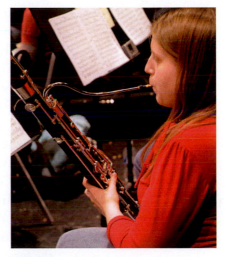

Photo by Lisa Pesavento

String Quartet	Woodwind Quintet	Brass Quintet
1st Violin	Flute	1st Trumpet
2nd Violin	Oboe	2nd Trumpet
Viola	Clarinet	Horn
Cello	Horn	Trombone
	Bassoon	Tuba

Fig. 7.19 Instrumentation of Standard Chamber Groups

From all of this, it is easy to see the relationship between timbre in music and color in art. Great variety exists in both areas to give the artist/composer vast tools to create wonderful works. Combining timbre with the other elements, we are ready to consider how music is put together.

FORM

The final element of music that we will study is *form*. The form of a piece refers to how the piece is organized. The details of form can be very complex. There are many different ways to put a composition together. We will primarily be concerned with three concepts, *repetition*, *contrast*, and *variation*. This simplifies the process of deciphering the composer's intent. Any of the previous elements can be organized using these three concepts.

Repetition is simply repeating what has just been stated. If it is a melody, then that melody is repeated. This can apply to a chord progression, dynamic organization, or instrumentation. First, listen for repeated elements.

Contrast is anything that is different from what was just stated. The most obvious contrasts occur in the melody. The composer can try to deceive the listener, for example, by repeating the melody but changing the chord progression or the instrumentation. Generally, when following the form of a piece, the melodies and the harmonies are the elements that determine repetition and contrast. (As I said, this can get very complex!)

The last element is variation. This can be more difficult to determine. Is the current melody the same or only slightly different? Is the melody the same but the accompaniment different enough to consider this a variation? The more experience gained with listening, the easier this is to determine. This element is one of the more advanced thinking processes involved in music listening. It requires a judgment to be made by the listener. As you practice this process, try to make your best judgment.

There is one final aspect to basic formal understanding. Often, composers will write a very long piece of music that is divided into a number of related sections, called **movements**. A *movement* is a complete, self contained, and often large section of a much larger work. A *symphony*, for example, usually consists of three, four, or even five movements. Some works may have as many as 13 movements. Each movement is different in character, tempo, and expression. Often, the composer will use music or themes from one movement in one or more of the others. As the art of composition developed, composers became more conscious of unifying the work by using music from one movement in another.

Over the centuries, composers have created a wide variety of forms. Becoming familiar with these forms will help in understanding the composer's intent in organizing the sounds that you hear. In the next chapter, we will spend some time looking at some standard forms and listening to examples of these forms.

The elements of music are numerous and varied. Many of them are familiar and easy to understand. As you listen to any music, whether it be Jazz, Metal, Classical, Country, Rap, or Popular, begin thinking about the music in terms of the elements. Don't just let the music wash over your ears as you listen. Focus on different concepts. What instruments are playing? What part do you like? How did the composer do that? Is anything repeated? Does the music get loud and soft or is it all just one level? By doing this, the music begins to come alive. Sometimes music you like may have elements that you never expected. You may begin to realize that your favorite music uses certain elements to a greater degree. Perhaps this is why you like the music.

Another advantage to this way of listening to music is that new music is not completely foreign to you. You can listen for the musical elements and begin to understand the composer's intent from the first listening. Sometimes we are overwhelmed by certain types of music because of the unfamiliarity. With these tools, the level of unfamiliarity will be lower and our musical experiences will begin to grow in totally new directions.

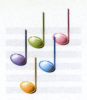

Chapter 7
Elementary, My Dear Watson

1. Name two familiar pieces of music, one with a conjunct melody and one with a disjunct melody. Use melodies from folk songs, movie themes, classical music, or patriotic songs.

2. Name two familiar pieces, one with a duple meter and one with a triple meter. Again, use folk songs, movie themes, classical music, or patriotic songs.

3. Name one style of music (Classical, Rock, Country, etc.) that tends to keep the same tempo throughout. Name one style that tends to change tempos.

4. Name two familiar pieces, one that is consonant and one that is dissonant. (Do not confuse dissonance with loudness).

5. In your own words, briefly explain why instruments sound different from one another.

8

MUSICAL ARCHITECTURE

Musical Architecture is the overall form of a piece of music. Understanding the form will help in understanding the composer's intent. This chapter looks at different forms of music that may be heard in a variety of pieces of music. As the chapter unfolds, the forms will move from simple to more complex. However complex the form, the composer's art is not one that is intended to be hidden, but one that is intended to be discovered by the listener.

Before we begin our look at different forms, it may be useful to have a system of labeling them. First, let's consider how a piece is divided up. For most pieces, there are a number of different sections that make up the whole piece. For an analogy, consider architecture. When you observe architecture, you see a foundation, walls and supports, a roof, etc. Each piece has its own unique appearance that adds to the overall design. When put all together, the effect is often overwhelming. Even then, each individual part or section can be seen as a unique part of the whole.

The same idea happens in music. However, the sections in a piece of music occur by themselves over a period of time. As we consider these sections of music, we see how they relate and how they affect the piece as a whole. In effect, the composer "builds" the composition from the ground up every time the piece is performed.

A section of music is one that uses similar melodic and harmonic material. When listening for different sections, one good strategy is to listen for main melodies. Often you will know that the section has ended when the melody comes to a cadence followed by material that has a different melody or harmony. As you remember, cadences are points of rest or "musical punctuation marks." Cadences will help you find the end of each section.

Music theoreticians will use letters of the alphabet to label sections of music. When the first section is presented, that can be labeled as "A." Remember our three characteristics of form, which are repetition, contrast, and variation. If the section is repeated, our map of the form would be A A. If the second section is contrasting to the first, the labeling would be A B. If the second phrase is a variation of the first, the labeling would be A A'. The only possibilities are 1) second section repeats, 2) second section is in contrast, or 3) second section is a variation of the first section.

Let's consider a piece with 3 large sections. The first is labeled A. Suppose the second section is in contrast to the first and the third section is a repeat of the first section. (You can see how this is already getting difficult to describe verbally.) This piece would be labeled A B A. Now, suppose there is a piece that is in 5 sections. The second section is in contrast to the first; the third is a repeat of the first; the fourth is in contrast to both the first and second (are you following this?!); and, finally, the fifth is a repeat of the first. If we had to describe the music like that, everyone would quickly become confused. And this is only a 5 section piece! It is much easier to represent this music as A B A C A.

Be careful that you do not become overwhelmed with this process. As you practice this new way of listening, take time to enjoy the sounds as well. By hearing and remembering the music, you will begin to hear multiple levels of music. You may even begin to anticipate the composition. The idea is not to lose the ability to listen emotionally, but to add a new dimension to your listening. Let's get started!

BASIC FORMS
The One and Only!

The first formal architecture we will consider is called **strophic form**. This form can be labeled as A A' A" A''' etc. A typical use of strophic form is a hymn such as "Amazing Grace." A section of music with lyrics (A) is heard. Then the same music is repeated with new words for the second verse (A', that is, a variation of A because of the different words.) This continues to the end of the song. The music may be varied further by changing elements while using the same melody. For example, the first verse might be accompanied by the organ. The second verse may be sung without accompaniment. (This would be a change, or variation, in timbre.) The third verse may be sung with *forte* dynamics. (This would be a change, or variation, in dynamics.) The harmony may be changed on the fourth verse, or a variation in harmony. By using these changes, the music does not become dull and routine.

Understand, the same music is being repeated. Even though different elements may change, the melody is always the same. This consistent melody will be useful as you are learning to follow the form. If you study some very advanced compositions, the composer may even change the melody and keep the harmony. To understand this type of composition requires a great deal of experience listening for form and is beyond the scope of this text.

These same ideas are used in Popular songs that are in *strophic form*. The song may start soft with an acoustic guitar and solo singer. On the second verse, other guitars and the drums might be added; thus, a change in timbre. The third verse might be louder, that is, a variation in dynamics. The possibilities are endless.

Many popular songs in strophic form consist of a verse followed by a chorus. This structure is repeated throughout the song. This may seem confusing because the chorus usually has a different melody than the verse and, thus, sounds like two different parts. The reason for analyzing the music as strophic is based on the extent of the verse and chorus. Theorists will break down a large "A" section into smaller parts, that is, "a b." So, even though the phrases contrast, they are not substantial enough to be considered a "section." With more experience, this will become clearer. If you happen to make a mistake as you are trying to listen to this level of music, do not give up. By virtue of the fact that you are using this information, you are already adding to your musical experience.

Another strophic form that occurs in jazz is **12 bar blues**. This form is based on a chord progression that repeats throughout the composition. Each section is 12 **bars**, or measures. A good example of 12 bar blues from popular music is the 1954 song "Shake, Rattle, and Roll" written by Jesse Stone and made famous by Bill Haley and the Comets in the same year. There are many other examples of this type of music. As a matter of fact, a whole genre of music, the Blues, uses this type of structure.

Two by Two

The second form we will consider is *binary form*. As the name implies, a piece in binary form has two contrasting sections, or AB. Often, the sections may be repeated, which would be labeled AABB. A specialized type is called *rounded binary*, which is labeled AABA. A clearer way to label uses the musical notation called a *repeat sign* and would look like this:

‖: A : ‖: B A' :‖

In rounded binary, the second section ends with material from the first section. One well known example of this in the jazz genre is Gershwin's *I Got Rhythm*. The first two phrases have the same melody and different lyrics. The third phrase has a contrasting melody. The fourth phrase is the same melody as the first two.

Three by Three

The third form is called *ternary form*. You may think this form would be labeled ABC, but actually, it is labeled ABA. The first and third sections are identical or very nearly so. The middle section is contrasting. In the music of the Baroque Era, the middle section was sometimes called the *trio*. When a structure is labeled as ABA, it is called simple ternary form. If each of the three sections is longer and has a structure within itself, for example ABA CDC ABA, the form is called *compound ternary*. It should be clear that there are still three equal length sections, the first and third being identical and the second contrasting. A good example of compound ternary is a Minuet and Trio from the Baroque Era.

Arch Form

Arch form is structured in the same way as an architectural arch. The labeling could be ABCBA or ABCDCBA or something similar. The music begins with a section and adds contrasting sections to a point. Then the sections return in reverse. (See Fig. 8.1)

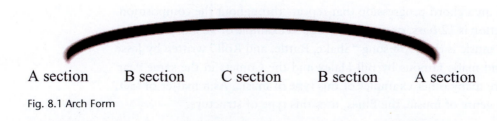

A section   B section   C section   B section   A section

Fig. 8.1 Arch Form

Much about the March

The March is one of the best known forms of music, especially in America. The March is the mainstay of patriotic music of Americana. Marches are usually written in major keys and are lively and rhythmic. They elicit foot-tapping and clapping. Marches have a unique form that the composer uses either to fulfill expectations or to move away from expectations creating a mind game between the composer and the listener.

Marches have specific names for the different sections of the music. The "typical" march form begins with a four bar *introduction*. Following the introduction, there are two contrasting sections, each of 16 bars. These are called the *1st strain* and the *2nd strain*. Both of these are usually moderately loud to very loud and are usually repeated. Following the 2nd strain, the key is changed and the *trio* is presented at a much softer level. Then comes a section that is commonly called the *dogfight*. The dogfight is very loud and consists of alternating instruments playing short phrases. The name comes from the feeling that different groups of instruments are "fighting" for dominance. The third strain follows the dogfight, both of which are usually repeated. If labels were to be attached, it might look like this: Intro AABBCCDEDE. However, the form of the March is usually labeled as in Fig. 8.2. A good example of this form is John Philip Sousa's *Stars and Stripes Forever*.

Where Have I Heard That Before?

The next form to be considered is called *rondo form*. Rondo form has a characteristic repetition of one section of the music. This section is the first to be heard. Between the repetitions of this A section are contrasting sections. Thus, the form can be labeled as ABACADA etc. The A section is usually distinctive and its return is obvious. Whenever you see a rondo on a concert program, listen for this repetition and see if you can determine how many contrasting sections there are. Sometimes the composer may try to throw you a curve by presenting an altered rondo, for example, ABACABA. This begins to approach an arch form, but the repeated A sections make it a rondo.

Intro ||: 1ˢᵗ strain :||: 2ⁿᵈ strain :|| Trio ||: Dogfight   3ʳᵈ Strain :||

ff   f   ff   p   ff   ff

Fig. 8.2 March Form

But It's All Different!!

Finally, we come to a form that is designed to be less obvious. Sometimes a composer will write a section, say A, then a contrasting section, B, then a contrasting section, C, etc. When a piece is in this form, we say it is *through-composed*. With this type, the composer works to avoid any repetition whatsoever. Although there may be similarities in some of the material, each section is contrasting.

OK, Take a Breath

At this point, the idea of listening for form may be a bit overwhelming. It does take some practice but there are always clues that the composers will give. It may be that your first attempts to hear different sections fall short of success. Do not give up. It takes practice to develop this level of listening.

LARGER, CLASSICAL FORMS

This section will address some larger forms that are used by composers of Classical music (as opposed to Popular and Jazz music). These sections will be longer. Some of them may even include one of the basic forms as a *section* of this form. The more you learn about music, especially music theory, the easier these will be to hear. Some composers will work to make them very obvious while others will work to make the form very obscure. That is one aspect that makes listening so fascinating. Will the composer try to help you hear the form or will she or he try to make the form hard to hear or try to trick you?

The Minuet and Trio

The **Minuet** was a dance in the Seventeenth and Eighteenth Centuries. The music for this dance, the **Minuet and Trio,** followed a strict form, as illustrated in Fig. 8.3. It was typically in a triple meter and was in three large sections. Each of these large sections was in *rounded binary* form and in different keys. The diagram for the Minuet and Trio is as follows:

||:   A   :||:   B   :|| A ||

||:   a   :||:   b   a   :|| ||:   a   :||:   b   a   :|| || a || b   a ||

Fig. 8.3 The Form of the Minuet and Trio

The Fugue

The first large form we will consider is the *fugue*. Many theorists believe that the fugue is not a form but a compositional process. For our purposes, we will consider the fugue just as we do different forms of music. The idea is to learn to follow the parts of the fugue.

The fugue most often occurs in instrumental music. In the discussion below, the terms "soprano," "alto," "tenor," and "bass" will be used. These are used to indicate high or low pitches, not necessarily human voices. Many fugues have been written for keyboard instruments in which all parts are played on the same instrument. However, the distinction in the "voices" will help to determine if the notes are high or low.

The most important part of the fugue is called the *exposition*. This section is used to present the melody or melodies that are important in the piece. In the fugue, the exposition has a definite structure, as it does in other forms. The fugue begins with a melody called the *subject*. The subject is the main melody that is used to compose the entire piece. It is presented alone, that is, monophonically, in one voice. For our example, let's say that it is presented in the soprano voice. After the subject is presented in its complete form in the soprano voice, it is then presented in another voice, let's say the alto. The soprano will then continue with contrasting music called a *countersubject*. The following is a diagram of the beginning of a typical fugue:

Soprano	SUBJECT	countersubject
Alto		SUBJECT
Tenor		
Bass		

This pattern continues. For our example, let's say the next subject appears in the tenor and the last subject appears in the bass. The following would be a diagram of the entire exposition:

Soprano	SUBJECT	countersubject		
Alto		SUBJECT	countersubject	
Tenor			SUBJECT	countersubject
Bass				SUBJECT

Sometimes, the composer uses additional countersubjects. This music is different from the subject and the countersubject and is labeled as the 2nd or 3rd countersubject. The following is an example of how this would work:

Soprano	SUBJECT	countersubject	countersubject II	countersubject III
Alto		SUBJECT	countersubject	countersubject II
Tenor			SUBJECT	countersubject
Bass				SUBJECT

As the exposition is presented, there are many different ways for the composer to present the subject. The subject does not always begin in the highest instrument. Also, there are not always four voices. Sometimes there are 3 or 5. The most important aspect is that the subject is played in its entirety.

The second large section of the fugue is the *episode*. The episode includes fragments of the music of the subject and countersubjects but never states the entire subject.

The next section is called the *middle entry*. In the middle entry, the entire subject is presented in at least one voice. This is then followed by another episode, which is followed by another middle entry until the composer brings the work to a close.

The best strategy for listening to a fugue is to listen for complete statements of the subject. The composer gives the complete statement at the beginning of the piece so that part is obvious. Following this, does the composer have four statements of the subject or three or five? Once in the episode, listen for *complete* statements of the subject. That will indicate a middle entry. Many times the composer will try to trick the listener with a partial statement. When a complete statement is heard, the middle entry has just been stated. The following represents a diagram of the entire fugue:

Exposition | Episode | Middle Entry | Episode | Middle Entry | Final Statement

This is a fun, compositional process to listen for. It may take some practice but the more fugues heard, the easier the listening process becomes.

Sonata Allegro Form

The next large form considered is the *sonata-allegro form*, sometimes called simply *sonata form*. One may run across this form in the first and last movements of symphonies or in musical works that are called "sonatas." We will discuss where to expect this type of form further in the next chapter.

As with the Fugue, Sonata form also begins with an *exposition* but this exposition is different from the fugue. In the sonata form, the exposition consists of four major parts. The exposition can be represented as follows:

Sonata Form

	Exposition			Development			Recapitulation	
Dyn	Part	Key	Dyn	Part	Key	Dyn	Part	Key
f	1st Theme	I						
f	Transition	I to V						
p	2nd Theme	V						
f	Closing Theme	V						
	Repeated?							

Note: The left-hand column indicates the expected dynamics; the right-hand column indicates the expected key of the section.

All of the Exposition is new material, although often the composer will use music from the 1st Theme in the Closing Theme. The first few times you hear a piece in sonata form, there will be a temptation to label the Exposition as A B or possibly as a rounded binary, that is, A A B A because of the similarity of the 1st theme and the Closing Theme. Also, be patient when listening to each section. It is quite easy to listen for very small parts of the Exposition. However, as the piece progresses, you will hear the structure of sonata form.

Many composers, especially in earlier works in this form, will repeat the Exposition. That gives the listener a second chance to hear the entire Exposition. It also helps the listener to hear the beginning of the next section.

Following the Exposition is the *Development*. In music, the term *development* is used to indicate that the composer is going to break up material from a previous section and use little fragments of it everywhere. In Sonata form, the composer can use pieces of melodies from the 1st Theme, the 2nd Theme, and the Closing Theme. The development area is where the composer becomes the most creative because anything goes. The structure of the exposition is set but the development can go anywhere.

Sonata Form

Exposition			Development			Recapitulation		
Dyn	Part	Key	Dyn	Part	Key	Dyn	Part	Key
f	1st Theme	I	*p* to	Fragments of				
f	Transition	I to V	*f*	music from	Many			
p	2nd Theme	V		Exposition. . .				
f	Closing Theme	V						
				Dominant				
	Repeated?			Preparation. . .				

The Development ends with a very strong cadence back to the beginning of the Exposition. The composer will often work very hard to help you hear the ending of the development. Many times, the composer uses dominant preparation to prepare the listener to hear the return of the music from the Exposition. This helps in the listening process. When you hear the Exposition again, you know that you have arrived at the Recapitulation, or simply, the Recap.

Sonata Form

	Exposition			Development			Recapitulation	
Dyn	Part	Key	Dyn	Part	Key	Dyn	Part	Key
f	1st Theme	I	*p* to	Fragments of		*f*	1st Theme	I
f	Transition	I to V	*f*	music from	Many	*f*	Transition	I to I
p	2nd Theme	V		Exposition. . .		*p*	2nd Theme	I
f	Closing Theme	V				*f*	Closing Theme	I
	Repeated?			Dominant Preparation. . .				

The Recapitulation basically states all of the music from the Exposition. The major difference is that the *keys* used in the Recap are different than those in the Exposition. Many years ago, the audience was keenly aware of the differences in the tonal centers. Today, music students spend many hours listening to gain this ability. Basically, the music of the 2nd Theme and the Closing Theme are played at a higher or lower pitch level. Listen carefully to see if you can hear the difference.

It is possible for one to think of the Sonata form as a very large A B A. However, because the music in the development comes from fragments of the Exposition and the fact that the parts of the Recap are in different keys from the Exposition, labeling the form as an A B A is not accurate.

Sometimes, a composer would use the audience's knowledge of form to try to deceive them. There might be an unexpected section added in the middle or end. Sometimes, the composer would add complete sections that did not fit the form. An example of this occurs in Beethoven's Symphony #5. After the Recapitulation, Beethoven adds a Coda, or ending. In this ending, he introduces a new theme that is in the wrong key. Then, it appears as if he moves to a second Recapitulation. This quickly moves to the final chords, but the effect was to keep the audience guessing.

Theme and Variations

The next form to be considered is a Classical form called *Theme and Variations*. This form would be diagrammed as follows: A A' A" A'" etc. At first glance, it looks exactly like the strophic form discussed earlier. However, this is a different form in several ways. First, it is a much larger form than strophic. Also, it is typically an instrumental form. A piece in strophic form is basically the same music with different lyrics. The variations are based solely on the text.

In the Theme and Variations, the composer begins with a single Theme, much in the same fashion as the Fugue or the Sonata. After the theme reaches the cadence, or rest point, it is often presented again with another melody decorating it. The composer may vary the theme by changing to another key. Sometimes the composer will play the theme upside-down. The intent of the composer is to find many ways the theme or melody can be changed or accompanied without becoming boring. It is fascinating to listen to this form unfold almost magically using the same melodic material.

Multi-Movement Works

Composers will often write pieces that are *multi-movement*. In the Seventeenth Century, composers would often write collections of dances with similar themes. By the Eighteenth Century, composers were writing symphonies with three and four movements. Each of the movements was self-contained and could be performed alone. Each movement would have a different form and the keys of the works would be related. As the Symphony developed, composers often used similar forms for different movements. This allows us to anticipate the form of a movement which makes hearing that form easier.

Let's consider an example related to the Symphony, which has been a standard compositional form since the Eighteenth Century. From this time, the symphony is typically (but not always) a four movement composition. The expectations for each movement of the Eighteenth Century symphony are shown in Fig. 8.4.

	Tempo	Meter	Dynamics	Form
Movement I	Fast	Duple	Loud (overall)	Sonata Form
Movement II	Slow	Duple or Triple	Soft	Theme & Variations Sonata Rondo
Movement III	Moderate	Triple	Moderate	Minuet & Trio
Movement IV	Fast	Duple	Loud	Sonata Rondo

Fig. 8.4 Eighteenth Century Symphony—Expectations for Movements

Sometimes composers would write something unexpected to use the audience's expectations to deceive them, as mentioned before. For example, the beginning of the first movement of Beethoven's Symphony #1 is slow. The knowledgeable audience member would be confused as to tempo and the composer's intent. Shortly after the beginning, the tempo is fast and the movement unfolds as expected. This is the same formal deception used within the form, as discussed earlier with Sonata form.

Another example of a multi-movement work would be the *concerto*. A *concerto* is a multi-movement work for solo instrument accompanied by orchestra, piano, or other ensemble. This form was established during the Seventeenth Century, but became more standardized in the Eighteenth Century. A concerto typically has three movements. The expectation for the movements of the concerto are given in Fig. 8.5.

	Tempo	Meter	Dynamics	Form
Movement I	Fast	Duple	Loud (overall)	Sonata Form
Movement II	Slow	Duple or Triple	Soft	Theme & Variations Sonata Rondo
Movement III	Moderate or Fast	Triple	Moderate	Rondo

Fig. 8.5 Eighteenth Century Concerto—Expectations for Movements

Final Thoughts

Composers have developed many other variations in these forms. Some types of forms might be combined. Some composers wrote music in a form called *sonata rondo* form. This form combines the Sonata form and Rondo form and can be labeled as follows: ABA Development ABA. It is clear that there are elements of both the sonata form and the rondo form. As you gain experience with hearing form, you will be delighted to hear how a composer can set you up and suddenly change directions from what you expect. It is not unlike a great writer who can convince the reader of what is about to happen and suddenly changes directions.

Keep an open mind as you listen. Be aware of the form and see how successful you can become in following the composer's intent. This is a whole new dimension of music awareness that will help you to enjoy music at a new level while developing your ability to concentrate on different planes of thought.

Chapter 8
Musical Architecture

1. What is the difference between the exposition of a fugue and the episode of a fugue?

2. What is the difference between the exposition of a fugue and the exposition of a piece in sonata form?

3. What is the difference between the exposition of a piece in sonata form and the recapitulation?

4. How is a Theme and Variations different from a strophic form?

5. What tempo would you expect for each movement of a four-movement symphony?

9

GENRES OF MUSIC AND THE CONCERT EXPERIENCE

At this point, you have learned a great many new concepts and strategies for future listening. This chapter will help you to anticipate different venues of music and different genres of music. What should you expect when you attend a jazz concert? How do people react differently at a rock concert and a Classical recital? Just what does all this information in the program mean and how does it help me?

Rock and Popular Concerts

This area of concert attendance is more familiar to the younger generation than any other type of concert. A number of different types of music might fall in this category type, even though they are not technically "rock" music. A concert of popular music might include rock, heavy metal, country, rap, or even contemporary Christian. Most people who attend are dressed very casual as dress is not an issue at this type of concert. Sometimes there is no seating and the crowds either sit on the floor or ground or stay standing during the concert. Often, the crowds entering the music venue can be very large and great care must be taken to insure the safety of the audience.

At the beginning of the performance, there is usually an opening act that performs. This individual or group is usually a young, talented novice to the concert stage. This could even be the first public performance for the opening act. Following this, the main attraction arrives and the main concert begins. Many times, the production is accompanied by very large light shows and pyrotechnic displays. The audience is very vocal and may even sing along with the performers. The need for quiet in order to hear the music is usually not necessary because of the great amplification of the performers. The audience at this type of concert actually becomes a part of the performance through clapping, yelling, singing, and cheering during the songs.

The popular performance usually consists of a series of songs. Sometimes the most well-known songs will be played last in an effort to tease the audience. Because most of the songs are familiar, the crowd will usually react loudly at the very beginning of each song as they recognize it. If you attend a popular concert and you know most of the songs recorded by the group, you may want to focus on familiar songs to see if they are performed exactly as they were recorded. Performers may add things to the music in live concerts. Another reason the music may be different at a live performance has to do with the recording industry. When manufacturing a CD, there is a limited amount of space on the disc for music. However, during a live performance, there are no limitations so the performers feel free to add to the music.

Jazz Concerts

A jazz concert will have a very different atmosphere. Jazz concerts usually occur on a concert stage or in a club and may be performed by a Big Band or a small jazz combo. The atmosphere is still casual for jazz, but the audience usually refrains from the loud noise and constant movement that often happens at rock concerts. The audience listens quietly to the music and gives applause at the end of the piece. One exception to this is applause for a well-played solo. As mentioned before, improvisation is an integral part of jazz music. When a soloist *takes a ride*, that is, plays an improvised solo, the audience will applaud at the end of the solo, especially if the artist plays with dazzling technique and great imagination. This applause during the song is not only appropriate, but it is very much appreciated by the performers. It is a way that the audience can encourage the performers while they are playing.

At a jazz concert, it is important to focus on the rhythm section. You will notice that each piece has a distinctive sound and rhythm. Rhythmic style is vital to a fine jazz performance. As each piece is played, focus on what is different from the previous piece and try to identify why it is different. Is the drummer playing in a different fashion? Are the instruments playing in different groupings? Is the bass player a dominant feature or is that part far in the background? How much input does the piano player give to the piece? These types of questions will help you discover style in jazz.

Formal and Chamber Recitals and Concerts

Recitals by individuals or small groups are a more formal activity than any of those we have discussed so far. A different level of audience behavior is required at a formal concert. Usually, the audience will dress a bit less casually. Dresses and Coat-and-Tie are often the norm. It is customary to arrive at the recital early to find your seat and to read through the program. Also, before entering a recital or concert, it is very important to turn off cell phones and pagers. Even the "buzz" of a cell phone set to vibrate can be distracting to audience members.

The program is a very helpful aid to the audience. It gives information about who is performing and what can be expected. On the front cover, the performer or performers are given. Also, the date, time, and place of the concert are listed. Inside the program, there are several things to note. The *program order* is listed. This gives the titles of the pieces, the composers, what movements are being played, and often the birth and death dates of the composers. You can use these items to help you follow what is happening during the concert. For example, if you see that one of the works is called "sonata," you already know what type of form you can expect. Consider the program entry in Fig. 9.1.

Rondo in D Major, op. 162	Justus Composers (1876–1931)	Fig. 9.1 An Example of a Program Entry

This entry indicates a number of important facts. First, the piece is a *rondo*, so we know that it is important to listen to the music at the beginning because it will return many times. As you remember, the form is labeled ABACADA or ABACABA, or something similar. Also, the key of the piece is given, in this case, D Major. That tells you what the tonic note is, but more importantly, it tells you the *mode* of the piece. In Western Classical music, there are two prominent modes—major and minor. A number of other modes are used but these two are the most often used. Some people label the *major* mode as "happy" or "pleasant." Music in a *minor* mode is often labeled as "sad" or "scary." These may or may not be accurate but they can be a starting point in listening for different modes.

From the above entry, we see "op. 162." *Op.* stands for the word *opus*, which literally means "work." From the given information, we would determine that this is the one-hundred-and-sixty-second piece of music that this composer wrote. In some cases, there are other letters that represent works. For example, for the music of Mozart, the letter "K" is used, as in K. 191. The letter "K" stands for Koechel which is the name of the individual who cataloged Mozart's works. The same conclusion can be made regarding the order of compositions, that is, K. 191 is the one-hundred-and-ninety-first work of Mozart. There are cataloging systems that are not chronological. For example, when you see a work on a program by Johann Sebastian Bach, it will probably be followed by the letters "BWV" followed by a number. These letters stand for *Bach Werke Verzeichnis*, which means "Bach Works Catalog" in German and lists works by theme rather than chronology.

Finally, the composer's name is given on the far right along with his/her dates of birth and death. Those dates help us identify the historical period of the music, which we will discuss later. From all we have learned from the printed program, we are ready to totally focus on the music and listen on several different levels.

If the work is a multi-movement work, it is listed with the movements indicated. Some composers will give names to movements. When this occurs, these names will appear on the program, as seen in Fig. 9.2.

Fig. 9.2 An Example of a Multi-Movement Work from a Concert Program

Of Sailors and Whales	W. Francis McBeth
Queequeg	(1933)
Ishmael	
Father Maple	
Ahab	
The White Whale	

The title of the piece is *Of Sailors and Whales* and there are five movements. It was written by W. Francis McBeth who was born in 1933 and is still living.

If the composer does not give specific names to the movements, they are listed with their tempo and/or style markings. This is helpful in following the program because the listener will know if a movement is fast or slow or medium and should be able to tell when each movement begins. An example of a program listing tempos for each movement is given in Fig. 9.3.

Symphony No. 2 in D Major, Opus 36   Ludwig van Beethoven
   Adagio molto; Allegro con brio   (1770–1827)
   Larghetto
   Scherzo: Allegro
   Allegro molto

Fig. 9.3 An Example of a Multi-Movement Work from an Orchestral Program

This entry tells the audience that this is the second symphony written by Beethoven, it is in the key of D Major, and it is his 36th work written. It also gives four tempo markings which indicate that there are four movements. The translations for these terms are given in Fig. 9.4.

Adagio molto; Allegro con brio	Very Slow followed by Fast with Spirit
Larghetto	Slow, but not as slow as *largo*, or very slow
Scherzo: Allegro	A fast movement in triple meter: Fast
Allegro molto	Very Fast

Fig. 9.4 Translations of tempo terms from Fig. 9.3

Because the tempo markings are given, the audience can follow the movements by listening for fast and slow music. As you read the program, you will gain more and more insight about the performance and will be ready to listen with better understanding.

There are a number of conventions that should be followed in a formal recital. As the performers enter the stage, the audience should applaud. While the music is being performed, the audience is expected to be completely quiet. One should not do anything to make a sound, including opening a wrapper, talking, or making noise with the chairs. The reason for this is that much of the music performed will be at a very soft level. In addition, the performer must have silence for total concentration, much as a tennis player expects the crowd to be absolutely quiet. Also, to listen to complex music on a number of levels, it is important that the audience members be able to focus without distraction.

At the end of a piece, applause is expected and appreciated. If the performer is playing a work of multiple movements, do not applaud between movements. Even though there are several breaks, the piece should be heard in its complete form. If ever in doubt as to applaud or not, wait until many other members of the audience applaud, but do remember, sometimes others will make mistakes. Usually, the performers will give some indication that the piece has ended, such as a nod of the head or completely relaxing. Following a piece, the performer will typically bow and acknowledge the applause of the audience. If the music is performed at a particularly high level, the audience will often continue applause after the performer has left the stage, encouraging him/her to return.

If arrival to a recital or chamber concert is after the musicians begin playing, it is considered *very* rude to enter the performance area during the music. The proper action is to wait until applause is heard, then enter the audience area. In the event that it becomes necessary to leave a recital, it is considered extremely rude to leave while the music is being performed. It causes a distraction to all around and to the performers. Wait until the piece ends and then quietly slip out during the applause.

During a recital and concert, it is inappropriate to use flash photography. This is true in every live performance. The performer must concentrate very hard for an extended period of time in order to perform well. If a flash goes off in the audience, it can cause the performer to lose concentration and may even cause them to stop completely. This is often given in an announcement before the recital or in the program. Often, this announcement or program note will also mention that audio and video recording of the concert is not allowed. This is primarily for copyright reasons. It is very important that these directives are followed as a matter of courtesy. In a professional situation, violation of these directives may cause the audience member to be removed from the concert and photography and recording equipment seized.

Many of these traditions and conventions may seem odd or even silly to the novice of formal concerts. However, the point of these conventions is to give respect to the music, the composer, and the performers. It also allows everyone in the audience to experience the entire atmosphere of the concert and every nuance of the music.

Large Band And Orchestral Concerts

All of the conventions for recitals and chamber concerts should be followed in a concert of a large orchestra or band. Even so, there are a few differences. When a concert is about to begin, the orchestra or band will play one last tuning note. At an orchestra concert, the *concertmaster,* or first chair violin, will enter the stage and signal the tuning pitch to be played. Usually an oboe or clarinet, or in some cases, a tuba, will give a single pitch. Each member of the orchestra or band will play the same pitch to bring the instruments in tune as closely as possible. There are many conditions, such as heat, cold, and humidity that affect each instrument differently causing them to be at different pitches. It is important to begin the concert with the instruments as close to the same pitch as possible. In the orchestra, it is normal to hear the tuning pitch two or three times. If played three times, the woodwinds tune first, then the brass tune, then the strings tune. This is done so that each group can hear themselves as they tune. This might not be possible when the entire group plays together.

When the concertmaster enters the stage, the audience acknowledges this important person with applause. The concertmaster is not only the best violin player, but also works as an assistant to the conductor. The concertmaster will often coordinate the bowing for all of the strings and is ready to step in for the conductor in the event of an accident or illness. This is a very important position and very deserving of applause at the beginning of the concert.

After the concertmaster sits down, the conductor will enter the stage and walk to the podium. Applause is expected and appreciated by the conductor. He/she will acknowledge the applause and then turn and begin the concert.

When attending a professional concert of a symphony, it is wise to have cough drops with you. Some concert halls even have bins of cough drops at the doors as you enter the audience area. A cough or sneeze during a concert may be unavoidable, but repeated coughing or other noise is very distracting. Also, many professional orchestras may be recording a concert for later release as a CD. Any extraneous sound from the audience is detrimental to the recording.

Opera, Ballet, and the Musical Theater

All of the conventions above for formal recitals and large band and orchestral concerts should be followed at a performance of these musical events. There are some other considerations for these theatrical performances. The most important is for you to prepare for the performance by learning about the work. If you are going to attend a performance of Turandot, look up the story and learn about the characters. If this opera is sung in Italian, you need to understand the story or you will be hopelessly lost in the performance. It would also be good for you to listen to some recordings of part of the opera to learn more about what to expect. The same is true for the musical theater, with the exception that most are performed in English. The more you understand the story line, the better you will enjoy an opera or a musical.

Some have wondered about the difference between opera and musical theater. Opera was developed in the early 1600s. Many of the more famous operas are sung in Italian, German, and French. One major difference between these two performing genres is that operas are entirely sung and, generally, musicals include spoken dialogue. This is not always true, however. An example of a famous Musical that does not include spoken dialogue is *Les Miserable*. Also, some modern operas include a device called *Sprechstimme*, which is singing, technically, but it approximates speaking.

In a Ballet, the type of performance is very different. In a Ballet, there is no singing or speaking. The whole performance is dance. The story is told through the dance and staging. In this case, it is also very important to know the story before the performance. This will allow the audience member to enjoy the beautiful expression of the dancers and understand the plot.

In all of these cases, most of the conventions of the formal concerts should be followed. You should arrive early enough to find your seat. Sometimes the theaters are very large and require quite a bit of stair-climbing. Once in your seat, you should review the story in the program. You may want to look at the different acts. Notice how many performers are involved, where the action takes place, and other information you can glean from the program.

The orchestra is often located in an area of the stage called the *pit*. The *pit* is near the front of the stage and often extends far under the stage. At the beginning of the performance, the orchestra will tune in much the same fashion as in orchestral concerts. The conductor will then come to the podium, but you will probably not be able to see the conductor for most of the entrance. Upon reaching the podium, the conductor will stand up in the middle of the pit so the audience can see him/her and acknowledge the applause. This may be the only time you see the conductor. Occasionally, you may see the baton above the level of the stage or you may see the conductor's head during the performance.

Following the entrance of the conductor, the orchestra begins the *overture*. The *overture* is music that presents many of the melodies you will hear in the performance. Immediately after the overture, the curtain will rise and the opera, musical, or ballet will begin.

Typically, the audience will applaud after each act. If the theater goes to black, it is appropriate to applaud. Also, following a well sung piece, the audience will often applaud. If you are uncertain, follow the lead of the rest of the audience.

When attending an opera, ballet, or musical, it is important to take in the whole performance. There is a great deal of artistic work done in these performances, not just in the music. Opera was considered as the ultimate art form because it involved vocal and instrumental music, drama, painting (the backdrops and props), sculpture (props and the set), and architecture (the set). For centuries, there have been complex and fascinating machines that do everything from moving a ship across a stage to building a revolving barricade on the stage. As you consider all of the different levels of music and drama happening, be sure to notice the machines and props. You will find a whole world of delight in this aspect of the theater.

Movies

One genre of music has become extremely important in our culture and many people are not even aware of its influence. The music written for movies has become some of the most interesting and unique music of our culture. Unlike music written simply to be heard, the music of the movies serves a definite function, that of enhancing the acting and the visual scenes. The greatest composers of movie scores can guide the observer through complex scenes and even help the moviegoer anticipate action that is about to happen. Consider a dark scene in a house. The music is a cue to what is about to happen. If the music becomes strident and dissonant, it is obvious that something important is about to happen.

Music has such a huge effect on the final movie, directors will often experiment with different soundtracks. The desired effect of a scene might be to make the audience sad, but the musical score might actually cause the audience to laugh. If the effect is to surprise the audience, the music will be written to illicit a certain emotion that is opposite of that which is about to happen. Most audiences do not realize that they are being manipulated by the music.

One of the most interesting uses of music occurred in the *Star Wars* movies. John Williams, one of the most famous writers of movie music, actually borrowed a technique from a composer from the Romantic Era. Richard Wagner used a melodic device called a **leitmotif**. A *leitmotif* is a melody or chord progression and is always associated with a particular person, place, object, or feeling. In Wagner's music, there were leitmotifs for characters, love, fate, and even paradise.

John Williams used the same device in *Star Wars*. For example, the first time Leia is seen in "Episode IV," a melody suddenly appears that is very different from the previous music. From that point, this melody occurs whenever Leia has an important appearance or function in the movie. Williams even used this device at the end of "Episode III." When the newborn baby is held in her adopted mother's arms for the first time, the name Leia is spoken and Leia's theme is heard.

When attending movies, listen carefully to the music. Experiment with your personal DVDs by watching the movie without the music, especially during dramatic moments. This will give you some insight as to the importance of the musical score to the dramatic action.

FINAL THOUGHTS

The most important thing in attending musical events is to actually attend. In our busy society, it is so easy to overlook some of the most fantastic experiences in our culture. During your life, commit to attend orchestra concerts, operas, musicals, recitals, rock concerts, jazz concerts . . . every type of musical event you can. As you attend more and more of each type, you will not only become comfortable, you will begin to experience the magic that is "art."

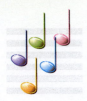

Chapter 9
Genres of Music and the Concert Experience

1. What information is in the following program entry?

    Symphony No. 35 in D Major, K. 385   Wolfgang Amadeus Mozart
        III. Minuet and Trio   (1756–1791)

2. When is it appropriate to give applause at a formal concert?

3. When is it appropriate to give applause at a jazz concert?

4. Why should flash photography be avoided in a concert or recital?

5. What does the "pit" refer to in an opera or a musical?

10

MUSICAL "BIGGIES"

In this chapter, some of the most famous musicians will be considered. Most, but not all, will be composers. Most, but not all will be "Classical." Hopefully, you will begin to see how all music relates and that there is great quality in the many different genres of music.

Before we begin, it is helpful to put musicians in a historical framework. Although all music of the world has legitimacy and each type has its own history, we will focus on the music of the Western culture, both "Classical" and "Popular." These classifications may be a bit confusing because the "Popular" music of the Seventeenth Century that has survived is now considered "Classical." An interesting question to consider is what music of today will be remembered 300 years from now.

The history of music will be divided into different time periods. Music historians use these classifications because of the musical activity during each time period. As with all of life, nothing simply stops one form of activity and suddenly begins another. In the art world, painters begin to experiment with new ideas. Other painters see these and begin to use some of these ideas. Soon, many are using these ideas. Finally, this becomes the "norm" for artists. But, of course, at this point, an artist may begin to experiment with a new idea. And so forth. That is typical of music as well.

The classifications that have developed are based on common practice. When the common practice becomes radically new, a new time period is established. There is nothing magical or hard-and-fast about any historical classification.

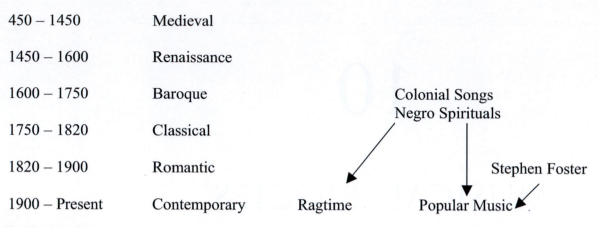

450 – 1450	Medieval
1450 – 1600	Renaissance
1600 – 1750	Baroque
1750 – 1820	Classical
1820 – 1900	Romantic
1900 – Present	Contemporary

Fig. 10.1 Eras of Music History with Significant Events in Jazz and Popular Music

Most consider the roots of Western culture beginning following the Roman Empire. Therefore, we will begin our time periods near this time, or 450 A. D. For the purposes of this course, we will identify the eras of "Classical" music as Medieval, Renaissance, Baroque, Classical, Romantic, Impressionistic, and Contemporary. Fig. 10.1 shows the dates for the different eras of Classical music along with events that influenced the beginnings of popular music and jazz in America.

The popular music and jazz music genres are both much younger than classical music. It is important to remember that classical music was the popular music of its day and that tradition has a great influence on what we call popular and jazz music today. The timeline of popular music and jazz music in America includes many different influences, both political and cultural. Fig. 10.2 lists a few of the important musical events in the development of these two musical forms.

WHO ARE THE "BIGGIES"?

Art Music

Evidence of music can be found dating back many, many years. Pictures of the Australian didgeridoo have been found in caves that have been estimated to be as old as 10,000 years old. Many musical references in the Bible indicate a rich and varied heritage of music. Psalm 150 lists a number of musical instruments to be used for praising God, including the flute, trumpet, lyre, and cymbals. In II Chronicles, 4000 Levites were assigned to play musical instruments in the Temple. Artifacts from ancient Greece and Rome have survived showing pictures of musicians playing various instruments. In Rome, specific musical instruments were used in the wor-

	Jazz	American Popular
1600 – 1776	West African Music Traditions	Ballads, Political Songs, Religious Music
1776 – 1860		Negro Spirituals, Folk Music, Stephen Foster
1860 – 1900		Civil War Songs, Vaudeville, Work Songs
1900 – 1910	Ragtime	
1910 – 1920	New Orleans Style	Country, R & B, Gospel, Blues, Folk
1920 – 1930	Hot Jazz, Chicago Style	Bessie Smith, Ziegfield Follies
1930 – 1940	Swing, Kansas City Style	Mahalia Jackson, Electric Guitar, Musical Theater
1940 – 1950	Bebop	Billy Holiday
1950 – 1960	Cool, Hard Bop	Elvis Presley, Buddy Holly, Rockabilly
1960 – 1970	Modal, Free Jazz, Groove	British Invasion, Beatles, Jackson 5, Woodstock
1970 – 1980	Fusion, Modern Jazz	Disco, Heavy Metal, Punk, Southern Rock
1980 – 1990	Afro-Cuban, Post Bop	Techno, MTV premieres
1990 – 2000	Classicism, Smooth Jazz, Retro Swing	Grunge, British Pop

Fig. 10.2 The History of Jazz and American Popular Music

ship of each of the gods. In ancient Greece, there were games similar to the Olympics in which musicians competed with great displays of musical ability. Civilizations throughout history have included music in many of the most important ceremonies and activities of the day.

Our musical journey will begin after the end of the Roman Empire as the Western culture was just emerging. As music grew throughout the development of the Western culture, certain composers and performers became very famous and made great contributions to the genre of music that we call "Classical" music. We will begin with the music of the Medieval era.

MEDIEVAL MUSIC—THE BEGINNING OF WESTERN ART MUSIC

Life in the **Medieval Era (450–1450)** was very difficult. Disease was common, at times wiping out a third of the population of Europe. The life expectancy was low and death was commonplace. Most people worked the land and had hard lives. Even with all of the difficult times, great strides in knowledge were made during this period. Many scientific discoveries were made, including the development of the scientific method and advancements in calculus and trigonometry. During the Medieval era, the first universities were established.

This period of history saw the Church become a very powerful and influential part of society. Often, the clergy would have more power than kings or lords. This influence also existed because the clergy and the monks were often among the few who were literate. As a result, the main sanctuary of Medieval knowledge and learning was the Church. Much of our understanding of that era comes from surviving books that were copied in monasteries. Many unknown monks spent years of their lives in small, dark rooms copying literature and music manuscripts using a quill and ink on sheets of parchment. In these monasteries, the daily lives of the monks included a great deal of music written specifically for certain prayers and services. The parts of the Mass itself were established during this time and specific kinds of music were used for each individual part.

Pope Gregory the Great, who served from 590 to 604, helped to establish the music that was used in the church. A body of chants was collected and codified into a single collection of work that was to be used in all of the Catholic churches. The text of the chants came from the Bible and was sung in Latin. This body of work came to be known as *Gregorian chant*, named for Pope Gregory.

Music of the church was to be performed in a specific manner as prescribed by the Church. It was to be sung by men, as women generally did not have any part of the church service. Chants were contemplative and serene and were designed to bring the listener closer to God. Music was to be sung without the accompaniment of instruments. Because instruments had been used for the worship of pagan gods in the Greek and Roman Empires, the Church did not want there to be any references to those pagan religions. For example, the Aulos, a double-piped, double-reeded instrument similar to an oboe, was used in Greece to accompany the worship of Dionysus, the god of drunkenness and debauchery. Obviously, the Church would not want to make any reference to this pagan deity.

Gregorian Chant is characterized by a single line of music, which is monophony. The Church considered different aspects of music to appeal to different parts of the individual. Rhythm tends to appeal to the body and may cause one to move or clap to the beat. Music with a beat, then, was not to be used in the Church because it does not speak to the Spirit of

Man but to the physical body. In the same way, harmony, as an intellectual pursuit, spoke to the mind of Man. This was inappropriate because, again, it distracted from the focus on God. Only melody, which speaks to the Spirit of Man, was to be used. This absence of rhythm and harmony resulted in music that was monophonic, a single melody without accompaniment.

Although sacred music dominated society and was preserved by the Church, secular music did exist during the Medieval era. This music included the use of musical instruments and, thus, was often homophonic. Often, professional musicians, called *Troubadours* and *Treveres*, would travel from city to city to provide entertainment and to spread news throughout the land. These musicians were also poets, dancers, and even jugglers. They sang songs about everything from nature to romantic love.

By the 12th century, the music of the church began to change. In the Cathedral of Notre Dame in Paris, Leonin and Perotin began to use rhythm in church music. Chants began to expand to include *sequences*, which were short melodic phrases included within the chant itself to explain or expand on the idea expressed in the chant. As this practice continued, more and more music and text were added to the chants causing them to be less clear. This practice was stopped by the church in the first Council of Trent. The church eliminated all sequences with the exception of five. One of these five sequences, the *Dies Irae*, meaning the Day of Wrath or the Day of Reckoning, was used for references to death and judgment. It was often used in a Requiem Mass, the mass of the dead. This particular melody became very important in the Romantic and Contemporary eras as it was used to refer to death.

Most of the composers of the Medieval era were unknown. In some cases, a large body of music was attributed to a single composer but that composer was unknown. One of those composers has been named Anonymous IV. Leonin and Perotin were some of the first known composers of the Medieval era. Machaut was the first known composer of a Mass. Hildegard of Bingen was one of the few known composers of chant melodies and, was one of the first known woman composers.

RENAISSANCE—MUSIC EXPANDS

During the **Renaissance Era (1450–1600)**, the culture of the West made great new strides. The Renaissance was an age of continued expansion of philosophy, science, and thought. The previous era was considered the "Middle Ages" that bridged the gap between Classical Greece and Rome and the new "Rebirth" of culture in the fifteenth century. New innovations such as the invention of the printing press allowed knowledge to be more easily disseminated. The first important book to be printed on this new invention was the Gutenberg Bible in 1455. Names such as Michelangelo, Leonardo Da Vinci, Botticelli, Raphael, Donatello, and Brunelleschi were among the great artists and thinkers of this age. During the Renaissance period, Copernicus discovered that the earth was in orbit around the sun, going against the errant belief that the sun revolved around the earth. In religion, this was the age of the Protestant Reformation and the First Council of Trent. The Spanish Inquisition, led by Torquemada, tortured many people in the name of God. Nostradamus published collections of prophesies that are still studied today. Great exploratory adventures occurred, such as Columbus' voyage to the new world.

Music, too, made great strides in development. Although the Church was still a great force in the world, a subtle shift of focus was moving away from the Church. The focus was moving more toward humanity than God. The music of the Church continued to develop and became more and more polyphonic. This increase in complexity was considered a problem by the leadership of the Church because the message of the text had become less clear. The concern became so great that the Church made a major policy change in the First Council of Trent. In an effort to make the message of scripture more clear, music was no longer to be composed using complex polyphony. This change was instrumental in changing the style of music, effectively ending the Renaissance style of music.

Music in the Church and in society continued to become more important. Josquin Des Prez, Ockeghem, Isaac, Tallis, and Palistrina, to name a few, contributed to the advance of sacred and secular music in this era. In addition, composers of music were identified and became well known. Prior to the Renaissance, much of the music was written by composers who were unknown.

Instrumental music grew in importance, although not to the degree that happened following this era. For hundreds of years prior to the Renaissance era, instruments were used to make music, first to perform secular music and later in the Church. The common practice was for individuals to get together with whatever instruments they had to play music. One person might bring a recorder, another might bring a viol (predecessor of the violin), another might bring a sackbut (predecessor of the trombone), and another might bring a crumhorn (double-reeded instrument related to the oboe). Every rehearsal or performance would have a different group of instruments. They would divide up the parts of music and each would play a different line of music. Often singers would perform with them doubling the lines of music. These early instruments were being developed and they would eventually be improved to become the instruments we use today. Early forms of the oboe, bassoon, flute, lute, and violin were in common use. Some instruments, such as the *cornetto*, were completely different from their modern descendants. The cornetto looked similar to a recorder but had a trumpet-type mouthpiece. The crumhorn had a double reed like an oboe, but unlike the oboe, the reed fit completely inside the instrument.

In the 16th century, a major change in the use of instruments happened. Gabriele, a composer for the St. Mark's Cathedral in Venice, began to assign specific parts to specific instruments. This was the first time that this practice occurred. As a result, the composer could control the timbre of the music. This innovation would lead to the establishment of the orchestra over the next two eras of music.

As Renaissance music developed, different styles of music were established in different regions of Europe. For the first time, composers were reflecting the culture in which they lived. Now, for example, the music of France was clearly different than music of England. This trend toward nationalistic styles eventually led to music becoming more unique in style to individual composers. This individuality of composers caused some composers to become famous during their lifetimes and that fame continues today.

BAROQUE—GRANDEUR, EXUBERANCE, DETAILED

Just as in art, the **Baroque Era (1600–1750)** in music dealt with very large, elaborate compositions of great detail. Music in the church was still very important, but the music of the royal courts had gained importance as there was a subtle shift from the church to the courts. The works were larger than life. Beyond the large vision, the intricate detail was always present. The music was often long and very complex. Although these elements were more prominent in the Late Baroque music, the beginnings of this grandiose style did occur in the early Seventeenth Century.

At the beginning of the Baroque era, the style of music shifted from the complex polyphony of the Renaissance era to a simpler, homophonic style. This was partly due to the edict from the First Council of Trent in the mid-sixteenth century that declared that music of the Church should not be complex polyphony. This idea that music had become too complex was also promoted by other individuals. In the late 1500s, a group of intellectuals called the Florentine Camerata met with the purpose of discussing the musical trends of the day, a sort of "musical think tank." This group included a number of influential people such as Vincenzo Galilei, the father of Galileo Galilei. One of the ideas of the Camerata was that music should be simpler. As they experimented with this new style of writing and wrote about their thoughts, some major disagreements developed between members of the group and individuals who believed in the older style of writing music.

One new genre of music was created as a result of work of the Florentine Camerata. As the Camerata began to look back to Greece for understanding of "Classic" culture, they studied the Greek dramas. Because the Greeks believed that the recitations in dramas should have certain inflections, the conclusion was drawn that all Greek dramas were sung. Composers began to experiment with this new idea of telling a story through singing and a new art form was established and called *opera*. Opera quickly gained popularity in the Baroque Era and the genre has become an important part of the music of the Western culture over the centuries. Interestingly, this genre was established on an erroneous conclusion as Greek dramas were not all sung.

As the Baroque era continued, composers began to use more polyphonic writing. By the end of the era, music was extremely complex and was predominantly polyphonic. What began as an attempt to simplify music at the beginning resulted in complex polyphonic music at the end of the Baroque period.

Several characteristics of the Baroque Era developed from the above innovations. The beginnings of a standardized instrumentation for the orchestra occurred. The violin, viola, cello, and bass were all perfected at this time and became the prominent section of the orchestra. Other sections were still being established. The bass line of the music took on a much more important role which led to a particular sound that is still in use today. The harpsichord was very important both as a solo instrument and as a supporting instrument used to establish the harmonic structure of the music. Dynamics were more important and composers specified where music should be loud and where it should be soft. One type of dynamics characteristic of the age was called *terraced dynamics*. That term implies sudden changes in loudness rather than gradual crescendos and decrescendos.

In the Baroque Era, many new innovators were experimenting with music. Some notable composers of the time were Monteverdi, who was a transitional composer from the Renaissance to the Baroque, Corelli, Scarlatti, and Vivaldi. Of all the great composers of the Baroque age, two stand out as towering figures of this era: Johann Sebastian Bach and George Frideric Handel.

Johann Sebastian Bach

Johann Sebastian Bach was born in 1685 into a musical family. He learned to play the violin, harpsichord, and organ from an early age. Although his parents died before he reached his teens, he continued to study music with his brother and his uncle. He sang in several boys choirs and became very proficient on the harpsichord and the organ. Throughout his life, he made great contributions as a church musician, composer, and performer. He took his composition so seriously that before he began a piece, he would put the letters "J. J.," which stood for the Latin phrase *Jesu Juva*, meaning "Jesus, help me." Upon completion of the work, he would put the letters "S. D. G.," which stood for the Latin phrase *Soli Deo Gloria*, "To God Alone, the Glory." His output as a composer was so great, so innovative, and so typified music in the Late Baroque Era that the date of his death is considered to be the end of the Baroque Era, that is, 1750.

One of Bach's innovations was a work called "The Well-Tempered Clavier." The term *well-tempered* refers to a manner of tuning musical instruments. You may recall that the tuning of the musical scale was established by Pythagoras. The scale that he found did not divide the octave evenly but was based on mathematical proportions. Because of this, all tuning of instruments was relative which made playing in different keys impossible. The "well-tempered" system of tuning, or *even temperament*, is the same system we use today. Because of the structure of sound waves and frequencies, it is necessary to tune a keyboard instrument, such as a piano, with some notes slightly too high or slightly too low. Our ears can barely perceive this difference but this allows the piano to play in tune in many different keys. To prove this principal, Bach wrote "The Well-Tempered Clavier", which included a *prelude* and a *fugue* in each of the 12 keys. (The term *clavier* refers to a keyboard instrument similar to a harpsichord that predated the piano.)

Fugue Example.   The fugues of Bach were very innovative and highly polyphonic and, as such, they are good examples of Baroque music. One of

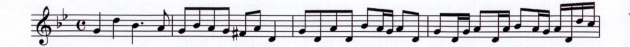

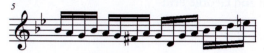

Fig. 10.3 Subject from Bach's Fugue in G Minor

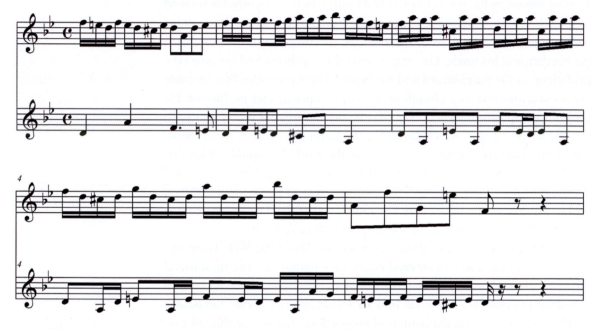

Fig. 10.4 Subject and
Countersubject from Bach's
Fugue in G Minor

his most famous is the Fugue in G Minor, also called the "Little Fugue."
(It might be beneficial to review the form of the fugue in Chapter 3.) The
subject of the fugue is given here in Fig. 10.3.

George Frideric Handel

George Frideric Handel was also born in 1685 and was also a great inno-
vator in the Baroque Era. Unlike Bach, Handel's father, a "barber-surgeon,"
did not approve of music as a career. Although Handel was allowed to take
music lessons, when he went to the university, he studied law. It was not
until his father died that Handel turned to a musical career. Like Bach, Handel was born and raised in Germany, but his career took him to Italy and
finally to London. Handel found great success in London writing operas

and, eventually, *oratorios*. An oratorio is similar to an opera except it contains no dramatic acting, costumes, or stage scenery and is usually based on a religious subject.

An Example of Handel's Work.   Handel's most well-known work is the oratorio *Messiah*. Handel wrote this work as a chronicle of the life of Jesus, from prophesy through His death and resurrection. It consists of 53 works divided into three parts. Handel completed this highly complex and diverse work in just 24 days. It is said that his servant would often find Handel in tears as music flowed from his pen and the experience overwhelmed him.

Of the many parts of *Messiah*, the most well-known is the "*Hallelujah Chorus*". One interesting characteristic of this work is the texture that Handel uses. In different phrases of this work, he uses different textures. As the work progresses, there are times of *homophony, monophony,* and *polyphony*. Handel uses this element and the different timbres of the choir and orchestra to create a very creative masterpiece. Listen carefully to the work and see if you can identify when the texture changes.

CLASSICAL—THE AGE OF ENLIGHTENMENT

The **Classical Era** in music (1750–1820) signaled a rebellion against the "gaudiness" of the Baroque Era. During the transition to the Classical Era, composers began to simplify the arts as a representation of a more refined and cultured society. During this time, men began to question the role of the Church in society. The Church had split into Catholic and Protestant factions and as the Church began to lose power, the State began to gain. Philosophers promoted new ideas of man's place in the world.

During the Age of Enlightenment, scientists and mathematicians made many new discoveries. These discoveries led to a divergence of thought in God's work in the world. Two main theories developed, that of Divine Right and of Natural Law. As these philosophies developed, society began to diverge into two separate worldviews.

During this great time of intellectual growth, the course of music composition changed from the Baroque Era. As culture moved to be more "refined," composers worked to make the music more refined as well. Many of the "standard" forms of composition were developed during this time. Compositions were less ornate and weighty. As in art, simple and dignified became the focus of the artists.

Mozart, Haydn, and Beethoven

During the Classical Era, some of the most important composers lived. Although many composers wrote during the Classical Era, including several famous sons of the great J. S. Bach, three composers were the most important and influential artists of this era.

Wolfgang Amadeus Mozart

Wolfgang Amadeus Mozart (1756–1791) was one of the towering geniuses of music. Although he died at a relatively young age, he made some of the greatest contributions to the art of music. He was considered a genius. He learned to play pieces on the clavier as young as age 4 and he wrote his first composition at the age of 5. By the time he was six, he was traveling throughout Europe performing for the great courts, such as Munich, Mannheim, Paris, and London and this travel continued until 1778.

Besides his great fame as a concert performer, Mozart was also a prolific composer. During his short 35 years, he composed 41 symphonies, 21 operas, 50 concertos for solo instrument and orchestra, and many, many other works for all occasions.

Mozart was very much an individual. He worked for a time for the court of the Archbishop of Salzburg, but left that post and moved to Vienna to work on his own. This was a new idea for composers for many maintained their livelihood by working directly for nobility. At first, Mozart was very successful. However, some of his later compositions were not successful and he began to fall on hard times. Ultimately, he died a pauper.

An Example of Mozart's Works. The style of Mozart's compositions reflects the style of the day in both the use of different forms and the balance of each of the sections in the form. As an example, we will consider the first movement of Symphony No. 40 in G Minor. This is one of the most famous of Mozart's 41 symphonies.

The form of this movement is Sonata Allegro form. As you remember, it consists of three main sections—the Exposition, Development, and Recapitulation. Within each of these sections, the organization of the work follows the "standard" formal plan, as discussed previously. In Mozart's writing, it almost seems that his intent is for the listener to be able to follow the form easily. Not only are the sections shorter in length, but his music often stops completely to identify a change in themes. That is the case with this movement. At the beginning, listen for the 1st Theme followed by the Transition at a louder dynamic level. The music stops before the 2nd Theme occurs, which makes following the form much easier. Remember the music at the beginning and listen for that same music at the beginning of the recapitulation. Listen to the movement and see how successful you are at following the form.

Franz Joseph Haydn

Another representative composer of this era was Franz Joseph Haydn (1732–1809). Haydn was also very well-known in his lifetime. Although born in Vienna, he did travel extensively; most notably, he made two extended trips to London. His compositional output was also extremely great, including 108 symphonies, 83 string quartets, 62 keyboard sonatas, as well as chamber music, cantatas, oratorios, operas, and masses.

Haydn's life was different from Mozart's. He became employed by the Esterhazy family, a Hungarian noble family. In this post, Haydn had a secure income throughout his life. At times, he lived in the palatial home in Hungary, along with the orchestra that was also in the emperor's employ. At other times during his employment, he lived in his native Vienna. Even his extended trips to London were approved by his noble employer. Mozart tried to live outside of the traditional court sponsorship and died in poverty. Haydn, however, kept the tradition of working in the court and his financial status was stable.

Ludwig van Beethoven

Ludwig van Beethoven (1770–1827) is one of the most recognized names in the history of music. Beethoven is often considered to be a bridge from the Classical Era to the next style period of music history, the Romantic Era. His music clearly reflects the Classical style in his early works. For example, his first two symphonies show the influence of Mozart in the 1st Symphony and Haydn in the 2nd Symphony. However, Beethoven's Symphony No. 3 was a ground breaking work that reflected a move from the more restrained Classical style to the more emotional Romantic style. Simply by considering Beethoven's nine symphonies, this move from balanced restraint to great emotionalism seems to grow with each new work.

Of course, Beethoven's works include much more than the nine symphonies. His astonishing creativity can be seen in all of his works, including piano and violin concertos, overtures, string quartets, piano trios, sonatas for violin and cello, variations, bagatelles, and an incredible output of remarkable sonatas for the piano.

An Example of Beethoven's Works.   Of all of his works, the Beethoven 5th Symphony is probably his most famous. This work was written at a point in Beethoven's life when he was wrestling with the fact that he was losing his hearing. This work is often called the "Fate" Symphony because Beethoven was dealing with this cruel twist of "fate." How can "fate" allow a successful composer to lose hearing? At times, Beethoven even considered suicide. With this symphony, however, Beethoven made a statement affirming the fact that, although he was dealt this cruel malady, he would overcome it and continue on. Before the end of his composing career, Beethoven went completely deaf. Even with this great handicap, he produced some of the most remarkable works of music in his last years.

The famous 4-note motive of the 5th Symphony is called the "fate" motive. Beethoven used this 4-note statement throughout the four movements of the symphony in various forms. To base a movement on a short motive had been done before, but to use that short motive for all four movements of a symphony was a new idea. Beethoven also introduced new instruments to the symphony with this piece. In the fourth movement, he uses the piccolo and the contrabassoon, both new to the standard orchestra.

The first movement of this piece is in Sonata form. Beethoven utilizes some very creative devices to deceive the listener. For example, the end of the piece should be in C Minor, but Beethoven actually wrote it in C Major. In the Coda (the ending of the movement), Beethoven introduces a new theme, which was also a new idea. The very end of the work sounds as if there will be a second recapitulation, which would be a radical move from previous composers. However, Beethoven quickly ends the piece, proving that it was just a playful teasing of the audience.

THE ROMANTICS

The **Romantic Era** (1820–1900) was truly an era of great expansion and divergence in Western music. During this era, composers began to expand every aspect of the Classical Era. Works become longer. Each movement of the symphony was expanded and additional movements were even added. Composers began to focus on the development sections of the music, expanding these creative parts and moving farther and farther away from the initial keys. Works became more complicated and more chromatic.

But Romanticism was far more than just an expansion of Classical ideas. It was a shift toward an emphasis on the middle class and against aristocracy. Basically, it was a move away from the "age of enlightenment" and its pursuit of reason and a move toward expression and imagination. Many influential philosophers made their contributions during the Romantic era, including Hegel, Schopenhauer, Kierkegaard, Karl Marx, Nietzsche, and many others. It was during this era that Darwin proposed his ideas about evolution. Many of the characteristics of Romantic thought were also important in music, such as Nationalism, emotionalism, individualism, and Exoticism.

During the Romantic Era, music became very diverse in every element. Composers began to develop individual styles. They pushed the limits of instrumental music almost to excess. Some works were performed by hundreds of musicians. Romantics were individuals who wrote from their own perspective. They were Nationalists who used music and experiences from their homeland to paint aural portraits of their country.

The Romantic Era included such "biggies" as Schumann, Schubert, Berlioz, Wagner, Tchaikovsky, Mussorgsky, Brahms, Liszt, Chopin, and many, many more. Some wrote exclusively for the piano. Some wrote mostly vocal music. Some wrote short, intimate works while others wrote large works that lasted for hours. One such work by Richard Wagner (RI-card VAG-ner), called the Ring of the Niebelung, consisted of four operas, each lasting several hours. The four operas told one story based on German mythology.

Hector Berlioz

There are so many "biggies" in the Romantic era, it is almost impossible to pick one that represents the musical composition of this era. As an example of one of the "biggies," consider Hector Berlioz. Berlioz (1803–1869) was a French composer who was well known for his orchestration, that is, how he combined orchestral forces to create new sounds.

Interestingly, Berlioz's father, a physician himself, sent young Hector to study medicine. His medical career was short-lived at his first visit to the dissection room. After just a few moments of revulsion, he ran screaming from the carnage. He stunned his parents by changing his chosen field to music. Berlioz's music was innovative and daring. His works are unique and unpredictable. He drastically expanded the size and timbre of the orchestra while creating powerful and dramatic works.

An Example of Berlioz's Music. The Symphonie Fantastique is one of Berlioz' most famous works. Although composed as a symphony, this work had some very unusual aspects. It was an example of *program music*, which can be defined as a musical work that describes a story, poem, idea, or scene. Although the music itself cannot convey a story or scene, the composer's notes or the title may refer to a particular story or idea.

In the case of the Symphonie Fantastique, the story is both fascinating and bizarre. Berlioz wrote this work about himself and his love for a famous actress, Harriet Smithson. Berlioz was so taken by her that he developed a story describing his unrequited love. In this "self-portrait," he describes himself as a "musician of extraordinary sensibility and abundant imagination." The story he writes describes an opium-induced dream in which his love appears in different settings. At one point in the dream, he kills his love and is executed by the guillotine. In the last movement, he encounters his love in a Witch's Sabbath as she taunts him.

In this work, Berlioz uses a new musical device called the *idée fixe*, or "fixed idea." This is a melody which represents someone and recurs throughout the work. In this case, the melody represents Harriet Smithson. As the circumstances change in the story, the *idée fixe* also changes.

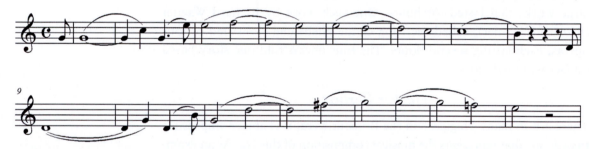

Fig. 10.5 Harriet's *Idée Fixe* from Symphonie Fantastique

Richard Wagner

One of the most important figures in Romantic music was Richard Wagner (1818–1883). Although he was considered a towering genius, his life was checkered by treachery and self promotion. Numerous times, Wagner piled up great debt, only to be helped by wealthy patrons. Some of his writings reflected an anti-Semite attitude which was a growing outlook in 19th Century Europe. But even though his character may be questionable, his musical genius cannot be questioned.

Wagner was not only a very gifted musician, but he also had a flare for great drama. His most well known works were operas, which he called *music dramas*. The stories for his music dramas were drawn from German and Norse mythology and legend. The works were monumental in size and scope. His greatest known work, the Ring of the Neibelung, took

26 years to complete and consisted of four operas which require a total of 15 hours to perform. For this work, Wagner not only wrote the music but he also designed costumes and stage backdrops. He was involved in every aspect of the performance of the Ring cycle. He even designed a theater in Bayreuth, Germany with specific acoustics that brought out the best in the performances of his music dramas.

One innovation of Wagner's music dramas was a musical device called the *leitmotif*. The leitmotif was similar to the *ideé fixe* of Berlioz, but Wagner used many different leitmotifs throughout his works. A leitmotif is a short musical melody that can represent a person, emotion (such as love), fire, objects, fate, or a number of other things. In the dramas, when a person was being discussed, that person's leitmotif would be heard. If love was mentioned, the leitmotif for love would be heard. In some situations, it was possible to predict who was being discussed even if their name was not mentioned. If one character was declaring their love for another, the leitmotifs for both characters and the leitmotif for love could be intertwined in the accompanying music. As discussed before, John Williams used leitmotifs in the musical score for the *Star Wars* movies.

Wagner and Berlioz are just two examples of a host of remarkable Romantic composers. Discussion of so many great composers cannot be covered in the scope of this text and further discovery of these composers is left to the reader.

THE IMPRESSIONISTS

An interesting movement in music had a direct parallel with a similar movement in art. The Impressionist period of music has been described as a transition from the Nineteenth Century Romanticism to the Twentieth Century. The primary work of Impressionist composers occurred in France and was primarily a move away from large, heavy Germanic compositional style.

Impressionist Art dealt with the effects of light, color, mood, and atmosphere and many of the subjects in Impressionism deal with water. The same can be said of the music of Impressionist composers. Many have programmatic titles involving water, such as *La Mer* (The Sea) or *La Cathédrale engloutie* (The Sunken Cathedral), a piece about a legendary cathedral that rises out of the sea. The music was fluid and flowed from one idea to another. Many different orchestral colors, or timbres, were used. Even though large orchestras were used, the music was not heavy or ponderous as was the case with many compositions from countries such as Germany or Russia.

IMPRESSIONIST COMPOSERS

Claude Debussy (1862–1918) and Maurice Ravel (1875–1937) are the two best known of the Impressionists. Although their music was very similar, even to the point that critics accused Ravel of plagiarism, both wrote very creative and individual music.

An example of Impressionist Music. Debussy wrote *Prelude to the Afternoon of a Faun* based on the Symbolist poet Stéphane Mallarmé's *The Afternoon of a Faun*. The piece begins very softly with a solo flute melody which seems to float. Different instrument colors and textures float in and out of the music to create a tapestry of sound. Although the form can be described as A B A', many elements of the piece are intentionally veiled, including the form. When listening to the work, strive to allow the music to create a mood in your mind.

CONTEMPORARY INFLUENCES

Composers of the Twentieth Century took a number of different directions in their composition. Some continued in the traditional Romantic Style of Germany and Russia. Some were influenced by the Impressionist movement and the music of Debussy and Ravel. Others continued to take music to extremes of timber, texture, dynamics, and form. As the Twentieth Century progressed, more and more musical experimentation took place.

Although the music of the Twentieth and Twenty-first Centuries have continued along vastly divergent paths, there have been some important works that have had great influence on the direction of music. Composers such as Stravinsky, Schoenberg, Berg, Webern, Bartok, Ives, Berstein, and Copland have made great contributions of highly influential compositions.

TWO EXAMPLES OF TWENTIETH CENTURY WORKS

One of the most influential composers of the Twentieth Century was Igor Stravinsky (1882–1971). Stravinsky was born and raised in Russia, but many of his compositions were written outside of Russia. His best known work, *The Rite of Spring*, was composed in Paris and performed as a ballet for the *Ballet Russe*, the Russian Ballet in Paris. During the early 1900s, Paris was a major intellectual center filled with writers, artists, and musicians, each influencing each other. As a result, many ground breaking works resulted.

The Rite of Spring is a long work based on a Russian legend of sacrifice to the gods of springtime. The work contains very dissonant sections with very complex rhythms. The subject was so controversial and the work was so radically different from anything previously performed that the first performance actually caused a riot and the composition could not even be completed. In many ways, this work set the tone for the music of the Twentieth Century.

Another highly influential composer of Twentieth Century music was Arnold Schoenberg (1874–1951). Schoenberg expanded ideas of the late Romantic Era creating new ways of composition. His most radical idea was called *atonality*. Using this technique, the composer worked to avoid the functional harmony. There is no feeling of a tonic chord or even a tonic note. All notes have the same importance.

Schoenberg is the best known of the *Expressionist* composers. Expressionism was a movement in art, literature, and music that stressed intense psychological emotion. Expressionists would often distort reality to explore inner feelings and shock and assault the audience with the deepest anguish of the human soul. Paintings from these artists did not attempt to portray "pretty" works, but instead depicted dark and frightening images. Composers would often write dissonant and harsh music to depict inner struggles.

One of Schoenberg's works, *A Survivor from Warsaw*, is a remarkable composition that represents the anguish and pain of a prisoner in a German concentration camp during World War II. The work, for orchestra, narrator, and male chorus, depicts an event at the camp when a number of prisoners were put to death. The narration is from the perspective of one prisoner who survived.

Schoenberg uses several interesting musical devices in this work to portray the frightening scene. The narrator speaks in different rhythms that help describe the scene. For example, when the narrator says "faster and faster," he speaks faster and faster. When he says, "it was painful to hear the groaning," the words are slow and drawn out, implying the pain and suffering. Schoenberg also uses orchestral devices that express the feelings given in the narration. This powerful and frightening work expresses the horror and fear of that dark time in world history.

Classical Music from the past has remained because it continues to invoke aesthetic feelings today. Great music is music that lasts not only for generations, but for centuries. It is important to understand that the music of the 20th and 21st Century "classical" composers has yet to be judged as being able to withstand the test of time. In our lifetime, we will never know what music will last.

POPULAR MUSIC
Important Popular Musicians

When considering the most important musicians of popular music, a great many styles of music could be discussed. A list of important popular musicians could include musicians of the British Invasion, the Blues, the Big Band Era, Country Music, Heavy Metal, Folk Music, Rap Music, Hip Hop, Jazz Music, Motown, Alternative Music, Punk Rock, Disco and many, many more styles. Beyond that, many of the composers of Popular Music are almost unknown. The performers are the stars. The music sung by Elvis can be listed by the devoted fan, but are the songwriters of those pieces remembered? Of course, in many cases, the performers are the song writers. Many of the songs recorded by the Beatles were written by Paul McCartney and John Lennon.

Certain musicians had a great impact on the course of Popular Music. Elvis Presley burst onto the scene and produced hit after hit and, as a result, set the tone for the future of Rock & Roll. His contributions included the Blues, Country, Rockabilly, Pop, Bluegrass, and even Gospel. His unique style made him an international star. Considering his success during his lifetime and the continued sales of his music, he is considered the single highest-selling performer in history.

Another significant event in Popular Music in America was the British Invasion of 1964 and 1965. British rock groups came across the ocean and had a great impact on the future of Popular Music in this country. Among the most notable groups were The Beatles, the Rolling Stones, Gerry & the Pacemakers, The Animals, The Yardbirds, The Dave Clark Five, and the beginnings of the Moody Blues. These groups sold millions of records that impacted a generation of young people. So great was their impact that some of these groups are still performing today. In 2006, the Rolling Stones announced a concert tour, a band of sixty-year-old rockers!

Later in the 60s, another musical event brought Popular Music to the forefront of the music world. Woodstock was a huge outdoor concert in August of 1969 that presented concerts by groups and individuals who would go on to great fame, including Joan Baez, Santana, Janis Joplin, Sly & the Family Stone, the Grateful Dead, Creedence Clearwater Revival, The Who, Jefferson Airplane, Blood, Sweat & Tears, Crosby, Stills, Nash, & Young, and Jimi Hendrix. Woodstock was a highly controversial event but this one event reflected the change that was happening in the culture of America and the music was a reflection of that change. Interestingly, a number of influential groups refused to perform at Woodstock for various reasons, including The Beatles, The Doors, Led Zeppelin, Tommy James and the Shondells, and Bob Dylan. With these events, the course of Popular Music moved away from Folk and Country music to Rock and Roll.

In 1964, a performer came on the scene that would make a huge impact on the Popular music world. The Jackson 5, consisting of Jackie, Tito, Jermaine, Marlon, and Michael, began performing in local clubs. In 1967, they performed in the famous Apollo Theater in Harlem and begin a professional performing and recording career. In 1971, Michael Jackson began his solo career and the world of popular music has never been the same. His meteoric rise to fame arrived following his 1982 album *Thriller*, which remains as the best selling album of all time, with 110 million sold. Michael's videos "Bad", "Billie Jean", and "Thriller" revolutionized the music video. They became the benchmark that everyone else tried to achieve. Over the decades, his popularity remained high with audiences all over the world. Although controversial as an individual, one cannot deny his great talent and influence on Popular music of every type.

In 1981, the world of Popular music began a new era with the introduction of Music Television, more commonly known as MTV. Prior to this time, Popular music shows such as The Midnight Special showcased a wide variety of Popular stars and bands. MTV began to present a new media type called the music video. With this new concept, all of Popular music changed. The music was no longer the only aspect of the performance, but now, the visual presentation of the music became as important, if not more important than the music itself. As a result, music producers no longer sought out talent based on musical ability alone, but now they looked for performers who were visually marketable, whether very attractive or very unusual. As a result, the music industry has changed greatly since that time.

Michael Jackson's "Thriller" was one of the remarkable early videos that brought about this change. Directed by John Landis, a well-known Hollywood movie director, the "Thriller" video was a short movie in itself. The use of makeup, costumes, elaborate choreography, and a storyline created a new genre of musical presentations, probably as remarkable as the emergence of opera in the beginning of the Baroque Era. Now, song writers and performers begin developing ideas for a video at the same time they are creating the music itself.

Throughout the 70s, 80s, 90s, and into the 21st Century, Popular Music has morphed and changed with society. Just as music of the 18th and 19th Centuries changed and as philosophy and culture changed, so the music of our century will continue to move in many different directions.

An interesting question arises concerning Popular Music. If Mozart and Beethoven wrote "popular music" of their day, what music of our culture will be considered as "classical" music 200 years from now? As mentioned above, the true test of great music is that it withstands the test of time. It would be interesting to walk through a time tunnel set 200 years in advance and see what "classical" music from the 20th Century was being performed.

THE "BIGGIES" OF JAZZ

Just as Popular Music has developed from Classical Music, the world of Jazz Music has grown out of the Popular Music of the 19th and 20th Centuries. When considering Jazz Music, it is also easy to become overwhelmed with the number of styles and famous artists. There are many, many different styles of jazz, including Big Band, Cool Jazz, Dixieland, Bebop, Latin, Funk, Fusion, and others. Although this diversity may seem staggering, the reason for the diversity is that there is something for everyone. Consider how many different styles there are in Classical and Popular Music.

Jazz Music is one of the few styles of music that has its roots in America, although it was influenced by music from other parts of the world. The earliest roots of Jazz came primarily from three sources. African slaves brought West African traditions of drumming and complex rhythms to America. Jazz was also influenced by folk music that came to America from traditional music from around the world. Finally, the melodic and harmonic structures, as well as the instruments from Western Europe, were a foundation for the development of Jazz Music. Just as America served as a "melting pot" of peoples from around the world, so Jazz Music resulted from a blending of different traditions brought by these peoples to the New World. Several cities became centers for the growth of Jazz Music, including New Orleans, Kansas City, and Chicago. In these cities, many musicians came together, began to share ideas, and jazz was born.

One of the first styles of Jazz from New Orleans to gain popularity was *ragtime*. Ragtime Music is a highly syncopated style of piano music performed primarily by African-American musicians who played in dance halls. The form was influenced by the syncopated rhythms of African Music and the traditional forms of the European march. The most well known composer of Ragtime Music, Scott Joplin, published a number of pieces in this style, including Maple Leaf Rag, The Entertainer, and Easy Winners.

Another popular style of early jazz that developed in New Orleans was called Dixieland. This jazz form is a highly individualized style of playing. Typically, the Dixieland band is made up of a *front line*, consisting of a cornet, a clarinet, a trombone, and sometimes a saxophone, and a *rhythm section*, consisting of any combination of drums, bass, tuba, piano, banjo, or guitar. There is a great deal of *improvisation* that takes place in Dixieland. As discussed earlier in the book, *improvisation* occurs when a musician adds notes and rhythms to the basic melody while following the harmonic progression. An easier way to explain this is that each musician "plays around" with the melody however he/she sees fit. Although it follows the music, this is a form of composition, as the musician is making up new ideas while performing the music. It is a quite remarkable feat!

The best known of the Dixieland musicians is Louis "Satchmo" Armstrong (1901–1971). Louis Armstrong was born to a poor family in New Orleans. He listened to the great jazz musicians in New Orleans, his favorite being Joe "King" Oliver. Oliver even gave the young Armstrong his first cornet and taught him how to play. From these humble beginnings, Armstrong became one of the greatest influences to generations of jazz musicians.

In the 1930s and 1940s, Big Band music was in its heyday. Names like Benny Goodman, Glenn Miller, Tommy and Jimmy Dorsey, Woody Herman, Duke Ellington, and Count Basie were the popular music stars of their day. Many of the songs made famous by their big bands are still popular today. It is not unusual to hear songs like "In a Sentimental Mood," "I Got Rhythm," "All of Me," "Sing, Sing, Sing," "April In Paris," "Chattanooga Choo Choo," "In the Mood," "Paper Moon," "Satin Doll," "Sentimental Journey," "String of Pearls," and many others in everything from movies to background music in restaurants.

One of the most influential jazz artists of all time was Charlie Parker (1920–1955). Parker grew up hearing every jazz style of music in clubs in Kansas City. He began to establish a unique solo style and his collaboration with Dizzy Gillespie helped to make this new style part of mainstream jazz. Gillespie and Parker, along with other innovators such as Miles Davis and Thelonious Monk, eventually moved toward a modern jazz style called *bebop*. *Bebop*, or simply *bop*, differed from the Big Band Swing style in a number of ways. It was usually played by a smaller group, called a combo. It was generally faster and more complex. The improvisation in bebop is much more complex and often diverges from the key or melodic material of the original song. At first, this style was not as popular as the Big Band music, but over the years, it has gained great popularity.

As with all popular forms of music, Jazz Music has continued to grow and develop. Different styles have developed and many jazz artists have contributed to the vast diversity of music heard today. Names such as John Coltrane, Herbie Hancock, Chick Corea, Weather Report, Jaco Pastorius, Spyro Gyra, and even some mainstream Pop groups such as Blood, Sweat, and Tears and Chicago have continued to develop styles of jazz using patterns from the past and new innovations to create new sounds. The best way to get to know this new musical "language" is to begin to listen to jazz and become familiar with the fascinating and varied music.

As you journey through life, make music a part of that journey. So many go through life without experiencing this most unique and wonderful art form created by interesting and innovative people. Music is an expression of the heart, the inner soul of the composer. The performer spends a great part of his or her life perfecting the craft of music-making in order to share the composer's music with you in a way that will move you to tears, joy, fear, exuberance, and a thousand other emotions. Make the time in your life to let this most glorious art reach you in its many forms. Never stop learning and experiencing all that is available in music. Listen to everything. Pay attention to how it moves you. Experience the joy!

Chapter 10
Musical "Biggies"

1. In general, what is the texture of the following:

    a. Medieval church music, or chant –

    b. Renaissance music –

2. What similarities do Baroque music and Baroque art have in common?

3. How is the music of the Contemporary era different from music from earlier eras?

4. What important soloists and groups did not perform at Woodstock?

5. In your opinion, what music of today will be considered the "classical" music in 200 years?

GLOSSARY/
INDEX

ART GLOSSARY/INDEX

Kouros: A term for a young male in Greek Statuary. p. 34

Lantern: A tower that allows light in over the alter in Romanesque architecture. p. 20

Line: The most commonly used basic element of art, the quality of the line is the most obvious element to the inherent style of any given artist. p. 54

Linear Perspective: When parallel lines converge, or come together as they recede in the image. p. 63

Monochromatic: A color scheme which uses primarily one color. p. 60

Mud brick: A mixture of mud and straw formed into bricks and hardened in the sun, used to make the early pyramids. p. 4

Narthex: Located at the end of the nave, the narthex is the entrance or lobby area of the Catholic Church. p. 17

Nave: Main body of the church. p. 17

Negative Space: In a sculpture, it's the area that has been carved away, such as between the legs of a figure. In painting or other art forms, it refers to space around an object. p. 34

Neo (new) Expressionism: Illustrates recognizable images such as humans, portrayed in a more violently emotional style. p. 107

Oculus: A round opening in the ceiling that serves to let light in the building. p. 14

Order: Within Greek culture, it represents the cosmos. It is the opposite of disorder. p. 7

Overlapping Composition: Created with shapes placed in front of other shapes. p. 63

Pantheon: Of Roman architecture, designed using a combination of geometric elements—a circle and a rectangle, means "every god" and was built as a pagan church, the only ancient building still in use today. p. 13

Parthenon: The largest temple on the Greek mainland. p. 8, 13

Pilasters: Egyptian architectural papyrus half columns. p. 9

Platform: The base foundation of a building upon which the column would sit. p. 8

Polykleitos: Wrote a treatise in which he created an advanced theory of symmetry. p. 36

Pont du Gard: An aqueduct that commissioned by Marcus Agrippa to carry water over thirty miles and is still in use today. p. 12

Portico: Front porch. p. 14

Pop Art: Popular culture images that were original works of art but looked mass produced. p. 106

Primary Colors: The basic colors found in the earth, they cannot be made by mixing other colors. Primary colors are yellow, red, and blue. p. 58

Radiating chapels: Small rooms located around the apse in Romanesque architecture. p. 20

Real Texture: Texture that is applied to a work. p. 61

Refinement: The appearance of stability due to the radical taper at the top of Doric columns. p. 8

Rotunda: Circular area of architecture. p. 14

Salons: Art galleries. p. 82

Secondary Color: Purple, green, and orange; made by mixing two primary colors. p. 58

MUSIC GLOSSARY/ INDEX

Aerophone: an instrument that produces sound by a vibrating column of air p.145

Alto: the lowest woman's voice part p. 146

Arch Form: a musical form that can be labeled as ABCDCBA; contrasting sections occur until the middle of the work and then repeat in opposite order, ending with the same material as the beginning p. 160

Atonality: music that avoids a tonic chord or note p. 203

Bass: the lowest men's voice part p. 146

Beat: the regular, recurring pulse of the music p. 135

Binary Form: a musical form consisting of two contrasting sections p. 160

Chord: two or more notes sounding at the same time p. 137

Chordophone: an instrument that produces a sound by a vibrating string p. 145

Concerto: a multi-movement work for a soloist accompanied by an orchestra or piano transcription p. 168

Conjunct: a melody that moves mostly in a step-wise fashion p. 133

Contra: word used to indicate "lower;" a contra bassoon would be an instrument like a bassoon but lower p. 146

Contrast: in form, a section that contrasts the previous music p. 152

Crescendo: to grow louder p. 143

Decrescendo: to grow softer p. 143

Development: the creative portion of the Sonata form which moves through various keys using material from the Exposition p. 165

Diminuendo: to diminish in loudness; grow softer p. 143

Disjunct: a melody that moves mostly by skips or leaps p. 133

Dominant Preparation: usually occurs at the end of the development; establishes the dominant of the original key anticipating the return of material in the Recapitulation p. 166

Double: this occurs when a sax player in a jazz band plays other instruments, such as flute or clarinet p. 148

Duple Meter: a pattern of emphasis that occurs every two beats p. 136

Dynamics: the relative loudness of the music p. 129

Electrophone: an instrument that produces a sound by the vibration of an electrical circuit p. 145

Episode: that portion of the fugue when there is not complete statement of the fugue subject p. 164

Exposition: 1) in a Fugue, the opening presentation of the subject by multiple voices; 2) in Sonata form, the large first section of the form which includes all of the thematic material p. 163

Motif: a very short musical fragment which is used as a basis for the composition of a larger work p. 133

Movement: a complete, self-contained portion of a larger work p. 133

Mute: a device usually used in a brass instrument with the main purpose being to alter the timbre or sound of the instrument; also causes the sound to be softer p. 149

Octave: the interval between two notes, the frequency of the second note being double that of the first p. 130

Oratorio: a type of music similar to an opera but without the use of staging, costumes, scenery, and acting; usually based on a Biblical subject p. 195

Orchestra: a large ensemble consisting of strings, woodwinds, brass and percussion p. 147

Overtones: (see Harmonics) p. 144

Partials: (see Harmonics)

Pianissimo: *pp*; very soft p. 143

Piano: in dynamics, *p*, soft p. 143

Pitch: a single sound frequency p. 130

Polyphonic: a texture consisting of two or more equally important melodies at the same time p. 140

Program Music: music that is based on an extra-musical idea, a story, poem, scene, or idea; the story, or "program" is usually indicated by the composer. p. 199

Recapitulation: the large section at the end of a Sonata form which repeats the material from the Exposition all in the tonic key p. 166

Repertoire: standard literature for a particular ensemble p. 151

Repetition: in form, a section that is repeated p. 152

Rhythm: organized music in time p. 129

Rhythm Section: the instruments of a jazz ensemble that support the music with the rhythm and underlying harmony; can consist of drums, bass, guitar, piano, or synthesizer p. 207

Rondo: a musical form in which the original material recurs between a number of contrasting sections; ABACADA. . . p. 161

Rounded Binary Form: a specialized binary form that can be labeled AABABA p. 160

Scale: consecutive notes in the Western musical system from which melodies and harmonies are constructed p. 131

Sonata: a large musical form consisting of the Exposition, Development, and Recapitulation p. 164

Soprano: the highest woman's voice p. 146

Staff: part of musical notation; the arrangement of five lines and four spaces on which musical notes are placed p. 132

Strophic: a musical form consisting of repeated verses and a chorus p. 158

Subject: the melodic material at the beginning of a fugue that is used for the entire composition p. 163

Symphony: 1) a large orchestral ensemble; 2) a large, often multi-movement piece of music p. 153

Syncopation: this occurs when the emphasis of notes in the music does not coincide with the emphasis of the meter p. 136

Tempo: the speed of the music p. 136

Tenor: the highest men's voice part p. 146

Ternary Form: a musical form consisting of three sections, the last being a repeat of the first; ABA p. 160

Terraced dynamics: sudden change in loudness; can refer to sudden increase or sudden decrease in loudness. p. 192

Texture: the melodic and harmonic "thickness" or density of a piece of music; indicates the number of melodies and/or harmonies that are layered upon each other p. 129

Theme: a longer musical statement, typically ending in a melodic cadence, which is used as a basis of composition in a larger piece of music p. 133

Theme and Variations: a large musical form made up of thematic material and a series of variations of that material p. 167

Timbre: that quality the distinguishes one instrument or voice from another p. 129

Tonic: the note or chord around which a piece of music is composed; "the home tone" of a work of music p. 133

Tonic Chord: the chord of "rest" or the "home" chord of a piece of music p. 138

Transcriptions: typically, works for orchestra that are rearranged for a concert band p. 151

Triad: three notes that are each the interval of a third apart p. 137

Trio: 1) an ensemble of three performers; 2) in Baroque and Classical music, this is the middle section of a larger form, the Minuet and Trio p. 161

Triple Meter: a pattern of emphasis that occurs every three beats p. 136

Variation: in form, a section of music that essentially repeats a previous section but varies that material to create a new section p. 152

Well-Tempered: a term used to indicate a particular tuning system developed in the Baroque era in which each note is an equal distance apart p. 193